Schools of Thought
in the Christian
Tradition

Schools of Thought in the Christian Tradition

Edited by
Patrick Henry

FORTRESS PRESS   Philadelphia

Library of Congress Cataloging in Publication Data

Main entry under title:

Schools of thought in the Christian tradition.

Bibliography: p.
Includes index.
1. Theology—Methodology—History—Addresses, essays, lectures. 1. Theology—Study and teaching—History—Addresses, essays, lectures. I. Henry, Patrick, 1939-
BR118.S36 1984   230'.09   84-47924
ISBN 0-8006-0730-9

42,499

K964C84   Printed in the United States of America   1–730

TO JAROSLAV PELIKAN
Sterling Professor of History
Yale University

with respect and affection and
in celebration of his sixtieth birthday
17 December 1983

Contents

Contributors

William S. Babcock
Associate Professor of Church History, Perkins School of Theology, Southern Methodist University

Francine Cardman
Associate Professor of Historical Theology, Weston School of Theology

Marcia L. Colish
Professor of History, Oberlin College

Melvin B. Endy, Jr.
Professor of Religion and Dean of the College, Hamilton College

Patrick Henry
Professor of Religion, Swarthmore College

E. Ann Matter
Associate Professor of Religious Studies, University of Pennsylvania

John Meyendorff
Professor of History, Fordham University
Professor of Church History and Patristics, St. Vladimir's Seminary

Albert C. Outler
Research Professor of Religion, Texas Wesleyan College

John M. Stroup
Assistant Professor of Church History, Yale University, The Divinity School

Robert L. Wilken
Professor of History of Christianity, University of Notre Dame

Abbreviations

NOTE: The system for citing Harnack's collected essays follows that in K. H. Neufeld, *Adolf von Harnack: Theologie als Suche nach der Kirche: "Tertium Genus Ecclesiae,"* Konfessionskundliche und Kontroverstheologische Studien 41, ed. Johann-Adam-Möhler-Institut. Paderborn, 1977.

AAWG.PH	Abhandlungen der Akademie der Wissenschaften in Göttingen, Philologisch-historische Klasse
AnBoll	*Analecta Bollandiana*
ASGW.PH	Abhandlungen der königlichen sächsischen Gesellschaft der Wissenschaften
AZH[1]	Agnes von Zahn-Harnack, *Adolf von Harnack* (Berlin, 1936).
AZH[2]	Agnes von Zahn-Harnack, *Adolf von Harnack*, 2d ed. (Berlin, 1951).
BECh	*Bibliothèque de l'école des Chartes*
BHR	*Bibliothèque d'humanisme et renaissance*
BHTh	Beiträge zur historischen Theologie
BLE	*Bulletin de littérature ecclésiastique*
BSt(F)	Biblische Studien (Freiburg)
ByA	Byzantinisches Archiv
BZ	*Biblische Zeitschrift*
CAr	*Cahiers archéologiques*
ChH	*Church History*
CChr.CM	Corpus Christianorum, Continuatio mediaevalis
CSCO	Corpus scriptorum Christianorum orientalium
CCM	*Cahiers de civilisation médiévale*
CCW	*Chronik der christlichen Welt*
CistSS	*Cistercian Studies Series*

DOP	*Dumbarton Oaks Papers*
FC	Fathers of the Church
GAW	Adolf von Harnack, *Geschichte der königlich preussischen Akademie der Wissenschaften zu Berlin*, 3 vols. in 4 (Berlin, 1900).
GG	*Geschichtliche Grundbegriffe*, ed. O. Brunner, W. Conze, and R. Koselleck (Stuttgart, 1972ff.).
GThW	Grundriss der theologischen Wissenschaft
HD	Adolf von Harnack, *History of Dogma*, trans. N. Buchanan, 7 vols. in 4 (New York, 1961).
HeyJ	*Heythrop Journal*
HJ	*Historisches Jahrbuch*
HR	*History of Religions*
HThR	*Harvard Theological Review*
IMU	*Italia medioevale e umanistica*
JAC	*Jahrbuch für Antike und Christentum*
JR	*Journal of Religion*
JThS	*Journal of Theological Studies*
KD (1811)	F. D. E. Schleiermacher, *Kurze Darstellung des theologischen Studiums* (Berlin, 1811).
KD (1830)	F. D. E. Schleiermacher, *Kurze Darstellung des theologischen Studiums. Kritische Ausgabe*, ed. H. Scholz, Quellenschriften zur Geschichte des Protestantismus 10 (Leipzig, 1935).
KKTS	Konfessionskundliche und kontroverstheologische Studien
LCC	Library of Christian Classics
LCL	Loeb Classical Library
Lenz	M. Lenz. *Geschichte der königlichen Friedrich-Wilhelms-Universität zu Berlin*, 3 vols. (Halle a.d.S., 1910).
MGH.Ep	*Monumenta Germaniae historica. Epistolae* (Hannover, 1887ff.).
MGH.PL	*Monumenta Germaniae historica. Poetae Latinae medii aevi* (Hannover, 1880ff.).
MGH.SS	*Monumenta Germaniae historica. Scriptores* (Hannover, 1826ff.).
MThZ	*Münchener theologische Zeitschrift*
NPB	*Nova Patrum Bibliotheca*
NPNF	*A Select Library of the Nicene and Post-Nicene Fathers of the Christian Church* (Oxford, 1887ff.).
OA	Orbis academicus

ODCC	*Oxford Dictionary of the Christian Church,* ed. F. L. Cross and E. A. Livingstone, 2d ed. (London, 1974).
PatSor	Patristica Sorbonensia
PG	J.-P. Migne, *Patrologiae cursus completus.* Series Graeca (Paris, 1857ff.).
PL	J.-P. Migne, *Patrologiae cursus completus.* Series Latina (Paris, 1841ff.).
RBen	*Revue Bénédictine*
RE	*Realencyklopädie für protestantische Theologie und Kirche,* 3d ed. (Leipzig, 1896–1913).
RevSR	*Revue des sciences religieuses*
RFNS	*Rivista di filosofia neo-scholastica*
RGG¹	*Die Religion in Geschichte und Gegenwart,* lst ed. (Tübingen, 1909–13).
RGG²	*Die Religion in Geschichte und Gegenwart,* 2d ed. (Tübingen, 1927–31).
RHPhR	*Revue d'histoire et de philosophie religieuses*
RSR	*Recherches de science religieuse*
RThAM	*Recherches de théologie ancienne et médievale*
RuA 1–2	Adolf von Harnack, *Reden und Aufsätze,* 2 vols. (Giessen, 1904–6).
RuA 3–4	Adolf von Harnack, *Aus Wissenschaft und Leben,* 2 vols. (Giessen, 1911).
RuA 5	Adolf von Harnack, *Aus der Friedens- und Kriegsarbeit* (Giessen, 1916).
RuA 6	Adolf von Harnack, *Erforschtes und Erlebtes* (Giessen, 1923).
RuA 7	Adolf von Harnack, *Aus der Werkstatt des Vollendeten,* ed. Axel von Harnack (Giessen, 1930).
RuA 8	Adolf von Harnack, *Ausgewählte Reden und Aufsätze,* ed. Agnes von Zahn-Harnack and Axel von Harnack (Berlin, 1951).
SC	Sources chrétiennes
SJTh	*Scottish Journal of Theology*
SpicFri	Spicilegium Friburgense
StT	Studi e Testi Biblioteca apostolica Vaticana
TaS	Texts and Studies. Contribution to Biblical and Patristic Literature
TMIE	Travaux et mémoires de l'institut d'ethnologie
TRE	*Theologische Realenzyklopädie,* ed. G. Krause and G. Müller (Berlin, 1981).

TThZ	*Trierer theologische Zeitschrift*
TU	Texte und Untersuchungen zur Geschichte der altchristlichen Literatur
ZKG	*Zeitschrift für Kirchengeschichte*
ZZ	*Zwischen den Zeiten*

Editor's Introduction

In the year 692 a church council admonished bishops to "become distinguished for their knowledge of patristic writings rather than for composing treatises out of their own heads." These days a theologian whose book is condemned for having nothing new to say is undone. The words of George Santayana, "Those who cannot remember the past are condemned to repeat it," have become a cliché, but it is instructive to imagine the form the truism would have taken on the lips of most Christians during the church's first millennium: "Those who cannot remember the past will be condemned for doing something different."[1] There is nothing we want more than to be innovative. There is nothing they wanted less.

How is a tradition preserved while being passed on? If "tradition is the living faith of the dead [and] traditionalism is the dead faith of the living,"[2] can we tell the difference between those new occasions that teach new duties and those that assault the very essence of the tradition? The question of *tradition* and its near corollary, the question of *authority*, are not the only theological and ecumenical questions in the forefront of Christian concern today, but it is safe to say that no significant issues can be sorted out, much less resolved, without attention to tradition.

No one in the late twentieth century has attempted a more comprehensive address to the problem of Christian tradition than Jaroslav Pelikan, Sterling Professor of History at Yale University. As the bibliography in the Appendix to this volume testifies, he has investigated questions across centuries, cultures, and languages with uncommon boldness. His work is culminating in his five-volume magnum opus, *The Christian Tradition: A History of the Development of Doctrine* (Chicago: University of Chicago Press). Volume 1, *The Emergence of the Catholic Tradition (100–600)* (1971); Volume 2, *The Spirit of Eastern Christendom (600–1700)* (1974); Volume 3, *The Growth of Medieval Theology (600–1300)* (1978); and Volume 4, *Reformation of Church and Dogma*

1

(1300–1700) (1984) have already been published. Volume 5, *Christian Doctrine and Modern Culture (since 1700)*, will appear soon. *Schools of Thought in the Christian Tradition* is offered to Professor Pelikan on his sixtieth birthday with thanks for all he has taught us and as a contribution to the work of historical investigation and interpretation of which he is a grand master. All of us have learned from him, eight as his students and two (John Meyendorff and Albert Outler) as close colleagues in ecumenical affairs over several decades.

As Robert Wilken notes in his chapter on the school of Alexandria, the term "school" is useful partly because of its imprecision; it can refer to a set of ideas, a way of interpreting the Bible, a form of spirituality, a style of pedagogy, a method of theological dialectics, an institution. This flexibility makes it possible to see connections between the "school of Alexandria" in the third century and the "school of Berlin" in the nineteenth century discussed by John Stroup, even though for the latter school we have information as detailed as the statutes of the theological faculty and for the former we are unsure whether it is accurate to speak of an "institution" at all. A school of thought is not necessarily limited to one place or one era, and some schools can be understood as stretching the usual definition of "thought." Francine Cardman's chapter on Jerusalem quotes Cyril of Jerusalem on the special advantage of those with access to the Palestinian holy places: "Others only hear, but we both see and handle." And Eusebius of Caesarea acknowledged the teaching power of the monumental church-building activities of Emperor Constantine: the structures themselves give "evidence of the refutation of godless tyranny."

Indeed, one of the characteristics of the chapters in this volume is their attention to the generally religious, and not exclusively theological, aspects of the Christian tradition. Patrick Henry discusses one of the ways in which liturgical practice shaped doctrine. William Babcock analyzes the conflicting claims to biblical images in the early North African church and reminds us that writing in that time and place was intricately tied to webs of personal relationships. John Meyendorff highlights the centrality for Eastern Orthodox Christianity of spiritual vision as the mark of authentic theology; to the question "Is knowledge of God independent of the sacramental nature of the church?" the Orthodox have answered an unflinching "No." In contrast, Marcia Colish recounts the processes in the West in the Middle Ages by which the teaching and learning of traditions became professionalized; indeed, her story of medieval Paris is an unfolding of patterns that, with certain modifications, are very familiar to professors and students today. Ann Matter shows how biblical commentary served generally as the language of instruction in the Carolingian Empire of the ninth century, not only where we might expect it, in theological advice to bishops, but also in political tracts. A king could be advised through a commentary on the prophets. And by way of contrast that highlights the main point, Melvin Endy tells of the spiritual liabilities in a tradition which emphasizes propositional theology to the virtual exclusion of the historical and affective dimensions of Christian experience.

This volume makes no claim to be a complete account of the ways in which the Christian tradition has been taught and learned. The imagination can have a field day listing other possible chapters: the Desert Fathers; the school of Antioch; monastic schools; Syriac, Coptic, Slavic, and dozens of other non-Greek/non-Latin traditions; Nestorian and Monophysite schools; the endless proliferation of Protestant traditions; the vast history of Christian missions; the scandalously neglected history of Christian women and their tradition. And then there are the chapters for which the materials are being developed in recognition of the sexist bias in the Christian tradition and in virtually all study of this tradition up to now. To counterpoint all the rest, there could be a chapter on the times when the tradition doubles back against itself. Stroup cites Franz Overbeck, who warned that the study of church history was the best school for learning to doubt the existence of God, and we can remember the Emperor Julian "the Apostate," brought up in the family of the first Christian world rulers, Friedrich Nietzsche, son of a pastor, and Josef Stalin, student in a theological seminary. And then there are the chapters for which the materials are being developed in our own time as Christianity's center of gravity shifts from the North Atlantic to the Third World. The historian of the Christian tradition does well to ponder the story, told by John S. Mbiti, of the young African theologian who goes to Europe to study and learns about demythologizing, and returns home to be greeted by a request that he exorcise a demon who is tormenting his sister.[3]

Still, while there is much more not in this volume than in it, these ten chapters illustrate many varieties of teaching and learning in Christian history, and readers may find that some current problems are not quite so unique as they thought. Marcia Colish notes that in the thirteenth century a dispute developed between the theologians and the arts faculty at Paris over who should control the teaching of philosophical ideas that had theological implications, and when financial stringency later beset the university, they started giving preference to students who could pay their own way, with the result that narrower national and personal interests began to control the academic atmosphere. William Babcock traces the influences that led Augustine, in opposition to the North African theologians before him, to draw the line between Christian and non-Christian, not at the border between church and world but through the human heart itself, and while Augustine's position may not be adequate for an age of such insistent pluralism as our own, it is instructive to see him making such a fundamental ground-shift in his own time. Robert Wilken and John Meyendorff tell of the importance of the personal qualities of the teacher; current debates over "objectivity" and "subjectivity" in the classroom can be informed by the examples of Origen and Symeon the New Theologian. In Ann Matter's study of ninth-century exegesis, we can see emerging the division between technical and homiletical commentary on the Bible, a division enshrined in our own time in the bifocal pages of *The Interpreter's Bible*, and a division which Origen would have found puzzling, for as Wilken points out, Origen did not make the distinction between preacher and teacher that seems so fundamental to us.

Several of the chapters warn against the temptation to see our own situations when we look to the past. If our experience is molded within the university, then when we read about teaching and learning in the past we almost unconsciously assume it was done pretty much the way we do it, or at least with the same underlying aims and convictions. Other chapters signal ironies that might slip past us. For example, in the twelfth century, when the West was reacquiring Greek learning with dizzying acceleration, the Christian East was becoming less and less Greek. In eighteenth-century America the Consistent Calvinists, who considered that Jonathan Edwards had constructed the necessary and sufficient edifice of theology for all time, lost touch almost completely with his appreciation for the religious affections and in so doing drained much of the life out of one of the most dramatic revival movements in Christian history.

If more of what is said in these chapters will seem familiar than some readers expect, there are nonetheless striking differences between the various "thens" and now. Teachers in the humanities who look with envy at enrollments in preprofessional courses will become wistful when they read that in medieval Paris theology outstripped medicine and law because of the prestige of the subject and because theology was of more utility than medicine or law for careers in state as well as in church. John Stroup's account of the varying intensity of German ecclesiastical and governmental intrusions in the affairs of the University of Berlin will strike many readers as being of a piece with today's newspaper, and there is wry amusement in the contrast with the situation at the Abbey of Ste. Geneviève in twelfth-century Paris, where the abbot was totally uninterested in the activities of the theologians he licensed to teach there—a sort of academic freedom by default.

Perhaps the most striking difference between the past and the present in Christian tradition is the catastrophic decline in our own time of a common core of knowledge. It is a risky business these days to make even the most commonplace of biblical allusions without identifying the source, and the web of classical Greek and Latin texts, which constituted a common culture up through the time of Adolf von Harnack, has been unraveled. Hope for even simple chronology seems to be in vain; what can be done when students refer to Calvin's (1509-1564) quotation of Milton's (1608-1674) *Paradise Lost*?

As Marcia Colish points out, Hugh of St. Victor instructed his pupils to "learn everything; you will see afterwards that nothing is superfluous," and John Stroup, tracing the Berlin tradition from Schleiermacher to Harnack, notes how those champions of the liberal tradition in theology insisted that one's own branch of learning, including theology, can be understood only in connection with all learning. Not every Christian teacher has agreed. The Consistent Calvinists acknowledged that nothing can be known in divinity without being known in connection with other branches of divinity and with the general scheme of divine grace, but this is a far cry from saying that theology must be set in conjunction with a whole university curriculum. It is worth remembering, however, as Melvin Endy notes, that these parsonage seminary instructors were limited to what they could find in rural parish libraries, and we who have ready access to millions of volumes should hesitate to sneer. Finally, it is important to remember the tradition of sharp protest by Christian theologians such as Tertullian, Søren Kierkegaard, and Karl Barth against accommodation to culture. Athens and Jerusalem are different places. If one is home, the other may be nice to visit, but you would not necessarily want to live there.

Albert Outler, who opens this volume with an evaluation of the place of Pelikan's *The Christian Tradition*, suggests a major paradigm shift in historical self-understanding to explain the difference between Pelikan's work and Harnack's *History of Dogma*. The emergence of what Outler calls "the ecumenical consciousness" gets us beyond the Athens/Jerusalem dichotomy and opens up perspectives on tradition that were simply blanked out by polemic (history will show that I am right and you are wrong) or by historicist triumphalism (history will show us the unqualified essence of the tradition, which has been lost for all these centuries until now).

Jaroslav Pelikan understands how often it is necessary to introduce statements about the history of the Christian tradition with words used by Francine Cardman in her chapter: "It is possible, though by no means either certain or provable, for instance. . . ." Professor Pelikan teaches the Christian tradition but also is always learning it, and it could not be said of him, as Melvin Endy notes was said of Nathaniel Emmons, that he has not grown dissatisfied with a single sentence he has written in the course of his long career. We thank him for teaching us how to learn and to keep on learning.

NOTES

1. Canon 19 of the Council *in Trullo*; see Chapter 5, by John Meyendorff, below. G. Santayana, *The Life of Reason; or The Phases of Human Progress* ("Introduction and Reason in Common Sense") (New York, 1906), 1:284.

2. J. Pelikan, *The Emergence of the Catholic Tradition (100–600)*, vol. 1 of *The Christian Tradition* (Chicago, 1971), 9.

3. J. S. Mbiti, "Theological Impotence and the Universality of the Church," in G. H. Anderson and T. F. Stransky, eds., *Mission Trends No. 3: Third World Theologies* (New York and Grand Rapids, 1976), 6–8 (reprinted from *Lutheran World* 21, no. 3 [1974]).

1

The Idea of "Development" in the History of Christian Doctrine: A Comment

Albert C. Outler

It would be appropriate if the fifth and final volume of Jaroslav Pelikan's *The Christian Tradition: A History of the Development of Doctrine* were to appear in 1985, the centenary of the publication of the first volume of Adolf von Harnack's famed *History of Dogma*. *The Christian Tradition* and the *Lehrbuch der Dogmengeschichte* invite critical comparison on at least three counts. First, there is the point of succession: Harnack (1851–1930) taught Wilhelm Pauck (1901–1981), who was in turn Pelikan's *Doktorvater*. Second, both histories are roughly equal in historical prowess and are monumental in their scope and substance, standing beyond less ambitious efforts. But third and most crucial, they reflect two very different outlooks, so that *The Christian Tradition* may be taken as a landmark in a major paradigm shift in historical self-understanding over the course of a century. This in turn suggests various reflections on the nature of historical inquiry (e.g., the "history of dogma," "history of doctrine," etc.) and most specifically on the idea of "development" as a clue to interpretation.

It may still be too early to attempt a comprehensive account of this shift, and at any rate this chapter is not such an attempt. But a "comment" on the shift and on its ecumenical significance might interest historians, theologians, and those church leaders who recognize historical perspectives as resources for their grapplings with current challenges.

An irony, deserving more consideration than it has had, is this: the inaugural classic of "modern church history," the *Magdeburg Centuries* of 1559–1574, was the brainchild of a bigot, Matthaeus

Flacius Illyricus (1520–1575), whose warfare against Rome was merely chief in a series of harsh contentions strung out over a lifetime. The *Centuries* were an outraged response to the cold-eyed cursings of Protestantism by the Council of Trent (1545–1563) and were designed to provide the Protestants with a historical brief both for their rejection of Rome and for their own self-congratulation. Inevitably, Roman Catholics such as Caesar Baronius (1538–1607), Robert Bellarmine (1542–1621), and J. B. Bossuet (1627–1704) also turned to history for aid in their rejoinders, and church history quickly became a potent weapon for attack and defense on all sides of an unrelenting conflict between irreconciled Christians. The great and more nearly balanced *Institutiones Historiae Ecclesiasticae* (1726) of J. L. Mosheim, whom Harnack called "the Erasmus of the eighteenth century," was untypical of this adversarial tradition, and it did not alter the atmosphere by much.[1]

These quarreling Christians shared the assumption that "pure doctrine" existed somewhere in a single authoritative system, the essence of "the faith once for all delivered to the saints" (Jude 3). Such pure doctrine would be the conceptual base on which the church depended (*articulus stantis vel cadentis ecclesiam*). For the Roman Catholics, this "apostolic faith" was lodged in Scripture, creeds, and dogmas and had been preserved through the centuries by the church's *magisterium*, its teaching authority. The Protestants found pure doctrine in Scripture *alone*, but the doctrine required explication in a series of rival confessions, and each tradition was equally confident of the pure truth possessed. The Lutherans had the Scriptures, *Augustana Invariata*, and the *Book of Concord*. The Reformed Christians had the Scriptures, Calvin's *Institutes*, and their several confessions. The Anglicans had the Scriptures, their *Book of Common Prayer*, the *Articles of Religion*, and the *Homilies*. The "Radicals," and after them the "Pietists," had the Scriptures and their *theologia cordis* (theology of the heart). Doctrinal pluralism was generally deemed reductionist and was abhorred by all, on principle. Church history's chief business was to bolster each church's ingrained triumphalism.

This conviction—that the fullness of Christian truth is embodied in this one church and explicated in this one system of pure doctrine—gave rise to what Bernard Lonergan and others have taught us to call "the classical consciousness." It was "classical" in the steadiness of its conviction of the perdurance in and through time of a *depositum fidei* essentially intact. The Scriptures were its

8

source, the dogmas its distillate, the church its *magistra* and trustee. This point was made variously: in the fifth-century Vicentian Canon ("what has been believed everywhere, always, and by everyone"), in the so-called Athanasian Creed, in the implicit boast of *semper eadem* ("always the same"—the motto chosen by Bossuet in the seventeenth century and by the rigidly conservative Cardinal Ottaviani in the twentieth). Something of this same "classical consciousness" persists in Cardinal John Henry Newman's *Essay on the Development of Christian Doctrine* (1845). For all his historiographical virtuosity, Newman centers "development" on the idea of a "full elucidation," *by stages,* of primal truth, "communicated to the world once and for all by inspired teachers."[2] It was this idea of development that helped clinch Newman's acceptance of Roman Catholic claims.

Protestant versions of "the classical consciousness" arose from Protestants' confidence that the two distinctive principles—*sola scriptura* and *sola fide*—could be validly and definitively interpreted. Their huge harvest of essays in aid of doctrinal consensus represents a heroic chapter in the history of Christian reflection. It is a pity that the labors of the great "dogmaticians"—from Philipp Melanchthon (1497–1560) to Martin Chemnitz (1522–1586) to Johann Gerhard (1582–1637), from John Calvin (1509–1564) to the Synod of Dort (1618–1619), to the Turretini (Benedetto [1588–1631], his son Francesco [1623–1687], and grandson Giovanni [1671–1737])—have been consigned to church-historical limbo. But the chief reason they were so consigned is instructive: nothing less than a massive shift away from the classical consciousness of the dogmaticians' world to something new that we may call "the historical consciousness."

This paradigm shift was the cumulative effect of the Enlightenment—of eighteenth-century revulsions against "orthodoxy," "dogma," "dogmatism"—and of nineteenth-century hopes that *history* could recover the essence of true religion while clearing away the debris of superstition, traditionalism, ecclesiasticism. Voltaire (1694–1778) is the archetype of this new consciousness; its specifically historical outlook is exemplified in Leopold von Ranke (1795–1886) and Wilhelm Dilthey (1833–1911). All kinds of study found a focus in the new idea of "progress"; terms like "modern," "new," and "recent scholarship" became sacrosanct. A new sort of study ("literary-historical") promised to disengage the Bible from traditional misconceptions. Hopes were raised that a fully credible biography of Jesus could reveal the primal gospel—namely, Jesus' personal religion. Teachings and practices that had later encrusted the religion of Jesus could be cataloged under various theories of degeneration, as in Martin Werner's scornful phrase *"Ersatzchristentum."* The way was opened for a radical reconception of the history of Christian thought, as in the work of Ferdinand Christian Baur (1792–1860) and Albrecht Ritschl (1822–1889). The bonus of it all was to have been the liberation of Christianity from the bonds of the past, especially from what was considered to be the dead hand of *Greek* metaphysics (*German* metaphysics was quite another thing).

One of the first-fruits of this reconception of the history of Christian thought was a new discipline that could scarcely have flourished or even been imagined earlier: *Dogmengeschichte.* There are many candidates for "founder" of the "history of dogma": Semler (1725–1791), Walch (1726–1784), Münter (1761–1830), Münscher (1766–1814), Lange (1802–1884), among others. But whenever and with whomever the new discipline began, its essential aim was clear: to provide historical vindication for the superseding of dogmas, in their patristic and medieval formulations, by reformulations based on "contemporary understandings" of Scripture and Christian experience. The new "historical consciousness" was not much less polemical—toward Rome *and* toward Protestant "orthodoxy"—than the older "classical consciousness" had been toward "heresy."

This historical consciousness came to its crowning glory in Harnack's great *Lehrbuch.* His unparalleled erudition and breadth of scope edified and intimidated even his most learned readers. But it can be too easily forgotten that, in Harnack's own judgment, the *Lehrbuch* was actually the prolegomenon to his famous lectures of 1899–1900, *Das Wesen des Christentums,* which he regarded as the truly definitive statement of his Christian self-understanding. As he wrote in the preface to the English edition, published in 1900 as *What Is Christianity?* "the theologians of every country only half discharge their duties if they think it enough to treat of the Gospel in the recondite language of learning and bury it in scholarly folios."[3]

While liberal Protestantism was enjoying its honeymoon with "modernity," Roman Catholicism continued its beleaguered way, insisting on *semper eadem.* Like Mosheim's work among Protestants a century earlier, J. A. Möhler's *Symbolik* of 1832 was an exception, but its real influence would come only much later. Pope Pius IX's *Syllabus of Errors* (1854) doggedly defied "modernity" and all its works. The First Vatican Council's definition of papal infallibility, *Pastor Aeternus* (1870), Pope Leo XIII's consecration of Scholasticism in *Aeterni Patris* (1879), and Pope Pius XII's condemnation of several modern developments, including existentialism, in *Humani Generis* (1950), form a clear series. Catholic mavericks, from Lamennais (1782–1854) to Buonaiuti (1881–1946), were hustled off the stage. "Ecumenism" and "indifferentism" were lumped together and condemned. Denominational triumphalism flourished all around.

Still, a new "ecumenical consciousness" *was* emerging, partly as a byproduct of new historical understandings of continuity and change, partly a fresh perspective for historical inquiry. This ecumenical consciousness found substance in exciting discoveries—on the mission fields, on university campuses, in Christian social action—of an implicit unity among Christians, a "common history" that transcended all separate, polemical histories. This new consciousness arose among liberals, but it moved beyond liberalism's typical anti-ecclesiasticism toward a balance between the critical temper of honest history and the ecclesial loyalty of honest faith. The ecumenical consciousness asks no sacrifice of a critical methodology on any altar of amiability, but it does encourage—indeed require—a shift in temper and aim: from polemics to irenics, from monologue to dialogue, from separation toward convergence.

At the heart of this new consciousness is the idea of *development*, an idea that has been in the air for a long time but is still seeking adequate articulation. Development presupposes an identity and continuity in and through cultural changes; it understands the limits placed on theological language by the irreducible mystery of God; its constants are tied less closely to single forms of words than to God's own self-communications in Christ and the Spirit. Something of this understanding of development was implied in Pope John XXIII's slogan *aggiornamento* (updating) and was the motivating idea in the distinctive documents of the Second Vatican Council (1962–1965). It was the avowed working thesis in the report entitled "Tradition and Traditions" by a Commission of the World Council of Churches Division of Faith and Order, a report developed in a full decade of collaborative study and presented to the Third World Conference on Faith and Order in 1963.

If the *Magdeburg Centuries* may be taken as ensign of the classical consciousness in Protestantism, and Harnack's *Lehrbuch* as a prime example of the historical consciousness, so also Pelikan's *The Christian Tradition* may be taken as the most impressive achievement to date of the ecumenical consciousness in the field of historical theology. There is nothing surprising here. Pelikan was born into a long line of Lutheran pastors, and his mother was a native of Orthodox Serbia. One of his early publications, *The Riddle of Roman Catholicism* (1959), appeared just three years before the opening of Vatican II and was awarded a prestigious prize by Abingdon Press, a Methodist publishing house. His education and academic career have been ecumenical by choice, and he was an active member of the "Tradition and Traditions" Study Commission, where he and I and the others had the fabled Russian Orthodox theologian, Father Georges Florovsky, for a colleague and mentor.

Harnack's familiar definition of "dogma in its conception and development" as "a work of the Greek spirit on the soil of the Gospel" was pejorative, despite his expression of admiration for dogma as "a great achievement"; the *Lehrbuch* is an elaborate exercise in the exorcism of that spirit in the interests of a recovery of an uncorrupted primal gospel, the *essence* of Christianity.[4] Pelikan's equivalent formula—"What the church of Christ believes, teaches, and confesses on the basis of the word of God: this is Christian doctrine"—recognizes a subtle dialectic between continuity and change in the historical process.[5] He sets no premium on innovation (*aliquid novi*); he will not settle for mere unfoldment (*semper eadem*). It might even be said that in preference to the familiar Vincentian Canon, Pelikan has promoted what we could call the "Diognetian Canon," derived from the anonymous second-century Christian document known as the *Letter to Diognetus*, which catalogs the paradoxes of the church in the world:

> Christians cannot be distinguished from the rest of the human race by country or language or customs. They do not live in cities of their own; they do not use a peculiar form of speech; they do not follow an eccentric manner of life. This doctrine of theirs has not been discovered by the ingenuity or deep thought of inquisitive persons, nor do they put forward a merely human teaching, as some people do. Yet, although they live in Greek and barbarian cities alike, as each person's lot has been cast, and follow the customs of the country in clothing and food and other matters of daily living, at the same time they give proof of

the remarkable and admittedly extraordinary constitution of their own commonwealth. They live in their own countries, but only as aliens. They have a share in everything as citizens, and endure everything as foreigners. Every foreign land is their homeland, and yet for them every homeland is a foreign land.[6]

Pelikan suggests that in style of life and in doctrinal development, Christians are *in* the world and therefore involved in its changes and chances, but not *of* the world because of their radically different ground and end. Thus, *The Christian Tradition* is more than a major landmark in the history of doctrine. It is a refocusing of the idea of development that opens up many a horizon for further fruitful inquiry.

We are grateful for Pelikan's reappraisals of such vexing questions as the import of Hellenization and the root causes of the tragic rifts between Eastern and Western Christianity. But the first three volumes of *The Christian Tradition* cover the easier part of his undertaking. The acid test comes when the idea of development-in-continuity is invoked to make what sense there may be in the radical discontinuities in Christian doctrine in the sixteenth, nineteenth, and late twentieth centuries. The problems for an ecumenically oriented historian of the epochs from Luther to Barth and from Trent to Vatican II are daunting. For three centuries history has been chiefly a solvent force in the tragic drama of Christian disunity. Can it be a healing force in our current struggles for convergence?

There is no way back to any ecumenical "square one," no realistic hope of the penitent return of members of self-acknowledged inauthentic churches into the embrace of the one true church. Vatican II recognized this ungrudgingly. By the same token, there is no unity worth having without a deep and honest consensus in shared beliefs, teachings, and confessions, based on the word of God and signified by genuine intercommunion. Cheap unity ("letting bygones be bygones"), like cheap grace, is self-deceiving.

The Christian Tradition is therefore somewhat more important than a prodigy of scholarship. Behind its intricate latticework of citations, narrations, and generalizations lies an informing vision that is, in a word, "traditional." Yet that "tradition" receives here a contemporary manifestation that is a good omen for a future in sore need of every kind of bolstering. The ecumenical import of *The*

Christian Tradition exceeds its virtuosity—noteworthy as that is. Its promise is that, from this sort of understanding of the Christian past, in both its constants and its changing contexts, Christians may gain a more adequately informed vision of their future as members one of another in the body of Christ.

NOTES

1. A. von Harnack, *History of Dogma*, vol. 1 (London, 1905), 26 (Prolegomena, sec. 2).

2. J. H. Newman, *Essay*, 5 (London, 1894), 169–206, which lists the "seven notes" by which *geniune* development may be contrasted with its "corruptions": 1) preservation of type; 2) continuity of principles; 3) power of assimilation; 4) logical sequence; 5) anticipation of its future; 6) conservative action; 7) chronic vigor. Interesting and fruitful as this outlook may be, it still poses the older problematic in a new guise. See also O. Chadwick, *From Bossuet to Newman: The Idea of Doctrinal Development* (Cambridge, 1957).

3. Harnack, *What Is Christianity?* (New York, 1957), vi.

4. Harnack, *History of Dogma*, vol. 1 (London, 1905), 17, Prolegomena, sec. 1 of English trans., but see also p. 21, where Harnack answers some objections to the definition.

5. J. Pelikan, *The Emergence of the Catholic Tradition (100–600)*, vol. 1 of *The Christian Tradition* (Chicago, 1971), 1.

6. *The Letter to Diognetus* 5.1–5, in C. C. Richardson, ed., *Early Christian Fathers*, LCC 1 (Philadelphia, 1953), 216–17 (slightly altered).

2

Alexandria: A School for Training in Virtue

Robert L. Wilken

In the history of Christian thought the notion of "school" has been remarkably durable. It is one of those elementary tools, the hammer or the saw, with which the historian constructs the edifice of the great movements of thought. As a category of investigation it is sensitive to the significance of ideas—a school is often distinguished by what its members taught—yet at the same time directs attention to the role of tradition in shaping theological conceptions. A member of a school can be in continuity with earlier thinkers and also be original. The notion of "school" is not bound to a peculiar time. It can designate modern theological movements, such as the school of Ritschl or the Chicago school, but it is equally appropriate to interpret the school of Antioch in the ancient world or the school of St. Victor in twelfth-century Paris. In other contexts it highlights the social or institutional setting of theological ideas, as when one speaks of the cathedral schools or of the scholastic theologians within the medieval university.

"School," then, is serviceable as an interpretative device in the history of Christian thought; it is nevertheless inherently ambiguous. It can refer to a certain set of ideas, a way of interpreting the Bible, a form of spirituality, a style of pedagogy, a method of theological dialectics, an institution—to name but a few of the more familiar uses of the term. Also, like all historical categories, it is shaped by the historian's experience, in this case by the type of education one has received and in what setting—that is, in what kind of school.

Most modern scholars who have written about the Alexandrian

school in the early church have had their homes in the university and have seen their own surroundings reflected in that ancient setting. Coming to the works of the Alexandrian theologians, Clement (c. 150–c. 215) and Origen (c. 185–c. 254), after studying the writings of the Apostolic Fathers, of Irenaeus (c. 130–c. 200), and even the first Apologists, historians have claimed to discover the first emergence of a "scientific" approach to theology in Christian thought. The school of Alexandria has been called the "first Christian academy" or the "first Catholic university."[1] It was seen as a school for advanced studies in Christian doctrine, an institute of higher Christian studies, a school for Christian philosophers whose purpose was to elevate faith to knowledge and to establish a scientific theology on the basis of faith. In the introduction to his section on Clement and Origen in the *Lehrbuch der Dogmengeschichte*, Adolf von Harnack wrote:

> The significance of the Alexandrian catechetical school for the transformation of the pagan empire into a Christian empire and of Greek philosophy into a churchly philosophy is immeasurable. In the third century this school overthrew polytheism by scientific means, while at the same time it conserved anything that was of value in Greek science and culture. The Alexandrians wrote for the educated of the whole world; they transported Christianity into the world culture.[2]

The phrase "catechetical school" comes from the description of the early teachers in the city of Alexandria in the *Ecclesiastical History* of Eusebius (c. 260–c. 340). "Now at that time there was a man of great renown for learning named Pantaenus, who had charge of the school of the faithful (*hē tōn pistōn diatribē*) at Alexandria, where it has been a primitive custom that a school (*didaskaleion*) of sacred studies should exist." Later, speaking of Origen, Eusebius notes that there was a succession of teachers in the school: "Pantaenus was succeeded by Clement, who directed the catechesis (*katacheseōs*) at Alexandria up to such a date that Origen was one of his pupils." And in another place he says explicitly that Origen became head of the "catechetical school (*katacheseōs didaskaleiou*) when he was eighteen years old."[3]

On the face of it, Eusebius's account seems straightforward enough, but in the last several generations serious doubts have been raised about its credibility. To take but one example: from Eusebius's own comments it appears that Pantaenus and Clement were both teaching at the same time in Alexandria—hardly likely if each, in turn, was the head of the school. Faced with these and other difficulties, some scholars have argued that Eusebius has confused the private teaching of men such as Pantaenus and Clement with the "official" instruction under the jurisdiction of the bishop. At the time, around the year 180, when Pantaenus first began to teach in Alexandria, it is unlikely that an "official" institution existed. Such a school was first established two decades later, around 202, when Origen was asked to take responsibility for teaching. Before that time Pantaenus and Clement functioned as private teachers (as did Origen after being relieved of his duties by the bishop), in the fashion of philosophers of the time, accepting as students those who wished to acquaint themselves with the Christian philosophy. "The catechetical school in Alexandria was founded after Clement. The schools of Pantaenus and Clement were free undertakings, which arose with their personal activity as teachers and ceased after them."[4]

This consensus, widely reflected in the literature on Alexandria, has been challenged by André Méhat in his masterful study of Clement's *Stromateis (Miscellanies).*[5] The difficulty with most discussions of the Alexandrian school, as Méhat sees it, is that scholars have approached it with too restricted a model of "catechetical." It has been assumed that "catechetical" means public and official in contrast to personal and private. But, he asks, is this distinction really appropriate in the church of Alexandria in the late second century? Furthermore, it has been thought that catechetical instruction was carried out by presbyters of the church—Bardy calls them "humble presbyters"—who were assigned the task of transmitting the rudiments of the Christian faith. But the stature of the men who we know engaged in catechesis in this period, Tertullian (c. 160–c. 220), Hippolytus (c. 170–c. 236), and Origen, suggests that the task of instructing new converts was given to the most learned in the community.

Méhat argues that the Greek term *katēchēsis* need not have the narrow sense of instruction leading to baptism; it can refer to instruction or teaching in general and hence is not inappropriately applied to the "private" schools of Pantaenus and Clement. Some people were attracted to Christianity through the "wisdom" of well-known teachers. As A. Knauber has emphasized, teachers such as Pantaenus and Clement were philosophical missionaries who brought Christian teaching to the attention of the larger society. Before Pantaenus settled in Alexandria he was, according to Eusebius, an "evangelist of the word" who had traveled as far east as India.[6] In Alexandria this private instruction by prominent teachers was eventually transformed into the ecclesiastical instruction associated with the catechumenate.

The merit of Méhat's work is that by suggesting continuity between the personal and individual instruction of the first teachers in Alexandria and the later catechists, he dispenses with the need to posit two distinct types of schools. His views, however, do not repudiate the basic insight of the early critics of Eusebius's account, for both he and they agree that the teaching of Pantaenus and Clement, and later Origen, is to be understood in the light of the model of the contemporary philosophical schools. "School" in the context of Alexandria at this time refers to a free association of students under the guidance and direction of a sage in a relation best described as master to disciples. "The authority exercised by the Head," writes Henry Chadwick, "was *auctoritas* rather than *potestas*: the authority of the expert, of the teacher whose reputation, learning and skill in teaching were sufficient to create his clientele."[7]

The phrase "school of Alexandria," then, is a way of speaking of the intellectual and spiritual activity of the early teachers in Alexandria at the time Christianity first comes into historical focus there at the end of the second century. If one wishes to discern what is distinctive about the school of Alexandria, one is perforce led to examine not an institution but the teaching style of Clement and Origen. Of Pantaenus, the first teacher, we know only what Clement and Eusebius say of him; none of his writings is extant.

The school of Alexandria, defined in this fashion, cannot be confined to the city of Alexandria for the simple reason that Origen left Alexandria around the year 230 and eventually settled in Caesarea in Palestine. There he established another "school," where he continued to teach until his death. Origen's activity in Caesarea must be taken into consideration in any discussion of the Alexandrian school. Many of his most important writings come from this period, and while in Caesarea Origen preached regularly. His preaching, as he says in his sermons, was really a form of teaching. Or to put the matter more correctly, he did not make the modern distinction between preaching and teaching. The term *didaskalos*, usually translated "teacher," describes his work as preacher.[8] But most instructive of all is firsthand testimony to Origen's teaching in Caesarea in the form of a speech of appreciation from one of his students, Gregory Thaumaturgus, which was delivered at the time Gregory left the school.[9]

Gregory's address, mistakenly called a panegyric since Jerome (c. 342–420) first designated it as such, was an expression of gratitude and admiration, and in the style of the rhetors it is filled with hyperbole. Everything is writ large, exaggerated, reflecting the characteristics of ancient orations, and Origen appears as a heroic, almost divine figure. What Gregory has to say is shaped as much by the conventions of Greek rhetoric and the ideal of a philosophical teacher as by Gregory's actual experience with Origen. As some scholars have observed, the distinctively Christian elements of Origen's teaching are not prominent in the address.[10] Nevertheless, if these reservations are kept in mind, the speech presents a picture of Origen that is not out of harmony with what we know from his writings, especially if we read it not so much as a handbook on Origen's theology as a book on Origen's teaching style, how he was perceived by one of his students, and what he considered the goals of his teaching. Further, what Gregory says of Origen fits remarkably well with what we know of Clement.

And this brings us back to the question posed at the beginning of this chapter. What precisely does the term "school" mean when we speak of the school of Alexandria? It is clear that the "scientific" model, or the example of the university, as used by Harnack and many others is far off the mark. Indeed, it is a mistake to describe the work of the school chiefly in cognitive or "scientific" terms. The teachers of Alexandria were not interested solely in conveying knowledge or transmitting intellectual skills.[11] They were interested in moral and spiritual formation. The course of studies was intellectual in the sense that students read and analyzed books and learned the techniques of debate and argumentation, but this activity was closely tied to moral training, self-analysis, and spiritual direction. These ancient teachers were, to use a modern cliché, interested in the "whole person," mind, heart, and will. Their goal was to form the lives of their students in light of the ideal set forth in the Scriptures and imaged in Christ. The school of Alexandria was a school for training in virtue.

Gregory introduces in chapter 5 the pattern of study under Origen's direction and indicates that the school was not an institution in the conventional sense, but rather a group of disciples gathered about a master. In the preceding sections Gregory had spoken about his own background and former studies and the specific circumstances that brought him to Caesarea. But toward the end of the section he says that he had only narrated the external circumstances; the true reason he came to Palestine was that he wanted to have "fellowship with this man (*hē pros ton andra touton koinonia*)" and through him to be led to "salvation (*sōtērian*)."[12] Gregory was attracted by Origen's great learning and his fame as an interpreter of Scripture, but in the speech he stresses Origen's spiritual and moral qualities. From the time he became a student, Origen urged him "to adopt a philosophical life (*protrepōn philosophein*)," for he said that "only those who live a life truly fitting reasonable creatures and seek to live uprightly, and who seek to know first who they are, and to strive for those things that are truly good and to shun those which are truly evil . . . are lovers of philosophy."[13]

Origen expected his students to adopt a new way of life, the philosophical life. To "philosophize" meant turning from one's former ways, fundamentally changing one's life—not simply to be "reformed (*emendari*)," said Seneca (c. 1–65), but to be "transformed (*transfigurari*)."[14] When Rogotianus, a senator, joined the school of Plotinus (c. 205–270) he renounced public life, "gave up his property, dismissed his servants, and resigned his rank. . . . He would not even keep his own house to live in, but went the round of his friends and acquaintances, dining at one house and sleeping at another (but he only ate every other day)."[15] The philosophical life required a choice, a conscious decision to embark on a new way. "The entrance to the philosophical life was a difficult inner battle between the old and the new life," writes Paul Rabbow.[16] As a consequence, Gregory Thaumaturgus resisted Origen's exhortations even though he had come to study under him. Though Origen's "words struck like an arrow," Gregory says he nevertheless "held back from practicing philosophy (*philosophein*), not allowing himself to be fully convinced," preferring instead to spend his time "in arguments and intellectual debate."[17]

Gregory uses the term "philosophy" in the sense current in the Greco-Roman world of his time, to designate a moral way of life.[18] Philosophers trained their students in the art of living, to seek justice and philanthropy, to cope with anger, lust, desire, fear of death, worldly goods, and ambition and showed them the way to a life of virtue and piety. One cannot be "truly pious (*eusebein holōs*) without leading a philosophical life (*philosophesanti*)," writes Gregory.[19] Galen (129–c. 199) uses the term in the same sense when he observes that Christians in their contempt for death, their restraint in sexual matters, their self-discipline in food and drink, and their pursuit of justice have "attained a pitch not inferior to those who live a truly philosophical life."[20] The themes of philosophical discourses (*diatribē*) were moral, personal, and religious. Philosophers sought not simply to instruct but even more to persuade people to take up a new and more rewarding way of life.

In the school of Alexandria, students were expected to submit to a moral and spiritual training that would transform their lives. The proper term for this is "conversion," and it is clear that this was Origen's goal. Those who came to him had undoubtedly shown an interest in Christianity and may even have had some prior association with the church, but they had not yet made the hard choice to adopt the Christian discipline. Hence students like Gregory initially resisted Origen's entreaties. Origen expected more than an understanding of his teachings; he wished to "move the soul" of his hearers, and he challenged them to give their hearts and to bend their wills. A student who heard his lectures and was not changed missed the whole point of his teaching. In Gregory's phrase: he "taught us to practice (*prattein epaideuse*) justice and prudence."[21]

Gregory makes clear that the key factor in helping the students achieve this goal was not a set of precepts or rules. Instead, Origen sought to change the lives of his students by establishing a personal and intimate relation with them. Gregory is speaking about spiritual direction, but it is significant that he calls it "friendship (*philia*)." Friendship, he says, is "not something one can easily resist, it is piercing and penetrating, an affable and affectionate disposition which is shown in the [teacher's] words and his association with us." Through Origen, Gregory learned to love the Word "whose beauty attracts irresistibly," but he also began to love Origen as well, "the friend and interpreter" of the Word. Only when he was "smitten by this love" was he persuaded to give up "those objects which stood in the way and to practice the philosophical life."[22]

Gregory compares his new relation with Origen to the friendship between David and Jonathan, one of the most beautiful stories of love and affection in the Scriptures. He was joined to Origen "as the soul of Jonathan was attached to David." What is remarkable about Gregory's comments on his relation to Origen is that he does not say the obvious, namely, that as a disciple he admired and cherished his teacher. Rather, he says that the affection originated with the teacher and that Origen was the dominant person in cultivating the friendship. "This David of ours [Origen] holds us, binding us to him now and from the time we met him; even if we wish, we are not able to detach ourselves from his bonds."[23]

It is clear that Origen's love for his disciples was part of the process of education. The master had first to know and love his disciples before he could cultivate their souls as a "skilled husbandman" and make an "uncultivated field" bear fruit. He had to know his students' habits and attitudes if he was to correct, reprove, encourage, and exhort them. This Origen did by "digging deeply and examining what is most inward, asking questions, setting forth ideas, listening to the responses" of his students. When he found anything "unfruitful and without profit in us," he set about clearing the soil, turning it over, watering it, and using all his "skill and concern" that we might bring forth good fruit.[24]

The agricultural metaphor is commonplace, but it helps shed light on an aspect of the philosophical schools of this period. The school was defined not by a fixed curriculum or course of studies but by the personal relation between master and disciple. To enter the school was to submit oneself to a system of spiritual direction, a "leading of the soul (*psychagoge*)," to use the phrase of Paul Rabbow. This period in history was "the epoch of the methodological leading of the soul (*Seelenleitung*)."[25] The school's method of teaching was chiefly oral and involved moral and spiritual exercises. One discipline was to meditate on the sayings of the sages, for example, the collection of sayings passed down under the name of Pythagoras (6th cent. B.C.E.). Galen describes how he used these sayings: "You may be sure that I have grown accustomed to ponder twice a day the exhortations attributed to Pythagoras—first I read them over, then I recite them aloud." For Galen the sentences were not seen as metaphysical or moral truths alone, pearls of wisdom on human life, but as instruments through which one learned self-control. They helped him overcome "voluptuous eating, carnal lust, drunkenness, excessive curiosity, and envy."[26]

A collection of sayings of this sort was put together by a Christian at the end of the second century. The *Sentences of Sextus* is a collection of over four hundred sayings on all phases of life: gluttony, loquacity, sex, marriage, death, sleep, wealth, pride, self-knowledge, happiness, fate, hypocrisy, ambition, self-love, self-control, wisdom, fame, and so on. There are close parallels between Sextus and Clement of Alexandria, and it is likely that the

Sentences of Sextus come from the same spiritual milieu.[27] Although some of the sayings deal with metaphysical and theological topics, the majority are moral and are designed to show the way to perfection. It is possible that in the day-to-day life of the school of Alexandria sayings such as these were used as aids for meditation as the sentences of Pythagoras were used by Galen. The *Sentences* not only set forth the virtues to which one should aspire, they served also as moral exercises and helped the students inculcate new attitudes and develop new habits. They also aided students in the task of self-examination. Self-knowledge, "to be attentive to one's soul" in Gregory's phrase, was one of the principles taught in the school.[28]

By the very nature of the goals of the school, instruction was largely individual. The teacher no doubt gave general lectures, but the real work of education took place in the one-to-one relationship between teacher and student, "soul to soul, spirit to spirit," as Clement puts it. This principle is echoed in the philosophical writings from the time. In one of the letters attributed (falsely) to Apollonius of Tyana (1st cent. C.E.), the author explains why he stopped giving lectures to large audiences: "No discourse can be really useful, unless it is delivered to a single individual." And Plutarch (before 50–after 120): "Admonitions to specific persons produce the most useful fruit."[29]

The teachers in Alexandria preferred oral instruction directed at specific persons. If one is able, says Clement, to address "those who are present," one can "test them in time and evaluate them according to one's judgment, . . . watch their words, their habits, their behavior patterns, the life, the movement, the attitudes, the look, the voice. . . ." For this reason Clement was wary of trying to teach through "one voice," the written. "To the one who inquires," written works "answer nothing beyond that which is written; for they require of necessity the assistance of someone else, either the author himself or another who has followed in his path." Ideally the teacher should have only one student, and for the gnostic, the one who truly knows and understands the truth of God, "it is sufficient if he has only one hearer."[30]

This emphasis on the one-to-one relationship between master and disciple, and the requirement that the master lead the student down a path he has already traversed, points to yet another characteristic of the school of Alexandria: the teacher was a model for the student. Origen taught us, says Gregory, by "his own moral behavior," for he was himself an "example (*paradeigma*) of the wise man." The reason for this principle is simple. Virtue cannot be taught by words alone. It can be learned only by observing the actions of good men and women. Consequently, in an effort to teach us to "gain control over our inclinations" Origen taught us "not only by words but also by his actions."[31]

The importance of example for teaching is an ancient principle familiar to any good teacher, but what must be emphasized here is that its centrality in Gregory's speech underscores that the purpose of school was moral formation. In the preface to his *Life of Pericles*, Plutarch explains that models "inspire us to attain our own proper virtue. . . . The examples and actions of good men implant an eager rivalry and a keen desire to imitate them. . . . Moral good . . . has a power to attract towards itself. It is no sooner seen than it rouses the spectator to action."[32]

Models are not simply ideals to emulate. They can also place before us a noble life which, when compared to our own, forces us to look inwardly at our own shortcomings. Seneca cites the words of Epicurus (341–270 B.C.E.): "Cherish some man of high character, and keep him ever before your eyes, living as if he were watching you and ordering all your actions as if he beheld them." To which he adds his own comments:

> We can get rid of sins (*peccatorum*) if we have a witness who stands near us when we are likely to go wrong. The soul should have someone whom it can respect—one by whose authority it may make even its inner shrine more hallowed. Happy is the man who can make others better, not merely when he is in their company, but when he is in their thoughts. . . . One who can so revere another, will soon be himself worthy of reverence. Choose therefore a Cato; or if Cato seems too severe a model, choose some Laelius, a gentler spirit. Choose a master whose life, conversation, and soul-expressing face have satisfied you; picture him always to yourself as your protector or your pattern (*exemplum*). For we must indeed have someone according to whom we may regulate our characters; you can never straighten that which is crooked unless you use a ruler.[33]

Although the idea of a model to which one aspires and against which to measure one's life is present within earliest Christianity, it does not play a major role.[34] Paul urged the Corinthians to be "imitators of me, as I am of Christ," and Ignatius of Antioch (c. 35–c. 107) exhorted the Philadelphians "to imitate Jesus Christ as he imitated the Father." The significant role of examples in Christian formation begins to become apparent only in the third century. Most of the earlier ethical material comes in the form of precepts, for example, the Sermon on the Mount, the maxims in the Book of James, the ethical sections in the Apologists and in the writings of Clement of Alexandria, and the *Sentences of Sextus*. Precepts, however, lack emotional power, and there are hints in the writings of Clement that precepts must be complemented by examples. One chapter in the *Paidagogos* suggests that examples (*eikones* and *hypodeigmata*) are the most effective means to teach virtue.[35] Within a generation of Gregory's appreciation of Origen, the deacon Pontius, a disciple of Bishop Cyprian of Carthage (d. 258), was writing the first Christian biography. His purpose in writing the work was to lift up the "noble pattern (*documentum*)" of Cyprian's life so that his deeds may be "kept alive in perpetual memory."[36] It would not be long before the writing of lives of holy men and women became the most popular means of teaching the Christian life.

By setting forth the necessity of examples in teaching, Gregory helps us see the importance of moral formation in the school of Alexandria. The highest praise he gives Origen as a teacher is that he showed his students how to live by his own life. Too many people, says Gregory, try to teach virtue by precept or by lectures on the meaning of the virtues. Origen, however,

> did not accustom us [to practice the virtues] by words which told us, for example, that prudence is knowledge of the good and evil or what ought to be done and not done. For this is a vain and useless study, if the word is divorced from acts, and if prudence does not do the things that ought to be done and shun those which should not be done, only giving knowledge to those who possess it, as we see with many persons.

This was not Origen's way of teaching. "Rather, he exhorted us by his actions and incited us more by what he did than by what he said."[37]

Ethics or moral philosophy is not the sole topic of Gregory's address. It also includes sections on the natural sciences, on philosophy, and on the Holy Scriptures. It is sometimes thought that in these passages Gregory is describing the various stages of study through which the student passed. But this gives a misleading view of the whole enterprise, for it suggests that ethics is simply one of the stages in the curriculum. A closer reading will show that moral formation was the reason the other studies were undertaken.

"The most important things of all," writes Gregory, "on account of which every philosophy school labors . . . are the divine virtues which concern the moral character (*ēthos*)." Gregory specifically mentions the four cardinal virtues—prudence, temperance, justice, courage—without which it is impossible to live a truly philosophical life. The section on the virtues is the longest in the address, and here more than in any other section he is not satisfied with general comments. He discusses the virtues in detail, and at the end of the section he sums up Origen's teaching: "This remarkable man, friend, and herald of the virtues . . . has, by his own virtue, made us love the beauty of justice, whose golden face he truly showed us." He also showed us prudence, wisdom, temperance, courage, patience, and above all "piety . . . the mother of the virtues."[38]

We miss the significance of Gregory's oration if we see ethics simply as one part of the curriculum. Clement of Alexandria's writings can help us see what lies behind Gregory's comments.

Clement's *Paidagogos* (*The Tutor*) is a treatise on ethics, the most extensive presentation in early Christianity of concrete rules for all areas of human life—eating, drinking, bathing, behavior at banquets, laughter, cosmetics, clothes, behavior in the baths, wealth, and so on. It is almost a guide to good manners. In the opening passage of the *Paidagogos*, Clement explains that the Logos has various roles. The first is to invite men and women to salvation (this is called *protreptikos*). Next comes his role as tutor (*paidagōgos*): "The role of the tutor is to improve the soul, not to teach, to train it in the virtuous life, not the intellectual life." The same Logos performs the several functions, but in the *Paidagogos* the Logos does not teach; he establishes us in the "moral life."[39]

This passage seems to suggest that training in the moral life will eventually give way to a more advanced level of instruction. This more advanced level has been thought to be presented in the *Stromateis*, where Clement deals with theology, providence, the theory of the sage (the gnostic), the Logos, the ends of human life, physics, and the relation of morality to theology. The implication then is that the *Paidagogos* deals with ethics, the *Stromateis* with theology and other lofty matters.

But as Méhat has shown in his study of the *Stromateis*, such a distinction is too neat, obscuring the relation between the two works rather than illuminating it. The separation between the *Paidagogos* and the *Stromateis* is not as radical as it would appear. "The Stromateis is also a work of morality," he writes. It is addressed to the same hearers as the *Paidagogos*, and it assumes that its readers have not reached moral perfection. The chief difference between the two is that the *Paidagogos* seldom gives reasons; it simply sets forth rules and precepts. The *Stromateis*, on the other hand, has few details, few specifics about the moral life, almost no precepts. Nevertheless, says Méhat, it is "always morality with which [Clement] is concerned." In the *Paidagogos* he is preoccupied with the more elementary duties, the realm of practical morality, lack of discipline in habits, evil conversation, pride, luxury; in the *Stromateis* his interest shifts to deeper concerns: ignorance, disobedience to the Logos in general, those virtues which lead to perfection, wisdom, and piety.[40]

Once again contemporary moral philosophy can help us understand the Alexandrian school's approach to education. In one of his letters, Seneca addresses a question concerning the role of precepts in moral formation. Someone asked whether the "parenetic" aspect of philosophy, that is, precepts for life, is sufficient if one is to become a wise person and live a life of virtue. Some argued: "The happy life consists in upright conduct; precepts guide one to upright conduct; therefore precepts are sufficient for attaining the happy life." Seneca, however, argues that precepts are not enough: one must also have what the Greeks call *dogmata* (doctrines), or what the Romans call *decreta* (doctrines), *scita* (tenets), and *placita* (opinions), for philosophy is "both theoretic and practical; it contemplates and at the same time acts." Philosophy is concerned about the place of one's actions within the whole universe. Without a consideration of this larger context, precepts are "weak" and "rootless." "It is the doctrines which will strengthen and support us in peace and calm, which will include simultaneously the whole of life and the universe in its completeness." It is difficult to change people's lives, says Seneca (he provides a whole string of illustrations), especially when they have grown accustomed to evil ways. For this reason something more is required than precepts, because "to root out a deep-seated belief in wrong ideas, conduct must be regulated by doctrines." Without such general principles, precepts are ineffective, for if we are to free persons from their bonds and tear them from the evil which clutches them, "they learn what is evil and what is good." Hence, he concludes, citing Posidonius (c. 135–c. 51 B.C.E.), that precepts alone are insufficient; to these must be added "the investigation of causes."[41]

So when Origen is said to have gone on to the "teaching of theology and spirituality (*theologias didaskalian kai eulabeian*)" after presenting ethics and to have instructed his students in the "knowledge of the cause of all things," or when Clement speaks of the "tutor" as giving way to the "teacher," this should not be taken to mean that they sought to elevate their students to a spiritual plane which transcended ethics or moral philosophy.[42] Rather, they were insisting that the goal of the Christian is perfection and that this cannot be achieved simply by presenting moral precepts or maxims. Whoever desires to "excel in every virtue" must also know and love God. The seeker after virtue must have an intimate relation with the one who is the source of virtue, the author of the precepts and commands. Both the elementary instruction in ethics and the more advanced teaching have the same end: to form the soul in purity that it may become "like God and remain in him." An examination of the school of Alexandria leads inevitably to a fuller consideration of the theology of the Alexandrian teachers, particularly the role of God's grace in forming the soul of the virtuous person. "The virtues are so great and exalted," says Gregory, "that none can be obtained by just any person, but only in the one in whom God has breathed the power."[43]

This last consideration, however, goes beyond the present assignment. We have seen that the school of Alexandria was a school for training in virtue, and what we have learned is that the life of virtue cannot be undertaken alone. We need guides. We must learn how to live virtuously, and the most effective teacher is another human person whose life shows us the way. As Leontius, Bishop of Neapolis in Cyprus in the seventh century, wrote in the introduction of his *Life of Symeon the Fool*:

> For those who are zealously devoted in soul to God, conscience is sufficient basis for teaching. It exhorts us to do good things and diverts us from evil things. To those who are more humble than these, there is need of the precepts of the law and exhortation. If, however, someone slips through the first or second way which leads to virtue, such a one can only be aroused to desire God . . . , and to pursue the hard and difficult way, by the zeal and devotion of those whose lives he sees or about whom he hears a story.[44]

NOTES

1. E. Molland, *The Conception of the Gospel in the Alexandrian Theology* (Oslo, 1938), 65; P. Léturia, "El primer esbozo de una universidad Católica o la escuela catequética de Alejandria," *Razon y Fe* 106 (1934): 297–314.

2. A. von Harnack, *Lehrbuch der Dogmengeschichte*, 5th ed. (Tübingen, 1931), 1:637.

3. References to the school in Eusebius, *Ecclesiastical History* 5.10.2; 6.3.8; 14.11, 15.1, 28.1; 7.32.30.

4. J. Munck, *Untersuchungen über Klemens von Alexandrien* (Stuttgart, 1933), 185. Among the more important articles are: G. Bardy, "Aux origines de l'École d'Alexandrie," *RSR* 27 (1937): 65–90; A. Knauber, "Katechetenschule oder Schulkatechumenat? Um die rechte Deutung des 'Unternehmens' der ersten groszen Alexandriner," *TThZ* 60 (1951): 243–66; M. Hornschuh, "Das Leben des Origenes und die Entstehung der alexandrinische Schule," *ZKG* 71 (1960): 1–25, 193–214.

5. A. Méhat, *Étude sur les "Stromates" de Clément d'Alexandrie*, PatSor 7 (Paris, 1966), 62–70. The consensus has been most recently stated by C. D. G. Müller, "Alexandrien I.3: Die 'Katechetenschule,'" *TRE* 1 (1978): 253–54.

6. Eusebius, *Ecclesiastical History* 5.10; Knauber, "Katechetenschule oder Schulkatechumenat?" 259.

7. H. Chadwick and J. E. L. Oulton, *Alexandrian Christianity*, LCC 2 (Philadelphia, 1954), 173.

8. Origen, *Homilies on Jeremiah* 5.13, in P. Nautin and P. Husson, *Origène: Homélies sur Jérémie*, SC 238 (Paris, 1976), 152.

9. Nautin believes that the name Theodore, which according to Eusebius is another name for Gregory, is in fact another person, and he attributes the speech to this Theodore, not to Gregory, Bishop of Neocaesarea in Pontus: *Origène. Sa vie et son oeuvre*, Christianisme antique 1 (Paris, 1977), 81–86.

10. W. Völker, *Das Vollkommenheitsideal des Origenes* (Tübingen, 1933), 230–33; P. Koetschau, *Des Gregorios Thaumaturgos Dankrede an Origenes* (Freiburg, 1894), x; H. Crouzel, "Saint Grégoire le Thaumaturge," *Dictionnaire de Spiritualité* 6 (1967): 1016. For Jerome's characterization of the text, see *Lives of Illustrious Men* 65.

11. A. Knauber, "Das Anliegen der Schule des Origenes zu Caesarea," *MThZ* 19 (1968): 182–203. For a discussion of Knauber, see H. Crouzel, "L'École d'Origène à Césarée," *BLE* 71 (1970): 15–27.

12. Gregory Thaumaturgus, *Panegyric* 5.70. I cite Gregory's speech in the edition of H. Crouzel. *Grégoire le Thaumaturge. Remerciement à Origène suivi de la Lettre d'Origène à Grégoire*, SC 148 (Paris, 1969).

13. *Panegyric* 6.75, 78.

14. Seneca, *Epistles* 6.1.

15. Porphyry, *Life of Plotinus* 7, trans. A. H. Armstrong, *Plotinus*, LCL (Cambridge: 1966), 1:27–29.

16. P. Rabbow, *Seelenführung. Methodik der Exerzitien in der Antike* (Munich, 1954), 261.

17. *Panegyric* 6.78.

18. On the term "philosophy," see A.-M. Malingrey, *"Philosophia": Étude d'un groupe de mots dans la littérature grecque, des Présocratiques au IVe siècle après J.-C.* (Paris, 1961). For its appropriation by Christians, see R. L. Wilken, "Towards a Social Interpretation of Early Christian Apologetics," *ChH* 39 (1970): 437–58.

19. *Panegyric* 6.79.

20. R. Walzer, *Galen on Jews and Christians* (London, 1949), 15.

21. Origen, *Homilies on Jeremiah* 20.6; *Panegyric* 11.141.

22. *Panegyric* 6.81, 84.

23. Ibid., 6.85, 92.

24. Ibid., 6.93, 95.

25. Rabbow, *Seelenfuhrüng*, 17.

26. Galen, *On the Passions and Errors of the Soul* 6, trans. P. W. Harkins (Columbus, Ohio, 1963), 49.

27. On the place of the *Sentences of Sextus* in early Christian "philosophy," see R. L. Wilken, "Wisdom and Philosophy in Early Christianity," in R. L. Wilken, ed., *Aspects of Wisdom in Judaism and Early Christianity* (Notre Dame, 1975), 143–68. See also the essay by W. Schoedel, "Jewish Wisdom and the Formation of the Christian Ascetic," in the same volume (pp. 169–99), on another collection of "sayings" from Alexandria, *The Teachings of Silvanus*.

28. *Panegyric* 11.141.

29. Clement, *Stromateis* 1.2.1; "Apollonius," trans. F. C. Conybeare, LCL (Cambridge, 1962), 2:417. *Epistles* 10; Plutarch, *On Listening to Lectures* 43–44.

30. *Stromateis* 1.9.1; 1.14.4; 1.10.4.

31. *Panegyric* 11.133; 11.135; 9.118.

32. Plutarch, *Pericles* 1.1—2.4.

33. Seneca, *Epistles* 11.8, trans. Richard Gummere, LCL (Cambridge, 1961), 1:65.

34. This is not to say that imitation is not a significant motif in early Christian literature, but during the first centuries imitation is seen chiefly in terms of imitation of Christ and God. See H. Crouzel, "L'Imitation et la 'suite' de Dieu et du Christ dans les premiers siècles chrétiens, ainsi que leurs sources gréco-romaines et hébraïques," *JAC* 21 (1978): 7–41.

35. 1 Cor. 11:1; Ignatius of Antioch, *Philadelphians* 7.2; Clement, *Paidagogos* 3.8.

36. A. von Harnack, ed., *Vita Cypriani*, TU 39/3 (Leipzig, 1913), 5.

37. *Panegyric* 9.123, 126.

38. Ibid., 9.115; 12.147–49.

39. *Paidagogos* 1.1.4; 1.2.1. On the opening passages of the *Paidagogos*, see Méhat, *Étude*, 71–95.

40. Méhat, *Étude*, 506–7.

41. Seneca, *Epistles* 95.4, 12, 35, 65, trans. Gummere, LCL, 3:61ff.

42. *Panegyric* 13.150; *Paidagogos* 1.1.4.

43. *Stromateis* 7.88, 101; 4.130; 4.55; *Panegyric* 12.149, 145.

44. PG 93.1669–71.

3

Christian Culture and Christian Tradition in Roman North Africa

William S. Babcock

Despite all that is known about the early history of Christian theology, the actual processes by which doctrine was taught and learned remain obscure. There is some evidence for the office of teacher in the earliest Christian communities, but that office, whatever its functions may have been, barely survived into the second century. Although such later Christian "teachers" as Justin Martyr (c. 100–c. 165) or Origen (c. 185–c. 254) may have been prized by the congregations with which they were associated, they do not appear to have held an ecclesiastical office. And in the middle of the third century, when Bishop Cornelius enumerated his clergy in Rome, he listed forty-six presbyters, forty-two acolytes, and fifty-two exorcists, but no teachers.[1]

The *Apostolic Tradition* of Hippolytus (c. 170–c. 236), written in Rome early in the third century, contains tantalizing hints of some kind of instruction designed for catechumens prior to baptism. Unfortunately, however, the scanty surviving evidence does not permit us to see how or even whether catechetical training, as a setting for the teaching and learning of Christian doctrine, significantly shaped the early church's theological tradition.

The case of Augustine is instructive. Augustine (354–430) grew up in a culture—the culture of post-Constantinian Roman North Africa—that was at least nominally Christian, and in a family that was linked to the church through his mother's unrelenting devotion. Yet nowhere in the autobiographical portions of his *Confessions* does he mention any training in Christianity sponsored or made available by the church itself. Including no Christian counterweight

31

to the traditional course of study, his education followed a standard Roman pattern, culminating in rhetoric, which launched his own career as a rhetor, first in Carthage, then in Rome, and finally in Milan.

By Augustine's own account, the chief moments in his intellectual development, and in particular the moments that marked the path of his return to catholic Christianity, appear to have happened almost by accident and quite apart from any ecclesiastical apparatus of teaching and learning. For instance, it was a mere acquaintance who supplied him, in Milan, with the famous *libri Platonici* that played such a critical role in shaping his theological outlook.[2] It is significant, too, that even after his "conversion," when Augustine wished to pursue his study of Christianity, he did so among a group of friends whom he had gathered for himself and in a retreat supplied by yet another friend. There was nothing specifically Christian or ecclesiastically sponsored about Augustine's leisurely studies and cultivated conversations at Cassiciacum. He was simply embracing the ancient ideal of a cultured retirement (*otium liberale*), with a Christian focus that he had given it himself.

Even after his ordination in 391, when Augustine felt a desperate need for additional study of Scripture to prepare himself for the priesthood, he did his reading and his thinking on his own. It is not too much to say that in the sphere of Christian theology and doctrine Augustine was an autodidact. Nor is there any reason to believe that Augustine's case, at least in this respect, was sharply at odds with the experience of other early Christian theologians. Whatever catechetical training they may have received remains largely hidden from our view.

While we cannot say with certainty what the teaching and learning of Christian doctrine in the early church was, we can say what it was not: it was not a scholastic enterprise in anything like the modern or even the ancient sense. With the possible exception of the so-called catechetical school of Alexandria or of schools that may have gathered around individual figures like Origen, teaching did not take place in anything that could be labeled an academic setting. Neither the patterns of early and secondary education nor the more advanced rhetorical or philosophic schools (if that is the right word) of late antiquity have any Christian analogues in the first centuries of the church's existence.[3] Consequently the early history of Christianity shows few signs of that tension between the academic theologian and the ecclesiastical hierarchy or the Christian community at large which became increasingly characteristic of Western Christianity after the emergence of the medieval university in the twelfth century.

In contrast, the theological tensions of the patristic era tended to be between bishop and bishop, community and community, rather than between church and academy. It is true, of course, that catechetical training appears to have become a major vehicle for the teaching and learning of Christian theology in the late fourth and early fifth centuries, for several major sets of catechetical lectures from this period have survived. But these lectures were delivered by the bishop himself, and they served to initiate new Christians into the local ecclesiastical community.

Thus, even where a specifically educational setting can be identified, it provided no independent standing or institutional support for an opposition theology. And in any case, such catechetical instruction lacked the characteristic features—for example, study of texts, student exercises—of more formal academic study, whether ancient or modern. So if we are to understand how doctrine was taught and learned in the early church, we must look to less clearly defined and less obviously educational factors in the life of patristic Christianity. We must look to the more subtle processes by which a culture is transmitted and a tradition given shape without benefit of the institutions of education, without benefit of a distinct class of teachers and learners.

Roman North Africa is no exception to the general rule. Here, too, the processes by which doctrine was taught and learned and shaped into an ongoing tradition remain obscure, and their setting is uncertain. We do have one large and relevant collection of evidence, both for North Africa and for patristic Christianity in general: the theological writings on which the study of early Christian doctrine is actually based. But the very clarity of the evidence may be misleading. We know what was written, but we know very little about how it circulated or who read it or what reading was like in that era. Augustine gives us a rare glimpse of a reader in late antiquity when, in the *Confessions,* he pictures Bishop Ambrose of Milan (c. 339–397) engrossed in study, reading to himself in the rare intervals between visitors.[4] Augustine feels obliged to search for some explanation for Ambrose's unusual practice of reading silently rather than out loud, and his uneasiness on this point reminds us how close to spoken discourse reading ordinarily was.

Augustine can also provide an example of the painful slowness

33

with which a work might circulate and reactions to it take shape. In a letter of 396 or 397 to Bishop Aurelius of Carthage, Augustine asks for Aurelius's opinion of Tyconius's *Book of Rules*, "as I have often written before."[5] Whether Aurelius ever replied is unknown, but it was not until some thirty years later that Augustine made open and acknowledged use of Tyconius's work. Were other copies of the book circulating and being read in the interim? Probably, although perhaps not very many. In any case, it is clear that we can assume no massive and nearly instantaneous spread of a written work through a given reading public in something like the modern manner. The progress of the written word was slow, uneven, and haphazard. We cannot think of an ancient writing as an instrument of instruction in any modern sense.

We may be misled in this regard by our own experience of books as essentially impersonal writings circulating among large and faceless audiences who read in silence to themselves. The writings of late antiquity were personal, directed to particular individuals or to specific groups, caught up in networks of personal relationships. Certain of Augustine's works provide clear and vivid examples. His early writings against Pelagianism amount virtually to an exchange of letters with Marcellinus, an imperial official in Carthage. Marcellinus submitted a list of questions to Augustine, and in response Augustine wrote *On the Merits and Forgiveness of Sins and on the Baptism of Infants* (412). Marcellinus was puzzled by one of Augustine's points; Augustine explained in *On the Spirit and the Letter* (412). Similarly *On Nature and Grace* (413–415), a reply to Pelagius's *On Nature*, was written specifically to the two persons who had sent Augustine a copy of Pelagius's work; and toward the end of the Pelagian controversy, the two treatises *On Grace and Free Will* and *On Rebuke and Grace* (426–427) find their immediate context in Augustine's correspondence with Valentinus, an abbot whose monks had raised questions about Augustine's teaching. Such "epistolary" writings—and the list could be expanded at considerable length—do not belong to the category of purely private and personal correspondence. They were meant to circulate well beyond their initial recipients. But they do show how patristic writings were often embedded in personal contexts. They must be located within the particular circles of friends and acquaintances to which they were directed and whose shared outlook they helped to create.

If we move back from Augustine to Cyprian (d. 258), Bishop of Carthage in the middle of the third century, we find the situation is not dissimilar. If Cyprian's writings are less obviously personal in form than Augustine's, their personal setting is still provided by the extensive collection of his surviving correspondence. In his case, of course, the "personal" setting, since it is chiefly defined by his relations with the clergy and laity of his own diocese and by his interaction with other bishops in North Africa and in Italy, has a more "official" cast than does Augustine's—which may account for the more anonymous tone of Cyprian's works.

Among North Africa's three great patristic theologians, it is only in the case of Tertullian (c. 160–c. 220), the earliest of them, that we cannot reconstruct an immediate personal setting for his theological writings on the basis either of a surviving correspondence or of the specific form of the writings themselves. Yet Tertullian's works are thoroughly rhetorical in character. In structure and in phrasing, that is, in both movement of thought and pattern of wording, they reflect the standard practices of classical rhetoric as classified and codified, for example, by Quintilian (c. 30–c. 100) a century before.[6] Even here then—and the same could be said of Cyprian and Augustine—we should think of the written works as spoken discourses, directed to the particular audiences that Tertullian had before him in imagination if not in reality (and at least some of his works may well have originated as sermons or as speeches). Consequently there is an immediacy of interaction between author and audience in the works of patristic theologians which we tend to overlook because we assimilate their writings to our own experience of the anonymous written word rather than to personal and spoken discourse. If reading in late antiquity stood close to oral discourse, so did writing—and we must learn to read the writings of the theologians accordingly.

Oral and personal discourse depend, in a special degree, on a shared context common to both speaker and hearer. The elements of that context—images, concepts, traditions, sayings—provide the common ground occupied by both parties. They are the features of the shared situation to which speakers can appeal with the expectation that their discourse will be understood and approved—or which they must array in their own favor if they are to win acceptance for unusual or controversial claims. They are the points which the hearer will recognize in what the speaker says, responding to them with a sense of familiarity and using them, virtually without thought, to interpret what is said. These elements of discourse mark the contours of the terrain within which understanding can be assumed or achieved. Or when they come themselves to be in dispute and begin to serve as boundary markers rather than con-tour lines, they locate the points at which the divergence between speaker and hearer will be most basic and most acute.

The common features of a shared context may function, then, in a variety of ways. They may bind a group together by supplying it with shared patterns of imagery, of thought, of experience, and of expression. They may link that group to other groups whose vocabularies of image and concept are substantially the same, or separate it from groups whose vocabularies do not overlap its own. And when they are interpreted or deployed in conflicting rather than common patterns, they may become the focal points for bitter controversy within the group itself.

It would be difficult and probably impossible, even if space allowed, to delineate fully the common context of North African Christianity in the patristic era. There is at once too much and too little evidence available. All the works of Tertullian, of Cyprian, and of Augustine, not to mention the minor authors and the declara-tions of various church councils, would have to be sifted from this point of view. At the same time, despite all the progress that has been made in the archaeology of Roman North Africa in recent years, we have relatively little access to such nonliterary forms of expression as visual imagery, funeral inscriptions, and graffiti. At most, then, we can hope to isolate a few of the common features of Christian culture in North Africa and to show how they, at least, helped to shape and define the complex tradition of North African Christianity.

There was, in the first place, a common imagery, a range of mental pictures to which appeal could be made in various circum-stances and for a variety of purposes. In large measure these images were drawn from Scripture, but they circulated and func-tioned independently, and their meaning or import cannot be fixed simply by referring to the biblical texts in which they occur.

Especially prominent were two images from the Book of Daniel: Daniel himself in the lions' den, and the three Hebrews in the fiery furnace. It is easy to see where the basic appeal of the images lay. Tertullian presents the three Hebrews as a "familiar example" of resistance to idolatry and reinforces his point by picturing a Daniel who "showed no more fear of the king's lions than they had shown of the king's fires."[7] But the same images could be deployed in vari-ous ways. Tertullian uses the three Hebrews to prove that one need not remove one's coat to pray and again, along with Daniel, to establish a contrast between the "old prayer" and the new. Christian prayer "does not establish the angel of dew in the midst of the fire" or "block the mouths of lions," but it does arm with endurance those who suffer.[8] Similarly, Cyprian finds in the three Hebrews an instance of what he calls the "law of prayer": that it should be offered in harmony to represent the unity of God's people.[9] But he can also appeal both to the three Hebrews and to Daniel as examples of the humility which ought to keep even those who have suffered persecution in Christ's name from supposing that they are now without sin or that they have no further need to make satisfaction to God.[10] Here, then, we have a classic case of shared imagery, linking speaker and hearer, functioning in a variety of contexts and serving a variety of purposes. In each case, however, it is the basic import of the imagery—the fundamental picture of loyalty to God in the face of idolatry and persecution—that makes the imagery effective and gives it persuasive power.

A second feature of the shared culture of North African Christianity is the heroic figure of the martyr. The earliest surviving literary evidence for Christianity in North Africa, apart from a Latin biblical text, is the account of the Scillitan martyrs, a group of Christians tried and executed for their faith late in the second century. The phenomenon of martyrdom left a deep and lasting imprint on North African Christianity. We can get some sense of its shape and impact from the *Martyrdom of Saints Perpetua and Felicitas*, a report of the martyrdom of several Carthaginian Christians in the year 203.

Perpetua, a young woman of some social standing, was one of the arrested Christians, and the document includes a kind of "prison diary" in which she herself records her experience in prison. It is a remarkable account. While in prison, Perpetua was visited by her father, who came to persuade her to save herself, for the sake of her family and especially her newborn child, by renouncing her Christianity. The interview ended, suddenly and dramatically, when Perpetua insisted that she could not be called "anything other than what I am, a Christian." Her father went away defeated, and she reports that for the next few days, "I gave thanks to the Lord that I was separated from my father and I was comforted by his absence."[11] The comment is rendered all the more poignant by Perpetua's belief that her father alone, of all her family, would not take pleasure in her suffering.

It would be hard to imagine a more vivid or a more penetrating demonstration of the way in which Christian belief could cut across and finally obliterate even the most intimate bonds of kinship and affection, breaking even the strongest ties that bind a person to the social order and give a person a familiar place within that order. By Cyprian's time, if not before, the commemoration of the martyrs had passed into the regular liturgical calendar of the Christian communities in North Africa. Such commemoration served to keep lively and constant the shared vision of a Christianity that would not yield to the intricate social and personal pressures that compromise belief and deflect the believer from God. Long after the era of martyrs and martyrdom had ended, Augustine was still preaching on Perpetua and Felicitas and appealing to their example.

If Christianity cut the bonds of kinship, it is no accident that it should itself have taken the form of an "alternate" kinship group. The theme stands out with particular clarity in the North African tradition, where it is clustered around two more of the common elements in the life of the church, the Lord's Prayer and baptism. To say "Our Father who is in Heaven" is, according to Tertullian, to bear witness to God, to position oneself among God's sons, and to fulfill the command that we are not to call anyone on earth father, "but only him who is ours in heaven." It is also to recognize the church as "Mother," the one in whom the Christian is begotten for God.[12] That such imagery should slip over into the area of baptism was only natural: baptism is the "washing of a new birthday," and the baptized now spread out their hands (i.e., in prayer) for the first time, with their brothers and in their Mother's house.[13]

The same syndrome of images appears also and more elaborately in Cyprian, who reiterates Tertullian's view of the "Our Father" and extends the range of the image of the church as Mother by making it a weapon in his battle against heretics and schismatics. Those who instigate heresy and schism separate the sons from their Mother and from their Father as well, for "you can no longer have God for your Father if you do not have the church as your Mother."[14] There is but one Mother: "of her womb are we born, of her milk are we fed, from her Spirit our souls draw life."[15] Such imagery lends itself easily to Cyprian's famous declaration that "there is no salvation outside the church," and it undergirds his conviction that heretics do not and cannot baptize, even when their baptismal rite includes the standard baptismal formula: "baptism cannot be common to us and to the heretics with whom neither God the Father, nor Christ the Son, nor the Holy Spirit, nor faith, nor the church itself are common." Christians have their nativity in baptism, but "Where and of whom and to whom was he born who is not a son of the church?" as if anyone could "have God for Father before he has the church for Mother."[16] If baptism is birth into a kin group, it cannot function—it cannot even be baptism—outside the range of the kin group itself. Shared imagery not only serves to bind a group together; it also severs it from other groups with whom it refuses to hold the images in common. Cyprian has turned the imagery of kinship into an instrument of division.

Christianity came late to Roman North Africa, and when it came it emerged with a sharp sense for the boundaries between the Christian and the non-Christian, the church and the world. All the major elements in the shared culture that it developed for itself— the dominant biblical imagery, the heroic figure of the martyr, the picture of the Christian community as an alternate kinship group—served to define and to reinforce that sense. All the great controversies that struck North African Christianity in its early history had to do with those boundaries: how and where were they to be drawn?

It is characteristic that Tertullian should have begun his literary campaign against the Gnostic and Marcionite heresies with a treatise, *The Prescription of Heretics*, in which he argued that the heretics have no right to claim possession of Christian Scripture and therefore can neither appeal to its authority nor pretend that they are rightly interpreting its content. They fall outside the boundary within which alone Scripture is legitimately and properly used. The same theme is sounded in another key when Tertullian finds in the birth and death of Christ—which are, in fact, the birth and death of God—a stark opposition to what, outside the Christian circle, constituted all reasonable expectation and ordinary plausibility: "The Son of God was crucified: I am not ashamed—because it is shameful. The Son of God died: it is immediately credible— because it is silly. He was buried and rose again: it is certain— because it is impossible."[17] And when Tertullian himself joined the heretical and schismatic Montanists, it was because he believed the catholic churches were no longer properly respecting the boundary between Christian and non-Christian in the discipline they exercised over their congregations.

Similarly Cyprian, when he faced the problem of dealing with those who lapsed in the face of Roman persecution by denying their faith, insisted that the lapsed had transgressed the boundary and were now outside the Christian community, and that it was his prerogative and responsibility, as bishop, to determine the conditions under which they could again enter the church. The discipline of penance provided a "border crossing" by supplying the means to overcome the act of defection and to transform the dispositions that had led to that act. Cyprian's position in the subsequent controversy over the rebaptism of heretics was yet another attempt to draw and defend the boundary between the Christian and the non-Christian. Because baptism is the point of transition from world to church, it can have no legitimacy or validity when it fails to lead into the church but leads instead into heresy. Such baptism is no baptism at all; it does not actually mark the boundary between Christian and non-Christian. Cyprian maintained that he was not rebaptizing heretics who deserted their heresy to come to the church, but was rather baptizing them for the first time.

In the North African setting, then, the teaching and learning of Christian doctrine—the forming of a Christian theological tradition—should be seen as a succession of sometimes conflicting efforts to marshal the elements of the church's common culture and imagery in support of or in defense of a particular way of drawing the boundary between the Christian and the non-Christian, between the area marked out by loyalty to the one true God and the areas marked out by heresy or by idolatry. That is the purpose to which the "spoken" discourse of Tertullian's treatises and Cyprian's letters was put.

But the trouble with borders is that they inevitably breed border disputes. The great crisis of North African Christianity was just such a dispute, provoked by the emergence of the Donatist movement in the early fourth century. The immediate occasion of the crisis was the ordination of Caecilian (d. c. 345) as Bishop of Carthage in 311, in the wake of the "great persecution" initiated by the Emperor Diocletian.

The Donatists claimed that the ordination was invalid because one of the participating bishops had been a *traditor*, that is, had yielded to persecution and had "handed over" a copy of Scripture to the Roman authorities. But the force and furor of the controversy far exceeded its initial episode, so much so that historians have attempted to account for the Donatist movement as a disguised form of national or social protest against the Roman political and social order in North Africa. Such interpretations are designed, of course, to reduce the discrepancy between the minor episode in which Donatism began and the power of its appeal as an alternative to "catholic" Christianity in the North African provinces. No squabble over the ordination of a bishop is sufficient to explain the lengthy history, rapid expansion, and social cohesion of the

Donatist movement. Something more must have been at issue. Yet the notion that Donatism must have set off impulses of protest against Rome faces severe difficulties, and it fails to recognize that there were more than enough fissiparous tendencies within North African Christianity itself for Donatism to activate. No matter how slight the initial occasion, any attempt to claim the support of the Christian tradition for a clear definition of the boundary between church and world was almost bound to evoke bitter and virulent dispute.

Donatism is known to us chiefly through the hostile witness of its ancient enemies. But even such anatagonistic sources make it clear that the Donatists did, in fact, appeal to just those elements of North African Christianity's common culture that we have already examined, claiming them entirely for themselves and using them to draw a boundary that finally excluded not only all other North African Christians but all Christians outside of North Africa as well. All non-Donatists were, in their eyes, infected by the apostasy of the *traditores* because they remained in communion with Christians who had not repudiated the *traditores*. Augustine took delight in ridiculing the vast pretensions of so intensely local a group. But the matter was not ridiculous, at least not in the North African context.

The Donatists found their support in the figures of Daniel and the three Hebrews, appealing to them not only as paradigms of resistance to idolatry but also as models for the rejection of political authority in the arena of religion. In this way they could turn the core of the North African tradition against the imperial legislation which supported the "catholic" bishops and the "catholic" churches. It was the Donatists, too, who continued to seek martyrdom after the persecutions had stopped, often resorting to bizarre forms of self-inflicted death which again invited Augustine's ridicule. But ridicule was not the answer, for here too the Donatists could claim that they alone were continuing the tradition of the martyrs and had rejected the enticing prospect of an easy accommodation between church and world, a blurring of the boundary between the Christian and the non-Christian. The same motif is present in the Donatists' practice of rebaptizing those "catholics" who joined their cause. They had drawn the boundary of true Christianity tightly around themselves, and following Cyprian, they believed that anyone who crossed that boundary to join them was becoming Christian and entering the true Christian community for the first time.

There is no need, then, to appeal to disguised movements of social and political protest to explain the force and staying power of the Donatist movement. It is enough to look to the shape and character of North African Christianity's common tradition itself. It was a tradition that drew boundaries. The Donatists simply activated all that tradition's force and power when they claimed those boundaries for themselves. What lay at the heart of the matter was not social protest against Rome but the social implications of Christianity itself.

When Augustine became first priest and then bishop at Hippo Regius during the final decade of the fourth century, he also became the chief spokesman for the "catholic" opposition to Donatism. The controversy dominated his writings and permeated his preaching for the next fifteen years. It would be impossible to reduce the intricate network of themes that Augustine wove into his anti-Donatist works to a single or simple formula. It is clear enough, however, that one element in his polemic was the attempt to meet and to counter the Donatist use of the common elements in the North African tradition itself. To divert these elements from the Donatist to the "catholic" setting, he had to remake the image of Daniel and the three Hebrews, to reinterpret the core of martyrdom, and to rework Cyprian's theology of baptism. The process is visible in his treatises and in his sermons.

At Augustine's hands, Daniel and the three Hebrews become figures of those who praise God even in the midst of adversity, ascribing the adversity not to God but to their own fault and treating it as part of the divine correction that will finally restore them to God.[18] More specifically, he turns these examples against the Donatists on the very question of resistance to political force and imperial coercion in religion. Once Daniel was saved from the lions' den, the king turned against Daniel's accusers, throwing them to the lions in turn, and made a decree in favor of Daniel's God. In the same way and with the same justification, the imperial power of Rome is used against the Donatists, and its legislation favors the "catholic" cause.[19] Such argumentation is not to be passed off as merely arbitrary, whimsical, or self-serving exegesis, no matter how strained it may seem. At stake were the questions of whether and how "catholic" Christians might claim the common tradition for themselves.

In similar style, Augustine insists that the core of martyrdom lies not in the bare fact of suffering but in the cause for which one suffers and dies. "It is not the penalty, but the cause that makes martyrs."[20] True martyrs are not those who are persecuted but those who are "persecuted for righteousness' sake" (Matt. 5:10). And the imperial legislation against the Donatists is certainly not an example of persecution for righteousness' sake; it is rather an example of the exercise of the civil coercive power against those who assault God's church.[21] Thus not only must "martyr" be distinguished from martyr, but also "persecution" from persecution. The case in which the righteous are persecuted by the unrighteous for unrighteous reasons is altogether different from the case in which the unrighteous are "persecuted" by the righteous for righteous reasons, and the two cases must be carefully held apart if we are actually to recognize what does and does not count as genuine martyrdom. The mere occurrence of the event itself proves nothing. In effect, then, Augustine has used the phenomena of persecution and martyrdom to blur the one thing that the figure of the martyr had seemed to make most clear: the sharply defined and dramatically visible boundary between the Christian and the non-Christian, between the church and the alien world.

Augustine adopted much the same approach in his response to the Donatists' use of Cyprian's theology of baptism. If baptism marks the border between the Christian and the non-Christian because it is the rite in which a person is born into the alternate kinship group of the church, a nativity which gives the person God as Father and the church as Mother, so the Donatists asked, does not the "catholic" failure to rebaptize returning Donatists amount to a tacit admission that Donatist Christianity does count as the true church and, therefore (since the church must be one), that "catholic" Christianity does not? Augustine's response has the effect of shattering the identification of baptism with the boundary between the Christian and the non-Christian and obscuring the connection between baptism and birth into true Christianity. He points to the case of Simon Magus (Acts 8:9–24) to show that baptism, even when administered by the church in its unity, can give birth to false Christians as well as to true Christians. The same womb, therefore, can give birth not only to those who ultimately fall within but also to those who ultimately fall outside the boundaries of the true Christian community:

> But those who are born within the family, of the womb of the mother herself, and then neglect the grace they have received, are like Isaac's son Esau, who was rejected, God himself bearing witness to it, and saying, "I loved Jacob, and I hated Esau" [Mal. 1:2–3; Rom. 9:13]; and that though they were twin-brethren, the offspring of the same womb.

In fact, Augustine complicates the imagery of birth and kinship groupings even further, imagining two lines of motherhood, one which gives birth to true Christians and one which gives birth to false Christians, while also allowing that the first may even give birth through the second as through a handmaid. When true Christians come to birth "through the instrumentality of those who preach the gospel not sincerely, Sarah is indeed the mother, but through Hagar."[22] Thus just as false Christians may appear in the true line of motherhood (as Esau from Rebecca), true Christians may appear in the false.

In the end, using the themes of Cyprian's baptismal theology itself, Augustine has so muddled the apparently clear picture of baptism as the boundary between the Christian and the non-Christian, and has introduced such complexity into the imagery of birth and kinship, that there remains no simple formula for linking the one to the other or for using either to mark a line of division between church and world. The true boundary between the Christian and the non-Christian is more hidden and more subtle than the North African tradition had suggested, and it runs, Augustine intimates, through Christianity itself, rather than between Christianity and its environing world.

To meet the Donatist crisis, it was not enough to divert or to dilute the apparent force of the common elements in the North African Christian tradition. The sense of boundaries, of sharply divided and starkly opposed societies, conveyed by those common elements was too strong to be dissolved in ambiguity and uncertainty. If the Donatist way of drawing the borders was to be defeated, it would have to be replaced by a new way of defining and locating the edges of the genuinely Christian community—a way which would not allow one Christian group to claim those edges strictly for itself. In this respect, Augustine was anticipated from the margin of the Donatist movement itself.

Tyconius (d. c. 400) was a disaffected Donatist, and his *Book of Rules*, ostensibly a treatise on the exegesis of Scripture, was actually a vehicle for a theology of the church that undercut the Donatist view at its center. For Tyconius the church, as the body of Christ, is bipartite. It includes both the true and the false, both children of God and children of Satan. In the sense it is, in the imagery of the Song of Songs, both black and beautiful: black in that part through which the name of God is blasphemed among the nations, beautiful in that part which the Lord has cleansed with his own blood.

44

But it is black as well as beautiful only because it actually does include the false brothers. If they were outside the church, they would not make it black.[23] Consequently the boundaries of the church do not, in Tyconius's view, correspond with the border between the true and the false, between those who are genuinely Christian and those who are Christian only in pretense.

With this imagery of the church as a bipartite society, Tyconius combined themes from Romans and Galatians which help to indicate how the border between the true and the false is actually to be drawn. The role of the law, he maintained, is to direct persons to grace by teaching them that they cannot fulfill what the law requires on their own. Those who do meet the law's demands, then, are those who in faith have received the grace of God. They have not made themselves, but have been made by God, for it is the Spirit of God that performs the law within them.[24] But the boundary between those who have received grace and those who have not received grace is no longer visible to the naked eye. It is a function of the divine foreknowledge of who will yield to faith and who will refuse to give up self-reliance—and not a function of any external mark such as baptism or acts of martyrdom. Consequently Tyconius restricts the idea of the separation of the true from the false to the end-time, when the "man of sin" will be manifested and the true children of God, like Lot, will depart from Sodom.[25] Short of the end-time, however, the boundary between the two parts of Christ's body can have no clear human representation.

Augustine took up what was adumbrated in Tyconius and perfected it in his massive vision of the two cities, the City of God and the City of Man. As is well known, Augustine's two cities, each a vast cosmic society, are formed by two loves, the one set in stark opposition to the other:

> We see then that the two cities were created by two kinds of love: the earthly city was created by self-love reaching the point of contempt for God, the Heavenly City by the love of God carried as far as contempt of self. In fact, the earthly city glories in itself, the Heavenly City glories in the Lord.[26]

For all its starkness, however, the opposition is still buried in the obscure, inward movements of the heart which are compatible with every manner and all modes of misleading and apparently conflicting outward behavior. As a result, no given earthly society can be strictly identified either with the City of God or with the City of Man. It is always likely that members of the one are present in any social grouping that, to all appearances, would seem to belong to the other. Furthermore, for Augustine the movement of the heart toward God is not under human control. It comes as a gift of grace which is not, in his view, awarded to foreknown faith, but is pure mercy to the utterly undeserving. It answers to nothing that a person has done or will do, but arises instead from the hidden and incomprehensible patterns of divine election.

Thus, following Tyconius's lead, Augustine has preserved the North African tradition's vivid sense for the boundary between the Christian and the non-Christian, but he has transferred that boundary to a terrain in which it is no longer under human control or subject to human definition. Neither the mysterious inner dispositions of the heart nor the ultimate riddle of divine election can be translated into external marks of social differentiation or claimed by one social group to the exclusion of another. For Augustine, as for Tyconius, the separation of the two cities so that each exists in pure form belongs to God's final judgment and not to any presumptuous human attempt to anticipate what God alone can do. On this point, too, the Donatists' claim to draw the boundary between the Christian and the non-Christian strictly and exclusively around themselves must be disqualified.

In the end, then, the answer to the Donatist crisis was not simply to dilute or to divert the force of the common elements of the Christian tradition in North Africa, but to let that force flow at full strength in a new imagery of two cities, accompanied by a new theology of divine grace and divine election and by a new sense that the prerogative of judgment belongs to God alone. In effect, what Tyconius and Augustine (and the others whom they were eventually able to enlist in their cause) did was to create a new common culture, a new shared context linking speaker and hearer in the more or less oral, more or less personal discourse of patristic theology. From this point of view, Augustine's subsequent struggle against the Pelagian threat to his doctrine of grace can be seen as an effort to protect and preserve the ground he had won in the Donatist controversy. What was at stake was not simply a particular point in theology, but a complex and still fragile Christian culture that was just coming to birth. Perhaps it can even be said that the Augustinian doctrine of grace, together with his vision of the two cities and his eschatology of divine control, is the disguised legacy of the North African tradition to Christian theology in the West, the anti-Donatist form of a pre-Donatist Christian culture.

The case of patristic Christianity in North Africa may yield no clear-cut correlations between the formation of Christian doctrine and well-defined patterns of teaching and learning. But it does provide a vivid instance of the way the themes and images of a shared culture shaped the tradition which that culture bears—and of the way a shift in the tradition requires a corresponding shift in the common culture's themes and imagery. New links between speaker and hearer must be created in order to shape new patterns of personal and oral discourse that will sustain a newly formulated theology.

NOTES

1. See Eusebius, *Ecclesiastical History* 6.43.11–12.

2. Augustine, *Confessions* 7.9.13.

3. The classic history of education in antiquity is H. I. Marrou, *A History of Education in Antiquity*, trans. G. Lamb (New York, 1956).

4. Augustine, *Confessions* 6.3.3.

5. Augustine, *Epistles* 41.2.

6. See R. Sider, *Ancient Rhetoric and the Art of Tertullian* (Oxford, 1971).

7. Tertullian, *On Idolatry* 15.10 (trans. S. L. Greenslade, *Early Latin Theology*, LCC 5 [Philadelphia, 1956], 101).

8. Tertullian, *On Prayer* 29 (trans. Ernest Evans, *Tertullian's Tract on the Prayer* [London, 1953], 39).

9. Cyprian, *On the Unity of the Catholic Church* 12–13.

10. Cyprian, *On the Lapsed* 31.

11. *Martyrdom of Saints Perpetua and Felicitas* 3 (trans. Herbert Musurillo, *The Acts of the Christian Martyrs* [Oxford, 1972], 109).

12. Tertullian, *On Prayer* 2 (trans. Evans, 5).

13. Tertullian, *On Baptism* 20.

14. Cyprian, *On the Unity of the Catholic Church* 6.

15. Ibid., 5 (trans. Maurice Bévenot, *Cyprian: De Lapsis* and *de Ecclesiae Catholicae Unitate* [Oxford, 1971], 9).

16. Cyprian, *Epistles* 73.21, 74.7 (trans. R. B. Donna, *St. Cyprian: Letters (1–81)*, FC 51 [Washington, D.C., 1964], 282, 290).

17. Tertullian, *On the Flesh of Christ* 5 (trans. Ernest Evans, *Tertullian's Treatise on the Incarnation* [London, 1956], 19).

18. See Augustine, *Exposition of Psalm 137* 14, and *Exposition of Psalm 91* 4.

19. Augustine, *Epistles* 185.2.7–8; 5.19–20.

20. Augustine, *Exposition of Psalm 34* sermon 2, 13.

21. Augustine, *Epistles* 185.2.9–11.

22. Augustine, *On Baptism* 1.10.13–14; 1.15.23—16.25 (trans. J. R. King, rev. C. D. Hartranft in *NPNF,* First Series, vol. 4: *St. Augustin: The Writings against the Manichaeans and against the Donatists* [New York, 1887], 418, 422).

23. Tyconius, ed. F. C. Burkitt, *The Book of Rules of Tyconius,* TaS 3/1 (Cambridge, 1894), 10–11.

24. For this line in Tyconius's thought, see the *regula tertia* of *The Book of Rules.*

25. See *Book of Rules,* 30–31.

26. Augustine, *The City of God* 14.28 (trans. Henry Bettenson, *Augustine: City of God,* ed. David Knowles [Harmondsworth, Eng., 1972], 593).

4

Fourth-Century Jerusalem: Religious Geography and Christian Tradition

Francine Cardman

"Let us review and analyze the times when gateways and sacred precincts, groves and temples in every city were constructed diligently for [the gods] and shrines adorned with a great variety of votive offerings," urges Eusebius of Caesarea (c. 260–c. 340) toward the end of his *Oration in Praise of Constantine*. "The esteem of the gods was common among tyrants then," he comments pointedly, but the fruit of their piety was only "wars, battles and revolutions," not the peace and prosperity of the present day. Indeed, the gods of old were not even able to foretell their own demise as a result of a "certain new epiphany" which would "extinguish their rites."[1] Sacred places and the activities peculiar to them had met their end in the coming of the true Sovereign, Jesus Christ, and the advent of his earthly servant, the sovereign Constantine (274 or 288–337). That oracles had ceased, temples had been emptied, and shrines had been neglected, while everywhere the power of the gods was brought to naught, had long been a standard theme of Christian apologetic. What was new in Eusebius's outlook was the confident identification of Constantine with the definitive end of "pagan" religious practices and places and, consequently, the certainty of the Christian church's triumphant place in the empire. What was new, too, though perhaps not yet apparent to Eusebius, was a future filled with Christian holy places—sacred precincts and all the ritual they would involve.

If the early Christian argument against the Greeks had made the appearance of Christian holy places seem unlikely, the concurrent polemic against the Jews made it even more so. Tertullian's (c. 160–

c. 220) treatise *Against the Jews,* one of the earliest in a long line of such works, illustrates not only Christianity's detachment from Judaism but also its separation from and rejection of the land and the places of the Jews. It was possible for Christians to look on the destruction of the Temple and the imperially encouraged dispersion of Jews from their land not so much with equanimity as with self-justification and a certain satisfaction. The church had displaced both the Temple and the holy city of Jerusalem:

> Let the Jews recognize their own fate—a fate which they were constantly foretold as destined to incur after the advent of Christ, on account of the impiety with which they despised and slew him. . . . Ever since we Gentiles . . . cast forth our idols, what follows has likewise been fulfilled. For "the Lord of Sabaoth hath taken away from among the Jews and from Jerusalem" [Isa. 3:1] . . . "the wise architect" too who builds the church, God's temple and the holy city, and the house of the Lord. For thenceforth God's grace desisted among them.

For having wrongly supposed that the holy land was "strictly the Jewish territory," they have lost, Tertullian argues, not only their earthly land but the heavenly things as well; even the Holy of Holies was lost to them.[2] What was new in Tertullian's outlook was simply the novelty of Christianity itself, a movement new enough, strong enough, and bold enough to thrive, at least for a time, on roots that were increasingly considered to be merely spiritual, while deriving its sustenance from elsewhere. What was new, too, and certainly unforeseen by Tertullian, was the deliberate turn of Christian attention, a little over a century later, back to that once-Jewish land and the places from which Christianity had sprung.

In distinction from both Jews and Greeks, therefore, the Christians' God was a God to be worshiped neither on Mount Gerizim nor in Jerusalem (John 4:21) nor in any other sacred precincts, groves, or temples. For the Christians of the first three centuries, the sacred space of Jew and Greek alike had been done away with, the pagan gods and their devotees vanquished. Christ was the victorious Lord of both cosmos and history, yet bound to neither. Christian teaching, however, required a context and a connection to the lives of believers and inquirers. The human need for the specific and the tangible thus came to demand that the tradition be given a location and center. So well had these exigencies been met by the end of the fourth century that the Risen Lord of the Christians had become closely associated with particular space, and a Christian map of the newly emerged "holy land" could be drawn in some detail.

W. D. Davies captures the sense of a center already to be found in the writings of the New Testament. His observations are appropriate to the situation of the following three centuries as well: "For the holiness of place, Christianity has fundamentally, though not consistently, substituted the holiness of the Person: it has Christified holy space." By so doing, it paradoxically supplied out of its own internal dynamic additional and specifically Christian motivations for the development of holy places. There is an inherent tension in this development. Having displaced previous and particular holy places by Jesus Christ, Christian faith had made all places potentially holy. Because Jesus had lived in a historically and geographically specific time and place, those places that had touched or been touched by him took on the contours of holiness: they became sacred spaces. "History in the tradition," Davies astutely argues, "demanded geography."[3] So, in time, Christianity developed its own saving geography, its holy places, its sense of sacred space in the land of the Jews, while also borrowing at will from the forms of the Greeks.

Because they looked to Christ as center, and because the center was both movable and local, Christians in the fourth century could attack Jew and Greek alike for their attachment to place at the same time as they appropriated from the religious geography and architecture of each. On the one hand, Christians could easily spiritualize whatever they valued in Judaism and thus sever any geographical or physical connections with it. On the other hand, they could not restrain the gradually growing interest of Christian teachers—and, later, of Christian pilgrims of all sorts—in the places of the incarnation.

Although the extant sources provide only a glimpse of this interest, the expressions used to record it are often telling. Justin Martyr (c. 100–c. 165), a native of Palestine (from Neapolis, near Shechem), provides the earliest testimony to a cave at Bethlehem in which the Savior was believed to have been born. His insistence that the cave had been foretold by the prophets, and that it was quite a different sort of thing from the cavelike place in which Mithraic initiations occurred, reflects the apologetic and polemical context of his remarks. Bishop Melito of Sardis (d. c. 190) journeyed to Palestine to ascertain the facts about the books of the Old Testament. A fragment from a letter of his is preserved by Eusebius: "So when I visited the East and arrived at the place where it all happened, and the truth was proclaimed, I obtained precise information about the Old Testament books, and made out the list which I am now sending you." It is also to Eusebius that we owe the story of Alexander, a bishop in Cappadocia, who was instructed in a dream to leave his own see and go to Jerusalem to share episcopal duties with the aging bishop of that city. Obedient to the revelation, Alexander set out around the year 213 "in order to worship there and to examine the historic sites." He subsequently became Bishop of Jerusalem. The last of the known pre-Constantinian visitors is Origen (c. 185–c. 254), who traveled to Palestine from his native Alexandria in about 230 and remained in Caesarea until his death. In his refutation of the pagan philosopher Celsus, Origen appealed, in a rather circular argument, to the cave and manger at Bethlehem as "further proof" that Jesus had been born there: "What is shown there is famous in these parts even among people alien to the faith, since it was in this cave that the Jesus who is worshiped and admired by Christians was born."[4]

It is interesting that there are no references to the tomb of Christ contemporary with the notices of the cave at Bethlehem. What can be gleaned from the information about those early visitors is the existence of traditions and the identification of sites that might have been more or less continuously present to the memory of the Jerusalem church. It is possible, though by no means either certain or provable, for instance, that the contemporaries of Jesus knew the locations of the crucifixion and tomb and that that information was preserved despite extensive changes in the city which brought those locations within the new city wall by the year 41 and later, after 135, covered them over with Hadrian's forum. The largely Gentile community that remained in the city after the First Jewish Revolt (66–73) centered its activity on Mount Sion, near the place of Pentecost. The "Mother of all the churches," as Sion was known, came to be the keeper of the Jerusalem traditions. Hadrian's buildings may have obliterated the site as far as Christian purposes were concerned, but they also preserved it for Constantine's workmen to uncover nearly two centuries later—with the assistance of the Bishop of Jerusalem.[5]

Identification of other biblical sites was often much less problematic than this one, and Christian visitors to Jerusalem were shown such indisputably authentic features as the Mount of Olives, Bethesda, or the Temple area. Various other Old and New Testament locations were more or less accurately identified and accessible—Nazareth and Capernaum, for instance, or Shechem and Jacob's Well. Apocryphal identifications also flourished as geographical features or convenient locales caused biblical events or stories to become attached to particular places. Thus Egeria (4th cent.) was shown the tomb of Moses, which she seems to have accepted as genuine, though she has to admit to her sisters, to whom she is writing, that at the place of the memorial to Lot's wife "what we saw . . . was not the actual pillar, but only the place where it had once been." In a moment of candor uncommon in most pilgrim accounts, Egeria reports that "the pillar itself, they say, has been submerged in the Dead Sea—at any rate we did not see it, and I cannot pretend that we did."[6]

Out of a mixture of necessity and curiosity, historical and theological motivations worked subtly on the Christian consciousness, preparing the ground for what would become, in Victor Turner's phrase, the "ritual topography" of fourth-century Palestine. Rejection and spiritualization of holy places was gradually giving way before the gathering momentum of what Davies terms "historical concern and sacramental concentration."[7] Christian sacred space was coming into being.

The concept of sanctification of time has long been a commonplace for students of Christian history, particularly though not exclusively in the area of liturgical studies. But the idea of sanctification of space has achieved much less currency.[8] Theological bias, whether liberal or evangelical, has sometimes reinforced inattention to this phenomenon from those who study the Christian tradition—and so has a kind of historical purism. In order to understand the emergence and meaning of the religious geography of early Christianity, particularly the development of the holy places and the role the Jerusalem church played in forming and handing on this way of touching and teaching the Christian tradition, we must draw on the resources of the history of religions, sociology, and anthropology, as well as the customary historical and theological disciplines.

Jerusalem had functioned as a sacred center—the *axis mundi*, or *omphalos* (navel) of the world—for Jews long before it became a similar center for Christians. The human need for orientation in space as well as in time motivated Jews to locate that center with increasing specificity:

> The land of Israel is the middle of the earth. Jerusalem is the middle of the land of Israel. The Temple is the middle of Jerusalem. The Holy of Holies is the middle of the Temple. The holy Ark is the middle of the Holy of Holies. And the Stone of Foundation is in front of the Holy of Holies.[9]

When Jerusalem became a Christian city in the fourth century, that same need for a center came to rest on the symbol of Golgotha, the rock of crucifixion. Of the place where Jesus "stretched out his hands on the cross, that he might embrace the ends of the world," Cyril of Jerusalem (c. 315–386) exclaimed, "This Golgotha is the very center of the world."[10] The holy places that developed in and around Jerusalem invited Christians not only to "come and see" but also to "come and touch," to stand at the center that had made all other centers, paradoxically, both superfluous and necessary. Thus, when access to Jerusalem became difficult or dangerous, other more localized "centers" would do as well. Because the center was both specific (Jerusalem) and ubiquitous (Christ), the map of the former could become more or less fixed, while the location of the latter shifted with remarkable fluidity, thus making it difficult to chart. Both maps were created out of the same human instinct that Mircea Eliade identifies as "the longing for transcendent forms—in this instance for sacred space."[11]

In the case of Christianity in general and Jerusalem in particular, the impulse for the creation of holy places derived a good deal of its energy from the fast-growing cult of the martyrs, on the one hand, and the politics of religion as practiced by the first "Christian" emperor, on the other hand. By "localizing the holy"—*hic locus est* ("this is the place") read the inscriptions of North African martyr shrines—the cult of the saints prepared Christian sensibilities to look to Jerusalem as a sacred center of special significance. In turn, the popularity of the Jerusalem holy places and the demand for relics and articles from them fed the more general desire for contact with the holy. The paradoxical result of this increased longing for the holy was that a multiplicity of centers sprang into being at about the same time as one center with particular claims of access to the holy *realia* that had been touched by the life of Christ took shape.

Thus, while the importance to Christians of particular places was increasing in the third and fourth centuries, a certain flexibility of style was developing in the ways that the tension between distance from and desire for proximity to the holy was managed. Both the cult of the saints and that of the holy places in Jerusalem evolved an attitude of detachment from "purely geographical setting," which made it possible to transcend place even while honoring it. Peter Brown describes the process:

> The holy could be brought ever closer through gestures of concord and gift-giving which the men [sic] of late antiquity and the early middle ages treasured as the cement of their social world. A network of "interpersonal acts" that carried the full overtones of late-Roman relationships of generosity, dependence, and solidarity came, in one generation, to link the Atlantic coast to the Holy Land; and, in so doing, these "interpersonal acts" both facilitated and further heightened the drive to transmute distance from the holy into the deep joy of proximity.

Pilgrimage was the most obvious means of overcoming distance, but the translation of relics ultimately proved the most practical. "By the early fifth century," notes Brown, "the strictly 'geographical' map of the availability of the holy . . . had come to be irreversibly modified." The balancing of distance and proximity applied equally to Jerusalem and to saints' shrines elsewhere in the empire. In addition, the need of persons in the West, facing the waves of barbarian peoples that were undoing the Roman world, to rely on the power of "invisible companions" and heavenly patrons, also drove many of those same persons to the East in search of refuge. Their continuing relationships with friends and family who had remained behind were the forces joining the holy places of Jerusalem with the Atlantic.[12]

In a different vein, it was by contributing the martyrium (martyr's memorial) to the vocabulary of early Christian architecture that the cult of martyrs furthered the growth of Christian holy places, not only in cemetery precincts but also in Jerusalem. Aside from meeting the needs of Christian funerary architecture, the martyrium was also an influential element in the design of the churches Constantine ordered built as memorials to the Savior's passion and resurrection. The other and perhaps dominant form guiding the buildings at Golgotha and the tomb was the basilica, the public meeting or imperial audience hall of antiquity. The Great Church at Golgotha, a basilica with porticoes and forecourts, was commonly referred to as the Martyrium, a name that could also be applied by extension to the entire complex of buildings at the heart of Jerusalem. There Christians could gather and pray, worshiping, as Jerome (c. 342–420) frequently remarks, "where his feet have stood." There they could be instructed in the Christian faith, being taught not only by their bishop but by the place itself as well. And there, near the very place where their Lord was raised from the dead, they could make their own journeys from death to life in the waters of baptism and then join the community in the celebration of the Eucharist in the Great Church. Through the memory, presence, and form of this sacred space the tradition was thus handed on.[13]

The buildings in which Jerusalem Christians experienced these mysteries were the outcome of a plan conceived by Emperor Constantine sometime after his surprising victory in 312 at the Milvian Bridge, when he had relied on the aid of the Christian God, and the issuing of the so-called Edict of Milan in 313, in which he announced religious toleration for Christians and for all others. His plan was simple yet sweeping in its purpose. Its aim, as Massey Shepherd characterizes it, was nothing less than "the sanctification of the temporal order through the Christian renovation of the empire." The restoration of churches damaged in the persecutions, the construction of new church buildings, and various other benefactions were expressions of imperial interest in the affairs and well-being of the Christian church. As Eusebius describes it, "At once in the very middle of the provinces and cities great works were raised on a royal scale, so that in a brief time these shone forth among every people, evidence of the refutation of godless tyranny." Constantine's intervention in the Arian controversy and his solicitous role at the Council of Nicaea in 325 went hand-in-hand with the generosity of his benefactions. By constructing magnificent new churches in Rome, Constantinople, Tyre, and Jerusalem in the years following the council, Constantine advanced both his ecclesiastical and imperial agendas.[14]

To Eusebius it seemed only natural that Constantine should turn his attention to Palestine, "inasmuch as in that place as from a fount gushed forth the life-bearing stream to all." Constantine's development and exploitation of the holy places was lavish, as Eusebius's description conveys:

> In the Palestinian nation, in the heart of the Hebrew kingdom, on the very site of the evidence for salvation, he outfitted with many and abundant distinctions an enormous house of prayer and temple sacred

to the Saving Sign, and he honored a memorial full of eternal significance and the Great Savior's own trophies over death with ornaments beyond all description.

Church construction of this sort served as advertisement not only for the Christians' Savior but also for their earthly sovereign who sought to rule securely by serving the Christian God well. In addition to the Anastasis or Church of the Holy Sepulchre, honoring the cave-tomb of Christ, Constantine caused churches to be built over the cave at Bethlehem and the cave on the Mount of Olives associated with the ascension, and a fourth church at the Oak of Mamre, where according to an early Christian understanding of Genesis 18 the Savior himself had appeared to Abraham in the company of two angels. Pagan cults of Venus at the tomb and of Thammuz/Adonis at Bethlehem, and an ancient tree cult at Mamre, were all overthrown and their traces obliterated by Constantine's churches.[15]

Despite the displacement of the pagan cults on these sites, physical features conducive to such cults remained: three caves and a sacred tree. In the case of the Holy Sepulchre, the cave was (re)discovered; at Mamre the oak stood clearly in a corner of the enclosure area around the shrine, and in each instance the archaic feature retained a place in the Christian reclamation of the site. Their presence in the biblical narrative dictated that they should remain and be honored. But their continuing presence also witnesses to the perduring sense of the holy that a physical object or geographical feature can attract and convey. The overlay of Christian meaning did not so much destroy the archaic significance of the symbol as add to it. Eusebius naively captures the continuity of symbolic structure in his remarks on the churches associated with the three caves:

> In this same region [Constantine] recovered three sites revered for three mystical caves, and enhanced them with opulent structures. On the cave of the first theophany he conferred appropriate marks of honor; at the one where the ultimate ascension occurred he consecrated a memorial on the mountain ridge; between these, at the scene of the great struggle, signs of salvation and victory.[16]

Constantine's construction of striking cultic centers at the holy places in and around Jerusalem had an appreciable effect on the form and style of the Jerusalem liturgy. The language spoken in those places was the language of imperial munificence; the style was that of the imperial court. The content of the liturgy, though in general common to the liturgical celebrations of other Christian churches, took on significance and substance specific only to Jerusalem.

The monumental character of Constantine's churches, wherever he built them, had the effect of emphasizing the historical as opposed to the eschatological situation of the church. The temporal order had acquired a new importance, no longer representing the merely transitory but now showing forth the "true image and copy of the eternal glory of the communion of the saints."[17] The importance of historical testimony began to prevail over eschatological hope as martyria—churches that were monuments either to victorious martyrs or to the Lord's own struggle and victory—were built in the Constantinian style.

Among the consequences of Constantine's church building were the "amplification" of the liturgy, occasioned by the new scale of the buildings in which it was celebrated, and the historicizing (or de-eschatologizing) of the Christian hope. The one saving Mystery of the Christian faith was fragmented into many separate mysteries; each of the resultant pieces tended to become anchored to specific places or objects.[18] The part the Jerusalem liturgy played in this process can be estimated from Cyril of Jerusalem's use of the holy places in the catechetical lectures he delivered around the year 348, as well as from the reports of the pilgrim Egeria on the liturgical situation as she found it in Jerusalem around 381.[19] These are not isolated witnesses. They mark the early stages of a movement by which baptismal catechesis, an expanded liturgical calendar, and the practice of pilgrimage to the holy places came to be incorporated into the life of the church as a whole.

For Cyril, likely a native of Jerusalem, the holy places are testimonies or evidences of the truth of the Christian faith. Whether buildings such as the Anastasis, physical features such as the rock of Golgotha (now encompassed by the adjoining basilica), or geographical points such as the Mount of Olives—these places were holy because they had witnessed the events of the Savior's life, death, and resurrection, and now offered their testimony to others who would come and see the place. Cyril speaks eloquently and often in the course of the lectures about the many "true testimonies concerning Christ" which are furnished not only by Constantine's buildings but also by places throughout the holy land:

> The blessed place of the manger bears witness. . . . Jordan is his witness among the rivers; the sea of Tiberias among seas. . . .

The holy wood of the cross bears witness, seen among us to this day, and from this place now almost filling the whole world, by means of those who in faith take portions from it. The palm tree on the ravine bears witness, having supplied the palm-branches to the children who then hailed him. Gethsemane bears witness, still to the thoughtful almost showing Judas. Golgotha, the holy hill standing above us here bears witness. . . .

The Mount of Olives bears witness, that holy mount from which he ascended to the Father.

Among the privileges Cyril counts to the Jerusalem church and to those who were able to stand "in this most holy Golgotha" and hear the story of the Lord's Passion and victory there, is this: "Others only hear, but we both see and handle." The faith that comes from hearing (Rom. 10:17) is thus strengthened, if not confirmed, by sight and touch.[20]

At the time of Cyril, therefore, a catechetical and apologetic function was being served by the holy places in and around Jerusalem. A period of catechumenate in preparation for Easter baptism was a time for instruction in the faith as well as for spiritual discipline in which the entire community was invited to join. Already the Lenten observance was longer in Jerusalem than in the West. By the time of Egeria's sojourn in the city, liturgical developments had progressed well beyond anything Cyril gives notice of in his extant writings, even though his episcopate was concurrent with the most creative period of development.

What is most notable in Egeria's account of the Jerusalem liturgy is the contrast between her report of a set form of devotion at numerous holy places (a prayer, followed by a lesson and appropriate psalm, another prayer, and a blessing if a bishop happened to be present) and her repeated expressions of surprise at the liturgical observances at the Jerusalem churches themselves, where "the psalms and antiphons they use are always appropriate, whether at night, in the early morning, at the day prayers at mid-day, or three o'clock, or at Lucernare (evening prayer)." Likewise, of the great feasts she remarks, "They have hymns and antiphons suitable to the place and the day, and readings too."[21]

From Egeria's reports it is possible to identify two levels of liturgical development in Jerusalem: the daily/Sunday cycle of observances, and the Lent/Easter cycle, to which the other feasts of the church year are related in form and content. On both levels the Jerusalem liturgy makes dramatic use of features of the sacred geography all around it. At the weekday service of Lucernare

(lamplighting, or evening prayer), for example, the already preg-
nant symbolism of light and darkness is carried a step further with
a gesture unrepeatable elsewhere: the lamps and candles are lit
from fire that is "brought not from outside, but from the cave—
inside the screen—where a lamp is always burning night and day."
On Sunday, too, the tomb takes a prominent part in the liturgy:
with the Anastasis filled with the smoke of incense, the bishop
stands behind the screen, at the door of the tomb, and proclaims
the Gospel account of the Lord's resurrection. Likewise during
Holy Week, or the Great Week as Egeria calls it, the events of the
Passion are commemorated at the places in which they occurred,
with psalms, antiphons, and readings appropriate to the day and
the place. So vivid was the sacramental imagination with which the
people entered into these observances that they became thoroughly
caught up in them. Egeria's comment on the reading of the arrest
narrative in Gethsemane on Thursday of the Great Week is typical:
"By the time it has been read everyone is groaning and lamenting
and weeping so loud that people across in the city can probably
hear it all."[22]

The approach to liturgical time and space embodied in the Jerusalem liturgy eventually came to influence the liturgy of the whole
church. The shape of the liturgical year, the rites of Holy Week (particularly the veneration of the cross), the celebration of Epiphany,
and the development of the stational observance are but a few of
the ways in which the holy places of Jerusalem contributed to the
development and diffusion of Christian tradition, teaching and
forming Christians through means more visual and tactile than
verbal, more dramatic than academic. As the influence and lure of
the holy places intensified, the numbers of people desiring to experience them firsthand increased proportionately. In turn, the presence of pilgrims both rich and poor left its mark on the city and led
to further development, even exploitation of the holy places. The
growing number of pilgrims also brought about the "exportation"
of the holiness they encountered there.[23]

After Constantine's buildings on Golgotha were well under construction, and before Egeria's visit or even Cyril's preaching, an
anonymous pilgrim journeyed to Jerusalem in the year 333. The
record left by the so-called Bordeaux pilgrim provides a useful
point of comparison to Egeria's account. From the two reports it is
possible to gauge the extent of the development of the holy places
and the "Jerusalem circuit" of sites shown to pilgrims in the fourth

century and later. What is surprising about the Bordeaux pilgrim's account is the number of places already accessible to interested travelers so soon after Constantine's first attention to the land. In addition to the central and obvious sites around Jerusalem, pilgrims in the early fourth century could evidently visit places in Galilee, as well as sites of peripheral importance in the Gospels or Acts. Significant Old Testament sites were also part of their itinerary. By Egeria's time these sites extended into Egypt and what is now Jordan.[24]

Later pilgrims, roughly contemporaneous with Egeria, evidenced an interest not shared by the pilgrim from Bordeaux: they were anxious to meet holy men and women who followed the ascetic way of life. These ascetics lived alone or in community, often dwelling near the holy places or, by their very presence, creating a new sort of sacred space of their own. It was not uncommon for pilgrims who had visited the holy places and the holy people later to undertake the ascetic life themselves. So, for instance, Rufinus (c. 345–410) and Melania the Elder (c. 345–410) established monasteries and guest houses on the Mount of Olives after having visited the monks of Egypt, and Jerome and Paula (347–404) journeyed through the ascetic communities of Syria and Palestine before establishing an ascetic community of their own near the cave of the nativity at Bethlehem. Subsequent monastic settlements in the Judaean desert owed some of their success to these earlier developments and to the women and men who sought sanctity in the environs of the holy places.[25]

Pilgrimage, patronage, and the expanding network of publicity did much to enhance the prestige of the holy places in and around Jerusalem. By the end of the fourth century other royal or aristocratic patrons had followed in the footsteps of Helena (c. 255–c. 330) and Eutropia (Constantine's mother and mother-in-law, respectively), who had set an example of active concern for the sacred places of Palestine when they first came into prominence in the early part of the century. Some built churches, others monasteries, and nearly all were acquainted with various of the ascetic communities and individuals scattered in the hills and desert of Judaea and beyond. The web of connections linking aristocratic Jerusalem pilgrims and expatriates with their friends and relations elsewhere in the Roman world inspired zeal for the holy places as stories and souvenirs from them were circulated throughout the empire.

Jerusalem thus became the goal of many Christians' longings, its

holy places the teachers and bearers of the story of the divine con-
descension in Jesus Christ. The meaning of the Christian religious
geography that took form in the fourth century in Palestine tended
to vary according to the circumstances of those who contemplated
it. Whether looked on directly or only imagined from afar, the holy
places called forth from Christians responses that ranged from the
renunciation vowed by those who undertook an ascetic life in their
shadows, to the chivalry and opportunism of those who crusaded
for their liberation from the "infidel," to the piety of those who
commemorated the finding of the cross or followed quietly along
its way in their own parish churches centuries after Cyril had
proclaimed the resurrection gospel from the threshold of the tomb,
or Egeria joined the procession down the Mount of Olives on the
Day of Palms.

NOTES

1. Eusebius of Caesarea, *In Praise of Constantine* 9.1, 5, trans. H. A. Drake
(Berkeley, 1976).

2. Tertullian, *Against the Jews* 13; *On the Resurrection* 26; Eng. trans. in
Ante-Nicene Fathers, vol. 3, ed. A. Roberts and J. Donaldson (Grand Rapids,
Mich., repr. 1973).

3. W. D. Davies, *The Gospel and the Land* (Berkeley, 1974), 368, 366.

4. Justin Martyr, *Dialogue with Trypho* 70, 78; Eusebius, *Ecclesiastical History* 4.26.14; 6.11.2, Eng. trans. G. A. Williamson, Eusebius, *The History of
the Church* (Harmondsworth, Eng., 1965); Origen, *Contra Celsum* 1.51,
trans. H. Chadwick (Cambridge, 1953).

5. For the history of the site and buildings of the Holy Sepulchre and dis-
cussion of the question of authenticity, see C. Coüasnon, *The Church of the
Holy Sepulchre* (London, 1974), 6–20; J. Wilkinson, *Egeria's Travels* (London,
1971), 39–46; idem, *Jerusalem as Jesus Knew It* (London, 1978), 178–97; J.
Murphy-O'Connor, *The Holy Land: An Archaeological Guide from Earliest
Times to 1700* (Oxford, 1980), 36–57; and C. Kopp, *The Holy Places of the
Gospels* (New York, 1963).

6. *Egeria's Travels* 12.7; all quotations of Egeria are from Wilkinson's translation.

7. Davies, *Gospel and Land*, 366.

8. See, e.g., M. Eliade, *The Sacred and the Profane* (New York, 1959); idem,
Patterns in Comparative Religion (New York, 1958); V. Turner, "The Center
Out There: Pilgrim's Goal," *HR* 12 (1973): 191–230; V. Turner and E. Turner,
Image and Pilgrimage in Christian Culture (New York, 1978). M. J. Hatchett,
Sanctifying Life, Time, and Space: An Introduction to Liturgical Study (New

York, 1982), is least successful in dealing with sacred space. For important analyses of the way these categories functioned in Judaism, see R. Cohn, *The Shape of Sacred Space: Four Biblical Essays* (Chico, Calif., 1981); J. Z. Smith, "Earth and Gods," *JR* 49 (1969): 103–27.

9. Midrash Tanhuma, Kedoshim 10, quoted in Z. Vilnay, ed., *Legends of Jerusalem* (Philadelphia, 1973), 6.

10. Cyril of Jerusalem, *Catechetical Lectures* 13.28.

11. Eliade, *Patterns*, 385.

12. P. Brown, *The Cult of the Saints: Its Rise and Function in Latin Christianity* (Chicago, 1981), 86, 90, 91.

13. A. Grabar, *Martyrium: Recherches sur le culte des reliques et l'art chrétien antique*, 2 vols. (Paris, 1943, 1946; reprint, London, 1972), is the classic work on the subject. His thesis is challenged by J. B. Ward-Perkins, "Memoria, Martyr's Tomb and Martyr's Church," *JThS*, n.s. 17 (1966): 20–37; reply by A. Grabar, "Martyrium ou 'vingt ans après,'" *CAr* 18 (1968): 239–44. The origins of the basilical church are likewise disputed. R. Krautheimer, *Early Christian and Byzantine Architecture* (Baltimore, 1965), 12–22, argues that the imperial audience hall was the model for Christian basilicas during and after the time of Constantine, but C. Mango, *Byzantine Architecture* (New York, 1975), 58–61, asserts that Christians were building basilical churches before Constantine took an interest in the church. For Jerome's use of the Septuagint version of Ps. 131:7, see his *Epistles* 47.2.

14. M. Shepherd, "Liturgical Expressions of the Constantinian Triumph," *DOP* 21 (1967): 59–78; Eusebius, *In Praise of Constantine* 9.15.

15. Eusebius, *In Praise of Constantine* 9.15, 16.

16. Ibid., 9.17.

17. Shepherd, "Liturgical Expressions," 72.

18. The concept of "amplification" is A. Schmemann's, *Introduction to Liturgical Theology* (Crestwood, N.Y., 1966), 93. I have discussed some aspects of these developments in more detail in F. Cardman, "The Emperor's New Clothes: Christ and Constantine," in *Above Every Name*, ed. T. Clarke, Woodstock Studies 5 (New York, 1980), 191–210, and "The Rhetoric of Holy Places," *Studia Patristica* 18 (Oxford, 1982), 18–25.

19. It is beyond the scope of this chapter to enter into the extensive debates on each of these dates, or those on the authorship of either the *Catechetical Lectures* or the *Mystagogical Catecheses*. For dating Cyril's episcopacy and for the argument that he was probably author of the *Catechetical Lectures*, see F. L. Cross, *St. Cyril of Jerusalem on the Sacraments* (London, 1966), xx–xxviii; and W. Telfer, *Cyril of Jerusalem and Nemesius of Emesa*, LCC 4 (Philadelphia, 1955), 19–30. Wilkinson, *Egeria's Travels*, 237–39, judiciously summarizes arguments for dating Egeria's journey to the years 381–384. The classic argument against Cyril's authorship of the *Mystagogical Catecheses* is W. J. Swaans, "A propos des 'Catéchèses mystagogiques' attribuées à S. Cyrille de Jérusalem," *Le Muséon* 55 (1942): 1–43. Cross, *St. Cyril*, xxxvi–xxxix, accepts their authenticity, as does E. Yarnold in a more

recent study, "The Authorship of the Mystagogic Catecheses Attributed to Cyril of Jerusalem," *HeyJ* 19 (1978): 143–61.

20. *Catechetical Lectures* 10.19; 13.22.

21. *Egeria's Travels* 25.5; 31.1.

22. Ibid., 24.4–5; 36.6.

23. See E. D. Hunt, *Holy Land Pilgrimage in the Later Roman Empire, A.D. 312–460* (Oxford, 1982).

24. See Wilkinson, *Egeria's Travels*, 153–63, for the Bordeaux Pilgrim, and *Jerusalem Pilgrims Before the Crusades* (Warminster, 1977) for other pilgrim accounts.

25. For the role of Melania and Paula (and their friends Rufinus and Jerome), see A. Yarbrough, "Christianization in the Fourth Century: The Example of Roman Women," *ChH* 45 (1976): 1–17, and R. Ruether, "Mothers of the Church: Ascetic Women in the Late Patristic Age," in R. Ruether and E. McLaughlin, eds., *Women of Spirit* (New York, 1979), 72–98. For later sojourner/settlers, especially the Empress Eudoxia, see Hunt, *Holy Land Pilgrimage*, 155–248. The origins of monastic establishments in the Judaean desert are treated by D. J. Chitty, *The Desert a City* (Crestwood, N.Y., 1966).

5

Byzantium as Center of Theological Thought in the Christian East

John Meyendorff

Established in the fourth century as a "New Rome" on the Bosporus to serve as the new capital of the Christian Roman Empire, Constantinople (Byzantium) gradually but inevitably became also the major intellectual center of Eastern Christendom. Amputated in the fifth century of its entire Western half, the empire survived for centuries, united by the three elements that are generally considered as constitutive of the "Byzantine" civilization: Christian faith, Roman political tradition, and Greek language. The use of Greek as the official language of the state and as the main channel of intellectual creativity, however, did not imply that the Byzantine Christian society was a Greek nation-state. Its multiethnic and multicultured character survived until the late Middle Ages. Armenians, Syrians, Slavs, Georgians, and representatives of other ethnic groups either found their way into the Byzantine social hierarchy or, when political circumstances allowed, formed independent states which nevertheless continued to consider themselves part of a Byzantium-centered Christendom and members of the canonical structure of the Orthodox church. It is from Byzantium also that the entire "Byzantine Commonwealth"[1] was receiving norms of tradition, patterns of religious thought, and criteria of worship and spirituality.

In the fifth century the Christian East was still polycentric: exegetical and theological traditions were distinct in Alexandria, in Antioch , and in Syriac-speaking Mesopotamia. However, the bitter antagonisms generated by the Christological controversies and the consequent Monophysite schism, adhered to by a majority of Syrians and Egyptians, weakened substantially the ancient intellectual centers of the Middle East. The Muslim conquest of the seventh century isolated them completely from Constantinople. The two Romes—the "old" one on the Tiber and the "new" one on the Bosporus—remained face to face within imperial Orthodoxy.

In the age of Emperor Justinian (527–565), a crucial period in the building up of medieval Byzantine civilization, the theology of the church of Constantinople consciously attempted to synthesize competing traditions coming from the past and to overcome their divisiveness. In Constantinople itself the prevailing influence had come from Antioch. The great John Chrysostom (c. 347–407; patriarch 398–404) and the ill-fated Nestorius (d. c. 451; patriarch 428–431) originated in Antioch, brought to the capital the exegetical and liturgical traditions of Syria, and established a solid tradition of the Christology that would eventually be known as "Chalcedonian." Nevertheless, for the sixth century, the Christology associated with Alexandria had to be accepted as normative because of the unionist (today we would say "ecumenical") policies of Justinian aimed at appeasing the Monophysites. These syncretistic trends were obviously the result of the worldwide unifying role played by the imperial capital. Just as Rome in the West, Constantinople could not exercise its "ecumenical" authority without attempting to reconcile and to arbitrate—a role which excluded the unilateral adoption of any particular theological trend. Remarkably, the result was not a hybrid compromise but an authentic synthesis.[2]

The imperial capital was the seat of institutions of higher learning: a university, organized in the year 425 by decrees of Theodosius II and continuing an intermittent existence until the late Middle Ages, and a patriarchal school for the education of higher clergy.[3] Schools existed in other cities, and some monasteries were centers of theological learning, but the influence of those schools—secular or ecclesiastical—could at no point be compared with the impact exercised by the medieval universities of the West after the twelfth century.

The imperial university of Constantinople contributed to the preservation, in a narrow and aristocratic circle of intellectuals, of the classical tradition of Greek antiquity. It taught "ancient Greek grammar and rhetoric" and graduated men "justified to serve in the *secrets* of the imperial administration and the upper echelons of the Church," but "their culture was impenetrable to a wider public because it was expressed in a dead language and presupposed a body of arcane knowledge."[4] With the exception of Patriarch Photius (c.

810–895; patriarch 858–867, 877–886), whose encyclopedic competence and ecclesiastical involvement influenced religious thought,
none of the intellectuals associated with the university can be listed
as an influential theologian. Like Michael Psellos (1018–1078), they
limited their writings almost entirely to philosophical or rhetorical
matters. And when they dared to express philosophical conviction
in theological terms, they faced ecclesiastical condemnation. Thus,

On the eve of the period when the West would commit its mind to the
philosophy of the ancients and enter the great epoch of Scholasticism,
the Byzantine Church solemnly refused any such synthesis between
the Greek mind and Christianity, remaining committed only to the
synthesis reached in the patristic period.[5]

But was theology advanced creatively through the means of the
patriarchal school of Constantinople, if not through the imperial
university? It does not seem so. The only period for which we have
historical evidence for an active role of "patriarchal" teachers in theological debates is the twelfth century, but these debates, while
conducted on a high level of sophistication, took place in a strictly
antiheretical and scholastic sphere.[6] Theological creativity, as we
will see below, was happening elsewhere.

These elusive facts concerning the relationship between theology
and learning in Byzantium explain the widely contradictory opinions expressed by historians concerning Byzantine Christian civilization. The historians of the Enlightenment (Voltaire, Gibbon)
despised Byzantium's "medieval barbarism" but credited it with the
very limited merit of having preserved the manuscript texts of
ancient Greek authors. In the nineteenth century the revival of
Byzantine studies was based on the same premises: in Byzantium
"Greek classical literature was the basis of public education,"[7] and
Byzantium was even recognized as the real source of the Italian
Renaissance, since it transmitted the Greek heritage to the West.
Recently, however, the systematically negative attitude of the
Byzantine church toward ancient Hellenism has been recognized
more clearly. What then was the real contribution of Christian
Byzantium? Was it only a backward, reactionary, and ultraconserva-
tive civilization, oblivious of antiquity and contemptuous of Catho-
lic Christianity?

According to a modern historian, "there can be no doubt that
behind the mock classical facade of Byzantium lay a reality that was

very different."[8] What was the reality? It is not the place here to answer this question in all its aspects, but we can speak to one: the nature of the Byzantine experience of the Christian faith and therefore of Byzantine Orthodox theology. We have noted already that this theology was not made primarily in schools. It was seen not as a scientific discipline, taught with an academic methodology, but rather as a system of truths, learned by reading Scripture (or listening to it in church), by praying either liturgically or personally, by hearing sermons, or by studying under a teacher whose competence was not only intellectual but also spiritual. Such was also the general attitude toward theology in the West, before Scholasticism. Augustine did not think otherwise. In a sense, Byzantium preserved the relationship between the Christian revelation and secular thought which existed in late antiquity.

I will illustrate this Byzantine and, more general, Eastern Christian understanding of theology by making three points.

1. *In the East, theology was always defined as experience or communion, not as a purely conceptual knowledge.* Indeed, "the eastern tradition has never made a sharp distinction between mysticism and theology; between personal experience of the divine mysteries and the dogma defined by the Church."[9] Already the Cappadocian Fathers, particularly Gregory of Nazianzus (329–389), used the term *theologia* to mean a contemplation of the divine Trinity rather than intellectual discourse about the Trinity. Thus the title *"theologian"* is reserved primarily, in Byzantine texts, to John the Evangelist, Gregory of Nazianzus, and also the mystic Symeon, known as the "New Theologian" (949–1022). What is clearly implied in the title "theologian" is not scientific erudition in theology, but a visionary awareness of divine Truth.

Evagrius Ponticus (346–399), a friend of the Cappadocian Fathers and the first prominent teacher of monastic spirituality, used a famous expression: "If you are a theologian you truly pray. If you truly pray you are a theologian."[10] For Evagrius himself this statement had a peculiar Origenistic and Neoplatonic meaning which we shall not discuss here, but in the later tradition of Eastern spirituality, the union of theology and prayer simply affirmed the experiential, or "mystical," character of Christian theology: the knowledge of God was seen as inseparable from holiness.

This approach to theology carried the danger of subjectivism and spiritualistic individualism. Was not the "theologian" actually understood as a gnostic, endowed with an esoteric privilege of knowing God? And indeed, the monastic circle of the fourth century within which the "mystical" understanding of theology was strongly affirmed also produced the movement known as "Messalianism." The Messalians rejected the sacraments of the institutional church, particularly baptism, and considered personal prayer the only necessary and efficient means of communion with God.[11] But the Byzantine church was aware of the danger. Messalianism was repeatedly condemned on several doctrinal counts, but particularly because it considered the knowledge of God a personal/ascetic achievement, independent of the sacramental nature of the church. The church affirms that, on the contrary, divine life and knowledge of God are gifts, both gratuitous and common to all the baptized, though also dependent upon personal spiritual effort.[12]

This debate around Messalianism and spiritual experience continued, implicitly or explicitly, throughout the history of Christian Byzantium. And although Messalianism was rejected in its heretical anti-ecclesial form, the prophetic and experiential nature of theology was never disavowed.

2. *Positive theological speculation was always confronted with Divine Transcendence.* In an often quoted comment on Eccles. 3:7 ("A time to keep silence, and a time to speak"), Gregory of Nyssa (c. 330–c. 395) writes:

> In speaking of God, when there is question of his essence, *then is the time to keep silence.* When, however, it is a question of his operation (*energeia*), a knowledge of which can come down even to us, *that is the time to speak* of his omnipotence by telling of his works and explaining his deeds, and to use words to this extent.[13]

The notion that the divine essence is totally beyond created knowledge or communion, and that God can be experienced only through his "grace" or "energy," was clearly expressed by the fourth-century Cappadocian Fathers, in the writings of Pseudo-Dionysius (beginning of the sixth century), and by Maximus the Confessor (c. 580–662). In the late Middle Ages it was more fully developed by Gregory Palamas (c. 1296–1359).

What was involved was not only "apophatic," or "negative," theology as such. Apophaticism was necessary as a liberation of the mind by means of the elimination of all concepts identifying God with that which he is not, that is, from all idolatry. But true experience, and therefore true theology, went beyond conceptual apophaticism; it was a positive experience of divine transcendence, or a "knowledge through ignorance." "The act of undergoing negation in spiritual vision, negation linked to the transcendence of the Object, differs from negative theology and is superior to it." Vision of God and communion with God can never imply *possession*: "In spiritual vision the transcendent light of God only appears *the more completely hidden*."[14] Therefore, vision and communion are not forms of natural created knowledge, but they are "life in Christ," in the deified humanity of the incarnate Logos.

This understanding of divine transcendence implies the experiential nature of theology, described above, but it also eliminates in principle the possibility of integrating theology into a preexisting philosophical system. Whatever influence Greek philosophy, particularly Neoplatonism, could in fact have had on particular aspects of Greek patristic thought, the official position of the church was negative. On the occasion of the trial in 1082 of a Neoplatonizing intellectual, John Italos, a special anathema, repeated annually in all churches for the first Sunday of Lent, condemned the "impious teaching of the Greeks."[15]

Seen in historical perspective, this formal renunciation in the eleventh century of the Greek philosophical inheritance in Greek-speaking Byzantium offers a remarkable contrast with the almost simultaneous "discovery" of Aristotle in the Latin West on the eve of the great synthesis between philosophy and theology known as Scholasticism. Paradoxically, in the Middle Ages the East was becoming less "Greek" than the West.

3. *The problem of doctrinal authority in the Byzantine Orthodox church*. There has never been any doubt that Scripture is the supreme criterion of Christian truth. The Fathers of the fourth and fifth centuries were primarily exegetes, as shown by the sheer volume of scriptural commentaries produced by them. The same tradition of exegesis continued in the medieval period. However, the Greek East took a longer time than the West in settling the problem of the *canon*: variations, particularly concerning the status of the "longer" canon of the Old Testament and of Revelation, existed until the eighth century. The Council *in Trullo* (692) accepted a canon that included books of the "longer" canon, even 3 Maccabees, but it omitted Wisdom, Tobit, and Judith. John of Damascus (c. 675–c. 753) failed to include Wisdom and Ecclesiasticus, although he considered them "admirable."[16] These hesitations, which ended with a general acceptance of the "longer" canon

(although Revelation never entered liturgical usage), did not cause much debate or controversy, which indicates clearly that the church and its tradition were not dependent on a fixed canon of God-inspired texts but were seen as sufficient sources of Christian truth, in continuity with the apostolic church.

The bishops were the normal witnesses to tradition. The episcopal council (or "synod") in a given geographic area, and the ecumenical council on the world scale, were called to solve difficulties, settle disputes, and take the necessary doctrinal options. It is significant, however, that every council of the Byzantine era emphasized that it was not changing anything in either the content or the meaning of the faith "once delivered to the saints" and that new doctrinal definitions were reluctantly made only to reject misinterpretations of the apostolic faith by heretics.[17] But this deliberately conservative attitude of the councils did not prevent them from sanctioning new terminologies (e.g., the doctrine of the "two natures" at Chalcedon in 451) or giving new interpretations to earlier definitions (e.g., the sanction given to a "Cyrillian" interpretation of Chalcedon at Constantinople in 553) or even formally claiming to "develop" the doctrinal formula of the past.[18]

The councils constituted, therefore, the normal means by which the church exercised its responsibility for maintaining the true faith. However, episcopal magisterial authority never suppressed—or substituted itself for—an understanding of the Christian faith as an experience accessible to the church as community and to each Christian as a personal experience of the Truth. This explains why the *liturgical tradition* was so often referred to as an authority, side by side with Scripture and the Fathers,[19] or why, in an extreme situation, a saint could oppose his prophetic experience and inspired conviction to that of the bishops. When confronted by his Monothelite judges with the fact that the entire episcopate, including apparently the Bishop of Rome, had accepted Monothelitism, Maximus the Confessor answered with a paraphrase of Gal. 1:8: "The Holy Spirit anathematizes even angels, if they utter teachings contrary to the (true) kerygma."[20]

This explains why in Byzantine Orthodoxy, doctrinal pronouncements made by councils still needed ecclesial "reception," not in terms of a democratic referendum but in terms of a sanction by the Holy Spirit speaking through the whole church.

It is primarily because theological truth could be neither conceived as a system of concepts to be taught as a scholastic discipline nor reduced to authoritative pronouncements of the magisterium that creative theologizing in medieval Byzantium was largely pursued in monastic circles. Starting with Maximus the Confessor, the great names of Byzantine theology are monastic names (Symeon the New Theologian, Gregory Palamas), whereas nonmonastic figures, like Photius, or the numerous anti-Latin polemicists, or the canonists of the twelfth century, limited themselves to a scholarly, intelligent, but essentially conservative preservation of the *depositum fidei*.

This conservative trend is reflected in the following solemn instruction issued by the Council *in Trullo* (692):

> It is necessary for those who preside over the churches . . . to teach all the clergy and the people . . . , collecting out of divine Scripture the thoughts and judgments of truth, but not exceeding the limits now fixed, nor varying from the tradition of the God-fearing Fathers. But if any issue arises concerning Scripture, it should not be interpreted other than as the luminaries and teachers of the Church have expounded in their writings; let them [the bishops] become distinguished for their knowledge of patristic writings rather than for composing treatises out of their own heads.[21]

However, when Gregory Palamas, in his controversy with Barlaam the Calabrian about the knowledge of God, solicited and obtained the support of the monks of Mount Athos, the *Haghioretic Tome* ("Tome of the Holy Mountain") issued on that occasion (1340) proclaimed the legitimacy within the New Testament community of a prophetic ministry, speaking authoritatively of the realities of the future Kingdom, just as Old Testament prophets announced the coming of Christ. This New Testament prophecy, a particular responsibility of the monks, was not necessarily bound by formulas of the past, but spoke of the Truth on the basis of direct spiritual experience:

> The doctrines [of the church] are suitably formulated, known to all and boldly proclaimed. However, at the time of the Mosaic law, these dogmas were mysteries foreseen in the Spirit by the prophets alone. So, the good things promised to the Saints [e.g., James 2:5] for the age to come are the mysteries of the Gospel community, granted to and foreseen by those who, at least in part, are possessing the vision of the Spirit, as first fruits [of the Kingdom].[22]

The creativity of monastic theology in Byzantium, whatever its one-sidedness in some respects, was therefore based on an "eschatological gnoseology," inseparable from the notion that the Christian community sacramentally anticipates the kingdom of God. This is why the concept of "mysticism," which in our modern usage designates individualistic and emotional religiosity, is inadequate when applied to Eastern Christian theology and spirituality, unless it refers to the *mystērion* of "Christ and the church" (Eph. 5:32) and implies the eschatological, sacramental, and ecclesial dimensions of theological knowledge.

NOTES

1. D. Obolensky, *The Byzantine Commonwealth: Eastern Europe, 500-1453* (London, 1971).

2. See J. Meyendorff, *Christ in Eastern Christian Thought*, 2d ed. (Crestwood, N.Y., 1975), 69–89; for similar evaluations of Byzantine theology, see also Meyendorff, *Byzantine Theology: Historical Trends and Doctrinal Themes*, 2d ed. (New York, 1978), and the article, "Byzanz," in *TRE* 7.4/5 (Berlin and New York, 1981): 500–532. For a remarkable general history of trends and ideas, see J. Pelikan, *The Spirit of Eastern Christendom (600–1700)*, vol. 2 of *The Christian Tradition* (Chicago, 1974). References and bibliography in H.-G. Beck, *Kirche und theologische Literatur im byzantinischen Reich* (Munich, 1959), and for the late medieval period in G. Podskalsky, *Theologie und Philosophie in Byzanz. Der Streit um die theologische Methodik in der spätbyzantinischen Geistesgeschichte (14/15. Jh.), seine systematischen Grundlagen und seine historische Entwicklung*, ByA 15 (Munich, 1977).

3. *Codex Theodosianus* 14.9.3; 6.21.1. F. Fuchs, *Die höheren Schulen von Konstantinopel im Mittelalter*, ByA 8 (Leipzig and Berlin, 1926); L. Bréhier, "Notes sur l'histoire de l'enseignement supérieur à Constantinople," *Byzantion* 3 (1926): 72–94, and 4 (1927/8): 13–28; and "L'enseignement classique et l'enseignement religieux à Byzance," *RHPhR* 21 (1941): 34-69; F. Dvornik, "Photius et la réorganisation de l'Académie patriarcale," *AnBoll* 68 (1950): 108–25.

4. C. Mango, "Discontinuity with the Classical Past in Byzantium," in M. Mullett and R. Scott, *Byzantium and the Classical Tradition* (Birmingham, 1981), 49–50.

5. J. Gouillard, "Le Synodikon de l'Orthodoxie—Édition et commentaire," *TMIE* 6 (Paris, 1976), 305–24; and C. Niarchos, "The Philosophical Background of the Eleventh Century Revival of Learning in Byzantium," in Mullet and Scott, *Byzantium*, 127–35.

6. Meyendorff, *Byzantine Theology*, 64.

7. R. Browning, "The Patriarchal School at Constantinople in the Twelfth Century," *Byzantion* 32 (1962): 167–202.

8. Mango, "Discontinuity," 50.

9. V. Lossky, *The Mystical Theology of the Eastern Church* (Crestwood, N.Y., 1976), 8.

10. *Chapters on Prayer* 60, ed. J. E. Bamberger, *Evagrius Ponticus: Praktikos and Chapters on Prayer*, CistSS 4 (Spencer, Mass., 1970), 65.

11. There is abundant secondary literature on Messalianism, but many issues connected with the movement are still controversial, particularly the meaning of the writings ascribed to Macarius the Great and identified as "Messalian" by several modern scholars, most recently H. Dörries, *Die Theologie des Makarios/Symeon*, AAWG.PH. 103 (Göttingen, 1978). For my view on the subject, see "Messalianism or Anti-Messalianism? A Fresh Look at the 'Macarian' Problem," in *Kyriakon: Festschrift Johannes Quasten*, ed. P. Granfield and J. A. Jungmann (Münster, 1970), 2:585–90.

12. On the teaching of Gregory Palamas on this point, see J. Meyendorff, *A Study of Gregory Palamas*, 2d ed. (London, 1974), 161–62.

13. Gregory of Nyssa, *In Eccl. Sermo* 7, in W. Jaeger, ed., *Works* (Leiden, 1962), 5:415–16.

14. Gregory Palamas, *Triads* 2.3.26 and 2.3.31, in J. Meyendorff, ed., *Grégoire Palamas: Défense des saints hésychastes. Introduction, Texte critique, Traduction et notes*, 2d ed. (Louvain, 1973), 2:439, 449.

15. Gouillard, "Le Synodikon de l'Orthodoxie," *TMIE* 2 (1967): 57.

16. John of Damascus, *De fide orthodoxa* 4.17, in *PG* 94.1180BC; also ed. B. Kotter (Berlin, 1973), 211.

17. E.g., the preamble of the Chalcedonian definition (451), *Conciliorum oecumenicorum decreta* (Bologna, 1973), 84.

18. The doctrine of "uncreated energies," formulated in 1351, was seen as a "development" (*anaptuxis*) of the decree on the two energies and two wills of Christ published by the Sixth Ecumenical Council (680), *Synodal Tome of 1351*, in *PG* 151.722B.

19. See, e.g., the liturgical references in the writings of Gregory Palamas against Barlaam, in Meyendorff, *Palamas: Défense* 2:746.

20. *Acta Maximi*, in *PG* 90.121C.

21. Canon 19, in K. Rhalles and M. Potles, *Syntagma tōn theiōn kai hierōn kanonōn* (Athens, 1852), 2:346.

22. Gregory Palamas, *Syggrammata*, ed. P. Chrestou (Thessaloniki, 1966), 2:567; see also *PG* 150.1225.

6

The Formulators of Icon Doctrine

Patrick Henry

The year 1987 will mark the 1200th anniversary of the Seventh
Ecumenical Council, the Second Council of Nicaea, the last of the
councils recognized by both Eastern and Western Christians as
authoritative. What we call the Seventh Ecumenical Council overturned the decisions of a council that had been held thirty-three
years before, in 754, and had called itself the seventh ecumenical;
and the decisions of what we call the Seventh Ecumenical Council
were themselves overturned twenty-eight years later, in 815, by a
council which reasserted the claim of the council of 754 to the title
of seventh ecumenical. Finally, after another twenty-eight years, in
843, the councils of 754 and 815 were anathematized and the Council of 787 was celebrated in what the Eastern church has ever since
hailed as the "Triumph of Orthodoxy."

Presented in this summary way, the period of the Seventh
Ecumenical Council may sound like a century of ecclesiastical
fruitbasket-upset, but the controversy exemplifies a dynamic process by which the Christian tradition was taught and learned. The
Orthodox teaching on icons, a teaching which received classical formulation at the council and in its aftermath, remains the most distinctive feature of Eastern Christian doctrine and practice. We in the
West are unaccustomed to "schools of thought" that persist for a
millennium and more. The Orthodox today do not think in exactly
the same terms or under the same conditions as their predecessors
of the eighth and ninth centuries, but the coherence in both form
and substance between what was written about icons then and
what is written about them now is striking.

From the perspective of subsequent Orthodoxy, the three great
literary defenders of the icons, John of Damascus (c. 675–c. 753),

Theodore of Studios (759–826), and Patriarch Nicephorus of Constantinople (758–828), do not appear to form a "school." They are simply the champions of Orthodoxy, the exponents in their own troubled time of the tradition of the Fathers. In their own view, the three do not form a "school." Theodore commended one of his own writings on the grounds that "I have introduced no thought of my own in the entire work." Moreover, modern study of the history of the use of icons in Christian worship has illuminated—and complicated—our understanding of the lines of influence between the Iconoclastic period and what came before it.[1]

Nevertheless, a study of the "Iconodule school" ("Iconodules" = icon worshipers) is an appropriate chapter in an account of schools of thought in the Christian tradition, not only because of the formal characteristics of the story but also because the implications of the Iconodule school's teaching reach right into our own time. The 1200th anniversary of Nicaea II will be an occasion for ecumenical celebration, but it may also provoke ecumenical awkwardness. Westerners, whether Catholic or Protestant, are traditionally ill at ease with the council's declaration that worship of images is not only compatible with orthodoxy but also an essential part of it, not merely an accidental and incidental liturgical curiosity. John Calvin says of the Seventh Ecumenical Council, "so disgusting are their absurdities that I am ashamed even to mention them," and he classifies the council's decree as "terrible blasphemies." While the Roman Catholic Church officially recognizes the council, Catholic attitudes are also shaped by the Council of Frankfurt of 794, which denounced Nicaea II (on the basis of an egregious misrepresentation of what had been decided there), and by the *Libri Carolini*, composed shortly before the Council of Frankfurt, which reject both claimants—the Iconoclast Council of 754 and the Iconodule Council of 787—to the title of "Seventh Ecumenical."[2] The Orthodox theology of the icon generates a radically different understanding of Christianity from what most of us in the West are accustomed to—indeed, a radically different experience of what it is to be a Christian, of what kind of world we live in, of how God comes to us and how we approach God.

In order to highlight ways in which the Iconodule position developed in response to shifting Iconoclast argument, I will first briefly outline the stages in the eighth- and ninth-century debate, primarily by reference to the works of Theodore of Studios, with citations from John of Damascus and Patriarch Nicephorus for comparison and contrast. Then I will suggest what lies at the heart of the Iconodule school's conviction about icons. Finally I will indicate ways in which Orthodox icon doctrine presents both problems and possibilities for ecumenical discussion.

Theodore, Abbot of Studios, wrote much in defense of icons, including scores of letters during the six years following the Council of 815, when he was in exile and his monastery's brotherhood, about one thousand in number, had been dispersed throughout the empire. The main source for our outline of the debate, however, is Theodore's best-known work on the subject, a set of three *Refutations of the Heretics*. The structure of his first two *Refutations* provides a stratigraphic record of the development of the Iconoclast argument from the time of Emperor Leo III to that of Emperor Leo V, that is, from about the year 730 to the year 815.

Refutation 1 opens with the Iconoclast's denunciation of "a practice which by some wile of the devil has been transferred from pagan tradition, bringing the veneration of idols into the catholic church." The sin of idolatry, outlawed by the Second Commandment, has been the charge most frequently leveled against the Christian use of images. It figures in Leo III's policy and in the dogmatic statement of the Council of 754, which said, "In the guise of Christianity [the devil] secretly brought back idolatry." John of Damascus devotes much attention to refuting the accusation, as does Theodore's contemporary, Patriarch Nicephorus, whose entire lengthy *Apologeticus Maior* is occupied with the idolatry question.[3] We might expect this charge to dominate Theodore's concerns too. In fact, he dismisses it in a single paragraph and takes it up further only briefly and incidentally. The idolatry accusation was "traditional," so Theodore had to notice it, but it was not current. The Council of 815 specifically excluded the charge from its general reassertion of the decision of 754: "In preserving without alteration what was expressed by [the Council of 754], we decree that the manufacture of icons is unfit for veneration and useless. We refrain, however, from calling them idols, since there is a distinction between different kinds of evil."[4]

Refutation 1 turns immediately to the issue that had been at the center of the controversy from 754: the Christological significance of icons. Nearly all students of the Iconoclastic controversy credit Emperor Constantine V (741–775) with a stroke of forensic genius in shifting the charge from idolatry to heresy—the icon either confounds the two natures of Christ (Monophysitism) or drives a wedge between them (Nestorianism)—and at first glance it does appear that the emperor, who relished theological debate, set the agenda for more than a millennium of discussion. The contemporary Orthodox theologian Leonid Ouspensky, following the historian George Ostrogorsky, argues to the contrary: Constantine V did not invent a Christological dilemma with which to trap the Iconodules, for a Christological defense of icons was already traditional, and Constantine was forced to counter it.[5] This debate over historical priority cannot be decided on the basis of our scanty sources for the origins of Iconoclasm, but in the view of Orthodox theologians the debate is not academic at all, for it touches on the fundamental claim that worship of images was a practice of the apostles, that is, image worship is given with the original Christian revelation. Theodore, however, does not dwell on the historical claim the way John of Damascus and Nicephorus and Ouspensky do. As we shall see, Theodore finesses the problem of historical ambiguity by grounding his argument in ontological and epistemological categories: in order to justify worshiping images of Christ, you do not have to establish that the apostles painted pictures, only that they really saw and honestly worshiped Christ.

Theodore spends much time on the Christological question. In so doing, he must have had his eye on popular attitudes and opinions rather than on official church policy, for just as the Council of 815 dissociated itself explicitly from the charge of idolatry, so it appears to have distanced itself implicitly from the Christological critique of images. The Second Nicene Council was called by the Empress Irene, who was regent for her young son, Constantine VI, and the *Definition* of the Council of 815 opens not with dogmatic solemnity but with a sneering rebuke of Empress Irene's "female frivolity" which had "undone the Church." The actions of 787 are attributed not to the council itself but to "her." When the Council of 815 gives its own reasons for banning icons, they are not couched in Christological formulas but are directed against injudicious veneration of icons. The Second Nicene Council "bestowed exaggerated honor to painting, namely, the lighting of candles and lamps and the offering of incense, these marks of veneration being those of worship." The *Definition* "banishes from the church the unwarranted manufacture of spurious icons" but appears more concerned with the icons' corruption of worship than with their distortion of dogma. That the center of gravity has shifted in this "second Iconoclasm" from what it was in the "first" is confirmed by Leo V's moderation, expressed in late 814: icons high up in the churches could remain, but all icons that were hung low enough to be venerated would be eliminated.[6]

The question of veneration cannot be entirely severed from the Christological dilemma, and Theodore is determined to show that the Iconoclastic position is an intricate web of impiety. The emperor's compromise, in Theodore's judgment, makes the heresy not only logically incoherent but also more starkly apparent. But Theodore must give more attention than previous Iconodules to the issue of worship of icons. His writings show the adjustments that the Iconodule argument must make when Iconoclasts start saying it is all right to make icons but not to use them. "Now that [the Iconoclasts] have been hemmed in by our proofs, they admit that our Lord Jesus Christ can be portrayed, but not that his icon should be set up and venerated."[7]

The relation of the worship of icons to worship in spirit and in truth is the central theme of *Refutation 2* and of the second half of *Refutation 3*. As readers work through the strata of the *Refutations* they uncover the three levels of the Iconoclastic attack on icons: (1) icons are idols, (2) icons are the outward and visible sign of Christological heresy, (3) icons are an abomination when improperly used. The third level is to some degree a circling back to the first level, for the charge of improper use is a variation on the charge of idolatry. "Then [the Iconoclasts] try to shake the understanding of the simple people by saying that in venerating the icon they are worshiping the creation instead of the Creator."[8] In both stages the dispute concerns worship, an activity which is as much a matter of practice as it is of thought.

One of the ideas Theodore holds to most tenaciously is that Christianity cannot be restricted to or by the claims of intellect alone. As so often in church history, it is a monk who takes seriously the need to consult the faithful in matters of doctrine and determines that the law of belief (*lex credendi*) will be set by the law of prayer (*lex orandi*). Theodore sees the attack on icons as an assault on Christian existence itself in the guise of a purification of worship. John of Damascus had written at length on various kinds and degrees of worship, but his discussion has a somewhat academic formality that reflects both the stage of the Iconoclastic controversy during which he was living (the basic assault was on icons themselves, and only secondarily on worship) and his location in a monastery near Jerusalem, in the Muslim caliphate where he was insulated from imperial censorship and reprisal (even though he had recently died, however, the Council of 754 anathematized him as one who "insults Christ and plots against the Empire"). At a later stage and in the thick of the fight, Theodore suspects that what the

Iconoclasts really want is a worship consisting entirely of pure mental contemplation and he says that if such were adequate, God would have revealed himself as an intellectually apprehensible abstraction—or, as one of my students once said, if God had wanted to appeal directly to our minds he would have had Mary write a book instead of bearing a child.[9]

Indeed, Theodore saw that the Iconoclasts had simply shifted the burden of holiness from the icons to the worshiper. The final words of *Refutation 1* suggest a last-ditch Iconoclast argument—even if the icons were holy, they could not help us: "Anyone who overextends the honor of Christ's icon and says they will not approach it, for it will not benefit them unless they are first purified from all sin, is a fool." Over against this perfectionism stands the example of Mary of Egypt, whose *Life* is quoted by John of Damascus at the end of his third *Apology*. She prays to the icon of the Virgin Mary:

> O Lady, Virgin and Mother of God, who gave birth in the flesh to God the Word, I know—how well I know!—that it is no honor or praise to you when someone so impure and depraved as I am looks upon your pure icon, for you kept your body and soul in purity, O ever-virgin. Before your virginal purity it is right that I inspire only hatred and disgust. But I have heard that God, who was born of you, became a human being only because he wanted to call sinners to repentance. Help me, for I have no other help.[10]

In each of the three levels of the argument—idolatry, Christology, worship—a fundamental decision was being made about the Christian understanding of the world. In refuting the charge of idolatry, the Iconodules reasserted a complex, paradoxical view of time that we find in Paul—the past is transcended but not obliterated. Idolatry was and is wrong, but with the incarnation of the Son of God the very preconditions for idolatry have been changed. To refuse to admit that Christ can be pictured is to make an idol of one's own ideas about what is and is not fitting for God. As John of Damascus said,

> In former times God, who is without form or body, could never be depicted. But now when God is seen in the flesh conversing with humankind, I make an image of the God whom I see. I do not worship matter; I worship the Creator of matter who became matter for my sake, who willed to take his abode in matter; who worked out my salvation through matter.[11]

The Iconoclasts considered history to be an opportunity for the church gradually to purify itself of remaining vestiges of paganism

and Judaism; the church is moving toward perfection. The Iconodules considered history to be the arena in which the church, established in purity and perfection at the beginning, must constantly
ward off attacks of the devil. The Iconodules, and by extension the
Orthodox generally, would find fault with both the classic Catholic
statement of Cardinal Newman, "To live is to change, and to be perfect is to have changed often," and the classic Protestant statement
of Adolf von Harnack, "No religion gains anything through time;
it only loses." They would see in both these observations a failure
to comprehend the manner of the church's existence *in* the world
but not *of* the world, a failure to integrate the scheme of shadows
and realities into the scheme of past, present, and future. The
Orthodox position, between Newman's "onward and upward" and
Harnack's "backward and downward," is neatly phrased by
Anthony the Younger, an Iconodule who in 843, on hearing of the
restoration of Orthodoxy, said: "Indeed, Orthodoxy has been established; but after a time things will only get worse."[12]

The Iconodule answer to the Christological dilemma is nothing
less than a reassertion of the scandal of the incarnation, with an
added insistence that the paradox of the incarnation cannot be
relegated to a period of thirty-three years several centuries ago. For
Theodore and the Orthodox, the relationship between God and the
world has been forever changed because of God's decision to
become flesh. The change is ontological, not simply epistemological or ethical. The icon is the answer to the skeptical query of Jew
and pagan (and of Christians themselves when their faith begins to
waver): "Where is the evidence that the kingdom of God is at
hand?" John of Damascus, who accused the Iconoclasts of
Manichaeism, devoted much of his *Apologies* to vindicating the
material world's claim to goodness. "Never will I cease honoring
the matter which wrought my salvation."[13] Theodore also levels the
Manichaean charge, but in a perfunctory way. He sees the real Iconoclast error elsewhere. It is not distaste for the material world that
motivates the Iconoclasts. They do not disdain the realm of ordinary experience, but make a sharp ontological distinction between
the spiritual world and the material world. For them, the human
attitude of reverence is limited strictly to the spiritual. Reverence
devoted to any material object would displace the proper order of
attitudes. By means of the category of relation, drawn mainly from
Aristotle, Theodore is able to counter this objection, not by denying
the distinction between the spiritual and material realms but by
demonstrating logical and intelligible connections between them.[14]

In the first *Refutation*, Theodore says that "as Christ has been proclaimed from the beginning, the proclamation about his image has followed according to its relationship with him." In *Refutation* 3 he develops this argument further:

> The prototype and the image have their being, as it were, in each other. With the removal of one the other is removed, just as when the double is removed the half is removed along with it. If, therefore, Christ cannot exist unless his image exists in potential, and if, before the image is produced artistically, it subsists always in the prototype: then the veneration of Christ is destroyed by anyone who does not admit that his image is also venerated in him.[15]

Underlying this statement is one of the most profound differences between the Iconoclasts and the Iconodules. The Iconoclasts, from at least the time of Constantine V, had argued that an image by definition must be *homoousios* (of the same substance) with its prototype. From this follows the Iconoclast assumption that when Iconodules claim that a picture is an icon they must be identifying the substance or essence (*ousia*) of the picture with the prototype. Theodore repeatedly insists that the image by definition differs in *ousia* from the prototype. What they share is a name:

> Is not every image a kind of seal and impression bearing in itself the proper appearance of that after which it is named? For we call the representation "cross" because it is also the cross, yet there are not two crosses; and we call the image of Christ "Christ" because it is also Christ, yet there are not two Christs. It is not possible to distinguish one from the other by the name, which they have in common, but by their natures.

The relation of prototype and image is active, not passive. Christ's image exists simultaneously with Christ, but the image does not sit still: "There could not be an effective seal which was not impressed on some material. Therefore Christ also, unless he appears in an artificial image, is in this respect idle and ineffective. This is absurd even to consider."[16] Icons keep worship of a God who acts from being itself both "idle" and "ineffective."

This dynamic activity of God, which seems to have been virtually unintelligible to the Iconoclasts, has its philosophic roots in Neoplatonic convictions about the fullness, indeed the pregnancy, of Being. "The seal shows its desire for honor when it makes itself available for impression in many different materials."[17] Theodore does not often quote Pseudo-Dionysius the Areopagite, but it is clear he had absorbed much of that anonymous Neoplatonist's understanding of the kind of world we live in. Theodore makes use of Aristotelian terminology, and even of some Aristotelian concepts. His defense of icons is not so richly endowed with the ontology and epistemology of shadows and realities as is that of John of Damascus, who frequently cites the most Platonic of all New Testament writings, the Letter to the Hebrews. But Theodore's fundamental attitudes and commitments, like those of John, are in the tradition of Plato. Both the Damascene and the Studite believe we live in a world that is mirrored better in dialogues than in syllogisms.

If Orthodox icon doctrine defines a Christian view of time and a Christian view of the relation between God and the world, icons through their impact on worship define a Christian view of what human beings are. The Iconoclastic controversy was not only about images of Christ; images of Mary and of the saints also came under attack. The Iconodules did not permit the Iconoclasts to divide the debate up into component parts, and this refusal is itself a key to the Iconodule position, and by the extension, a clue to a profound difference between Eastern and Western Christianity.

Human beings have been defined in countless ways, from rational animal to featherless biped, from angel to ape. Alexander Solzhenitsyn, a powerful if idiosyncratic exponent of Orthodoxy, makes a fresh and arresting proposal: what distinguishes human beings from the rest of creation is the gift of repentance.[18] Linked to repentance in the Orthodox view is the conviction that God became a human being in order that human beings might become God. We turn around not so much to face the God we have offended as to start on the road to becoming what God is. Western theology has something of this same motif in its various doctrines of sanctification, but they stop far short of the Orthodox claim about our capacity and our destiny. The East takes the identification of Christ as Second Adam and Mary as Second Eve far more seriously than does the West. The governing image for worship in spirit and in truth is not the angels in heaven, but Adam and Eve in paradise. Deification is not the transcendence of our humanity, but its perfection. As Ouspensky puts it, the "constructive role [of the icon] does not lie only in the teaching of the truths of the Christian faith, but in the education of the entire" human being, and "the goal of the icon is neither to provoke nor to exalt a natural human feeling. Its goal is to orient all of our feelings, as well as our intellect and all the other aspects of our nature, towards the transfiguration."[19]

This last reference points directly to the meaning of the icon in Orthodoxy: the "goal is to orient all . . . towards the transfiguration." The Gospel account of the Transfiguration (Matt. 17:1–8; Mark 9:2–8; Luke 9:28–36) has not played a major role in the formation of Western spiritual life. For the Orthodox, the Transfiguration is the heart of the matter, the revelation in light of which the rest of God's revelation makes sense. The center of gravity of Orthodox consciousness lies closer to Mount Tabor than to Golgotha. What Peter, James, and John saw and worshiped there is the warrant for what Christians claim to see and worship when they stand before an icon.

When they have anything at all to say about the Transfiguration, Western theologians usually classify the story as a misplaced resurrection appearance, so whatever meaning it has is specifically eschatological: the Transfiguration tells us something about the transformation of the world at the Last Day, not about the condition of the world here and now. For the Orthodox, on the other hand, while the Transfiguration reveals an essential truth about Jesus Christ, it simultaneously reveals a truth about human nature and its destiny in this world. To quote Ouspensky again: "Orthodox sacred art is a visible expression of the dogma of the transfiguration."[20] For this reason the icon cannot be relegated to a liturgical or theological role subordinate to that of Scripture. In a move decisive for all subsequent Orthodox piety, Theodore detects danger in the venerable Iconodule argument, put forward frequently by John of Damascus, that icons are the Bible for the illiterate. Pope Gregory I (590–604) had given this view currency in his rebuke of the Bishop of Marseilles, who had destroyed images in the churches of his diocese. "Pictorial representation is made use of in churches for this reason—that such as are ignorant of letters may at least read by looking at the walls what they cannot read in books."[21]

Theodore objects to this argument. In the first place, it presupposes distinctions between Christians on the basis of intelligence and learning, and while Theodore is well aware that such distinctions exist, he does not believe they should be legislated into ecclesiastical practice. A much more important objection, though, is the implication in this argument that icons are a provisional expedient, useful only so long as education is less than universal. As Gregory the Great had suggested, the Bible and the icons serve a similar function, but it is not that the one serves learned people and the other serves simple people.

> [Christ] nowhere told anyone to write down the concise word, yet his image was drawn in writing by the Apostles and has been preserved up to the present. Whatever is marked there with paper and ink, the same is marked on the icon with varied pigments or some other material medium.

The Bible and the icon are coordinate; the latter is not a tutor to lead us to the former. Theodore goes on to suggest that if there is a priority it belongs to the icon: "The disciples first saw the Lord and later wrote out the message. . . . However far back you go you would find the written word originating in observation."[22]

Just as Patriarch Nicephorus's extended refutation of the idolatry charge already has something of an antiquarian air, since the Council of 815 had explicitly removed that indictment from its brief against Iconodulia, so John of Damascus's use of the "Bible for the illiterate" defense is out of phase with the rest of his own argument. All our three formulators of icon doctrine believe that icons are not to be looked at in order to learn something—or that if we learn from them, it is a very special kind of learning. In the words of John of Damascus: "The icon is a hymn of triumph, a manifestation, a memorial inscribed for those who have fought and conquered, humbling the demons and putting them to flight." Icons are a gift of divine grace, one of the ways God comes to us. And because God is active in and through the icon, the Iconodules have a positive doctrine. In a judgment that is prejudiced but nonetheless sharply accurate, Nicephorus says of the Iconoclasts: "They define nothing. They demolish and reject the other view. . . . But they neither affirmed nor constructed anything of their own, for they had nothing to affirm. . . . Their *Definition* has only the power of denial and negation but possesses in no way at all a principle of affirmation."[23]

The approaching 1200th anniversary of Nicaea II prompts reflections on the continuing ecumenical significance of what the Iconodule school achieved. It may prove difficult for us in the West to understand fully that significance, not only because for over a thousand years Eastern and Western Christians have lived in separate worlds, but also because the study of history itself predisposes us to a certain reductionism. It is a modern historian's professional responsibility to be skeptical, to suspect that "the issue of iconoclasm was deliberately magnified by its opponents," so "we should treat their evidence with great circumspection." It is a modern historian's prejudice to judge, as does this same historian, that the administration of Emperor Michael II (820–829) "appears to have taken the eminently sensible position that the whole matter concerned nothing more than the correction of a devotional abuse."[24]

If we listen carefully to the voices from the eighth and ninth centuries, what would we learn?

We would learn that obsessive current Western Christological ponderings ("What can it coherently mean to worship an incarnate God?") need to be balanced by other questions (e.g., "What are the implications for worship of God's being incarnate?"). We ask, "Can we make sense of Chalcedon?" They asked, "What kind of sense does Chalcedon make of the world?" The translator of the Damascene's *Orations* says, "St. John's defense of the veneration of images safeguards the witness of the Orthodox Church, that the Jesus of history and the Christ of faith are one and the same."[25] This is an encouraging word for a Western Christianity whose theologians have left it virtually destitute of effective means for linking the Jesus of history and the Christ of faith.

We would also learn that the temptation to give intellect pride of place in worship and piety is really a temptation, not an advance toward worship in spirit and in truth.

We would also learn that Ouspensky's judgment ("The difference between Orthodox sacred art and Western religious art corresponds to a difference between the Orthodox and Western conceptions of holiness")[26] is both sobering (could anything be closer to bedrock ecumenical divergence than "different conceptions of holiness"?) and exciting (could anything be more interesting for Christians to learn from one another than "different conceptions of holiness"?).

NOTES

1. This chapter stands on its own, but it does include extensions and refinements of the argument I presented in "What Was the Iconoclastic Controversy About?" *ChH* 45 (1976): 16–31. Theodore's remark is in his *Letters* 1.43, *PG* 99.1064D (the work in question was not about icons, but the sentiment in the statement is fully characteristic of Theodore and the others). Particularly important modern studies of the background are E. Kitzinger, "The Cult of Images in the Age Before Iconoclasm," *DOP* 8 (1954): 83–150, with its argument that Iconoclasm was the response to a

recent explosive growth in "the everyday use made of religious images by private persons, by the clergy and by secular authorities, not only in devotional practices but also for the attainment of concrete and specific purposes" (p. 149); and S. Gero, *Byzantine Iconoclasm during the Reign of Leo III with Particular Attention to the Oriental Sources*, CSCO 346 (Louvain, 1973), which gives many historical features of early Iconoclasm a new and carefully grounded precision and discounts some erroneous "received truths" about the period. J. Pelikan, *The Spirit of Eastern Christendom (600–1700)*, vol. 2 of *The Christian Tradition* (Chicago, 1974), chap. 3, "Images of the Invisible," 91–145, makes clear the connections between piety and dogma, liturgy and belief, and restores to the study of the period a proper concern for its specifically religious import, which has been downplayed in much recent historical work.

2. The Seventh Ecumenical Council's *Definition*: J. D. Mansi, *Sacrorum Conciliorum Nova et Amplissima Collectio* 13.337C–380B, and anathemas, 397C–E. Calvin, *Institutes of the Christian Religion* 1.11.14–16, ed. J. T. McNeill, trans. F. L. Battles, LCC 20 (Philadelphia, 1960), 114–16. Canon 2 of the Council of Frankfurt: Mansi, *Concilia* 13.909D. *Libri Carolini* 4.9 and 4.4, in *Monumenta Germaniae Historica, Leges* 3, *Concilia* 2 *Supplementum*, p. 182 l. 22; p. 179 l. 20. For further discussion, see P. Henry, "Images of the Church in the Second Nicene Council and in the *Libri Carolini*," in K. Pennington and R. Somerville, eds., *Law, Church, and Society: Essays in Honor of Stephan Kuttner* (Philadelphia, 1977), 237–52; and S. Gero, "The *Libri Carolini* and the Image Controversy," *The Greek Orthodox Theological Review* 18 (1973): 7–34. I overlooked Gero's article in preparing the 1977 essay, but he is mainly concerned with the Carolingian attitude toward works of art, a different issue from the one I dealt with.

3. Gero, *Leo III*, 129–30, notes that "the various statements purporting to report Leo's reasons for his iconoclastic measures on the whole do not go beyond attributing to him a biblically-inspired antipathy to 'idolatry.'" Idolatry accusation in dogmatic statement of 754: Mansi, *Concilia* 13.221CD; text is also available in H. Hennephof, *Textus Byzantini ad Iconomachiam Pertinentes* (Leiden, 1969), 61–78, with indications of the Mansi columns. The entire *Definition* of 754, cited verbatim at the Council of 787, is translated by S. Gero, *Byzantine Iconoclasm during the Reign of Constantine V with Particular Attention to the Oriental Sources*, CSCO 384 (Louvain, 1977), 68–94 (quoted passage is on p. 70). John of Damascus, *De Imaginibus Orationes III*, PG 94: no. 1, 1232A–1284A; no. 2, 1284A–1317A; no. 3, 1317A–1420C (trans. D. Anderson, *On the Divine Images: Three Apologies against Those Who Attack the Divine Images* [Crestwood, N.Y., 1980]). Nicephorus, *Apologeticus Minor pro Sacris Imaginibus*, PG 100.833B–849B; *Apologeticus Maior pro Sacris Imaginibus*, 533A–833B; *Antirrhetici III adversus Constantinum*: no. 1, 205A–328D; no. 2, 329A–373C; no. 3, 376A–533A. On the interrelations of these texts and their general outlines, see P. J. Alexander, *The Patriarch Nicephorus*

of Constantinople: Ecclesiastical Policy and Image Worship in the Byzantine Empire (Oxford, 1958), 163–65, 167–73. Alexander also provides an extensive summary of Nicephorus's unpublished *Refutatio et Eversio* (pp. 242–62). Theodore of Studios, *Antirrhetici III adversus Iconomachos*, PG 99: no. 1, 328B–352B; no. 2, 352C–388D; no. 3, 398A–436A (trans. C. P. Roth, *On the Holy Icons* [Crestwood, N.Y., 1981]). The passage from *Refutation 1* quoted in the text is at 329BC (Roth trans., 20). Other writings of Theodore on icons, in addition to the many letters in PG 99 and A. Mai, *NPB* 8 (1871), are refutations of Iconoclastic poems, PG 99.436A–477A (Gero, *Leo III*, 113–26, argues that the poems themselves date from the earliest phase of Iconoclasm); *Questions to the Iconoclasts*, 477A–485A; *Seven Chapters against the Iconoclasts*, 485B–497C; a *Letter to His Uncle Plato*, 500A–505C.

4. Text of 815 in Hennephof, *Textus*, 79–82 (trans. in A. Bryer and J. Herrin, *Iconoclasm*, Papers given at the Ninth Spring Symposium of Byzantine Studies, University of Birmingham, March 1975 [Birmingham, 1977], 184).

5. L. Ouspensky, *Theology of the Icon* (Crestwood, N.Y., 1978), 146–47.

6. *Definition* of 815, as in note 4 above. On Leo V's compromise policy, see Alexander, *Nicephorus*, 128.

7. *Refutation 2*, 353A (Roth trans., 44).

8. Ibid., 353B (Roth trans., 44).

9. John of Damascus on worship: *Oration* 3.27–40, 1348D–1356C (Anderson trans., 82–88). Mansi, *Concilia* 13.356D (trans. in Gero, *Constantine V*, 94). Theodore, *Refutation 1*, 336D. Student's remark: Margaret Coulling, Swarthmore '81.

10. Theodore, *Refutation 1*, 352B (Roth trans., 41). *Life* of Mary of Egypt, quoted by John of Damascus in *Oration* 3, 1416D–1417A (Anderson trans., 105). P. J. Alexander, "The Iconoclastic Council of St. Sophia (815) and Its Definition (*Horos*)," *DOP* 7 (1953): 44, argues that according to the Iconoclasts of 815 the "only true image [of Christ and the saints] is the virtuous Christian worshipping God in his heart."

11. *Oration* 1.16, 1245A (Anderson trans., 23).

12. J. H. Newman, *An Essay on the Development of Christian Doctrine* 1.1.7 (New York, 1960), 63. A. Harnack, *History of Dogma* (London, 1898), 4:311. Remark in the *Life of Anthony the Younger* cited by C. Mango, "The Liquidation of Iconoclasm and the Patriarch Photios," in Bryer and Herrin, *Iconoclasm*, 139.

13. *Oration* 1.16, 1245B (Anderson trans., 23).

14. Alexander, *Nicephorus*, 189–213, articulates his thesis that sometime between 787 and 815 a new Aristotelian dimension was added to the Iconodule argument. It is true that Theodore and Nicephorus distinguish categories and connections with greater precision than does John of Damascus, and their argument can properly be designated "scholastic." As will be

indicated below, however, their attitudes are much less Aristotelian than their language.

15. *Refutation 1*, 337B; *Refutation 3*, 429CD (Roth trans., 28, 110).

16. *Refutation 1*, 337C; *Refutation 3*, 432D (Roth trans., 28, 112). Pelikan, *Spirit of Eastern Christendom*, 109–10, is a clear and helpful analysis of the Iconoclast claim about the *ousia* of the image.

17. *Refutation 3*, 433A (Roth trans., 112).

18. A. Solzhenitsyn, "Repentance and Self-limitation in the Life of Nations," in Solzhenitsyn et al., *From Under the Rubble* (Boston, 1975), 107.

19. Ouspensky, *Theology of Icon*, 210–11.

20. Ibid., 216.

21. John of Damascus, *Oration* 1, 1248C and 1268A; *Oration* 2, 1293C (Anderson trans., 25, 39, 58). Gregory I: *Letters* 9.105 (*PL* 77.1027B–1028A; trans. in *NPNF*, Second Series, 13:23) and 11.13 (*PL* 1128A–1129C; trans. *NPNF*, Second Series, 13:53–54), to Serenus. The quoted passage is from the first of the two letters, in which the pope also commends Serenus for his zeal against adoration of things made with hands. The second letter reiterates and further explains, in response to Serenus's evident distress on receiving the first letter. Gregory says (1129A) that the majority of Serenus's people have broken communion with him because of his "inconsiderate action."

22. *Refutation 1*, 340D; *Refutation 3*, 392A (Roth trans., 30–31, 78). "Concise word" appears to be a strained allusion to Rom. 9:28.

23. John of Damascus, *Oration* 2.11, 1296BC (Anderson trans., 59). Nicephorus, from the *Refutatio et Eversio*, cited in Alexander, "Council of 815," 46.

24. C. Mango, "Historical Introduction," in Bryer and Herrin, *Iconoclasm*, 5–6.

25. Anderson, trans., *On the Divine Images*, "Introduction," 11.

26. Ouspensky, *Theology of Icon*, 215.

7

Exegesis and Christian Education: The Carolingian Model

E. Ann Matter

The task of transmitting the Christian tradition has virtually always included the teaching of the Bible. In the ninth century the Bible played an especially versatile and important role in the schools. The culture of this age was overwhelmingly monastic; the tradition of such authors as Augustine (354–430), Jerome (c. 342–420), Gregory the Great (c. 540–604), and Bede (c. 673–735) was at the center of the intellectual world. No type of secular learning rivaled the place of biblical study in the Carolingian monasteries. It is therefore no surprise that biblical definitions, insights, and turns of phrase became the literary lingua franca of Frankish authors.

They spoke this language with fluidity and enthusiasm. A staggering number of biblical commentaries from the ninth century are extant—over twenty volumes of J.-P. Migne's *Patrologia Latina*. Few of these have been studied in any systematic way; indeed, only a very few have appeared in critical editions. As John Contreni has noted, "the field of Carolingian biblical study is not clearly mapped out terrain."[1] Any effort to speak on this subject is consequently an exercise in cartography. I intend here to add another piece to the map by focusing on the exegetical activities of two sets of related figures: Alcuin (c. 735–804), Hrabanus Maurus (776 or 784–856), and Walafrid Strabo (c. 808–849) at the beginning of the century, and Haimo (d. c. 855), Heiric (c. 841–c. 885), and Remigius of Auxerre (c. 841–908) at the end.

Each group of authors represents three intellectual generations in a direct line of descent. The careers of Alcuin, who died in 804, and

Remigius, who died in 908, clearly stand at the beginning and end of the century, a century dramatically opened by the imperial coronation of Charlemagne and ushered out by the dissolution of the Carolingian dynasty. It is my contention that, as the major intellectual activity of Carolingian culture, biblical interpretation shaped and was shaped by the educational needs of each generation. In topic, form, and relation to secular issues, exegesis serves as an index of the changing educational process and therefore of the intellectual life of the ninth century.

As is often the case in this period, the story begins with Charlemagne (742–814). Frankish monarchs were concerned with education, and traditionally supported scholars at their courts.[2] However, perhaps because of the relative breadth and stability of his kingdom, Charlemagne's educational innovations and the accomplishments of his teachers have merited the praise of medieval and modern historians alike.

Charlemagne actively recruited scholars from the fringes of his empire and beyond to supervise and guide the intellectual life of the court. The Italian Paul the Deacon (c. 720–c. 800), the Visigoth Theodulf of Orléans (c. 750–821), and the Anglo-Saxon Alcuin made of Aachen an intellectual center of remarkable sophistication. Perhaps the greatest achievement of Charlemagne's palace school was the bringing together of Paul, Theodulf, and Alcuin; as has always been the case at good schools, the faculty benefited greatly from their association with one another. Encouraged by their royal patron, these three scholars shared a concern for the Bible which began with the establishment of an official text from the welter of available Latin versions. As Bonifatius Fischer put it, "Care for the text of the Bible has a significant place in Charlemagne's cultural efforts."[3] Alcuin and Theodulf both undertook critical revisions of the Vulgate. Of the two, Theodulf understood his task more in the tradition of Jerome; besides the corrected Bible text, he provided prefaces for each book, which have been characterized as a *vade mecum* to his program of theological study.

Alcuin, who also provided prefaces to the books of the Bible, complemented his study of the biblical text with a large corpus of commentaries. Among the books he explicated are Genesis, Psalms (in several groups, treated separately), Song of Songs, Ecclesiastes, John, Titus, Philemon, and Hebrews, and perhaps the Apocalypse. In this he was following the school tradition of his native Northumbria, where the figure of that prolific exegete, Bede, loomed large.

Like Bede, Alcuin approached the Bible through the lens of the Fathers. The commentary on John, written and revised for Gisela and Richtrudis of Chelles in 800–801, demonstrates how deliberate this borrowing was, and for what purpose. Alcuin's dedication of the final redaction explains that this exposition is based on Augustine most of all, but also draws much from Ambrose (c. 339–397), the homilies of Gregory the Great and Bede, and any other interpretations of the Fathers he was able to find. A year earlier, in a letter acknowledging the first half of the commentary, which Alcuin had sent to Chelles as a Lenten gift, Gisela and Richtrudis admitted that they had a copy of Augustine's sermons on John but found the interpretation obscure in many places and too ornate for their learning. In other words, both the motivation and the procedure for Alcuin's commentary on John was explicitly to present the wisdom of the Fathers in a form accessible to contemporary students.

The same spirit is evident in the rest of Alcuin's exegetical works. The *Interrogationes et responsiones in Genesin*, made up of questions from Genesis and answers from Jerome and Gregory, is dedicated to Sigulf, an old friend at York who had followed Alcuin to Aachen and later taught with him at Saint Martin of Tours and at Ferrières. The tripartite *Enchiridion* on the Psalms was written for Arno, Bishop of Salzburg, a dearly beloved former pupil; the dedicatory epistle discusses the liturgical use of the Psalter and reminds Arno that a bishop's job includes the spiritual care of his flock. The prologue claims without pretense that the interpretations come from patristic writings. An exposition of Ecclesiastes, drawn from Jerome, was sent to three former pupils, Onias, Candidus, and Nathaniel, who had left Alcuin's fatherly care to serve the secular world at the court of Aachen. Three undedicated commentaries remain: the *Compendium in canticum canticorum* is based on Bede; the Expositions of Titus, Philemon, and Hebrews are based on Jerome; and the Apocalypse commentary attributed to Alcuin is heavily dependent on Ambrosius Autpertus (d. 784).

Because of the intellectual accessibility of these works and the widespread network of his disciples, Alcuin became the primary educational model for later continental authors. His place in the Carolingian intellectual tradition thus differs strikingly from that of Bede. While Bede always remained a venerable figure, he was nevertheless a remote one; Alcuin was the spiritual father of the next generation of Frankish cultural leaders, both within and without the church.

It is a tradition of modern scholarship to speak of the "Circle of Alcuin," a group of friends, associates, and former pupils who dominated the school life of the ninth century. Not many of these authors are known primarily as exegetes; indeed, it is not altogether fair to characterize Alcuin in this way, as he also wrote dogmatic treatises against the Adoptionists, basic educational works in the form of grammar, logic, and rhetoric texts, and copious letters. But it is Alcuin's exegesis which stands out as typical of what it is fair to call the "School of Alcuin." This is not a school bounded by the walls or curriculum of Aachen, Ferrières, or Tours, but a method and purpose of biblical study which remained an example for several generations and which can be understood only in an educational context. The flame was clearly passed to one of Alcuin's students, the most enthusiastic exegete of the age, Hrabanus Maurus.[4]

Hrabanus was an exemplary student of Alcuin, with whom he studied at Tours and perhaps at Aachen as well. He was also an exemplary monk, whose first loyalty was always to the monastery of his profession, Fulda. Already in his mid-twenties, Hrabanus was established as a teacher at Fulda; he became abbot about twenty years later, in 822. Although he felt that monks should avoid both ecclesiastical and secular politics, Hrabanus found himself in the midst of both. In fact, he played a major role in the condemnation of that troublesome misfit, Gottschalk (c. 805–c. 868). This high ecclesiastical profile brought with it a political role in the empire. Hrabanus never served at any Carolingian court, but he was confidant, adviser, and supporter to several monarchs, notably Louis the Pious (778–840) and Lothar I (795–855). After the collapse of Lothar's empire, Hrabanus fell into disfavor with Louis the German (804–876) and was forced to resign his abbacy. He moved to the Petersburg, not far from Fulda, where he wrote *De rerum naturis*, a collection of materials useful for the interpretation of Scripture. His reconciliation with Louis the German, an important step toward his ordination in 847 as Archbishop of Mainz, was sealed by a commentary on the Canticles of the Old and New Testaments, requested by and dedicated to the king.

By this time Hrabanus was over sixty years old. In the course of his long life he had written an astounding number of biblical commentaries: treatises on all the Old Testament historical books, Judith and Esther, Wisdom and Ecclesiasticus, the four major prophets (the Jeremiah commentary includes the first Latin exegetical treatment of Lamentations), the books of the Maccabees, the

Gospels of Matthew and John, the Acts of the Apostles, and the Pauline Epistles.

Space does not permit a detailed discussion of Hrabanus's biblical commentaries, which are not only many and varied but also extremely long. Like Bede and Alcuin, Hrabanus tended to expound his texts systematically, verse by verse, and to lean heavily on a variety of patristic authors. His use of sources has been the subject of modern study, and his exegesis has been seen as a guide to the state of original thought among, and the sources available to, Carolingian authors. But for the concerns of this chapter, Hrabanus's influence is of more importance than his originality or lack thereof. Hrabanus's exegesis was widely circulated in the ninth century and beyond—and this was by design, for these texts were written for an impressive variety of figures associated with the spread of Christian culture in Frankland.

De rerum naturis, a textbook of exegetical principles culled from patristic sources, was written at the request of Haimo of Halberstadt, who had also been a student of Alcuin at Tours, but the text was rededicated to Louis the German. In a similar manner, the commentary on Maccabees was written for both Louis the Pious and Geroldus, Archdeacon of Worms. Royal patrons also received the commentaries on the Canticles (dedicated to Louis the German), Jeremiah and Ezekiel (dedicated to Lothar I), and Chronicles (probably intended for Louis II [c. 822–875], the son of Lothar). The commentaries on Judith and Esther were dedicated to Ermengard, wife of Lothar. Among monastic and episcopal recipients of Hrabanus's treatises were his fellow student Freculph, Abbot of Lisieux (Pentateuch), Hilduin, Abbot of Saint Denis (Kings), Haistulph, Archbishop of Mainz (Matthew), his successor, Otgarius of Mainz (Wisdom and Ecclesiasticus), and finally Samuel, Archbishop of Worms and Lupus of Ferrières, to whom the commentaries on the Pauline Epistles were dedicated.

This list shows that Hrabanus habitually used biblical commentary as the language of instruction, whether the lesson was meant to be political, as in the exegesis of the prophets dedicated to the Carolingian monarchs, or expressly theological, as in the Matthew commentary written for Haistulph of Mainz. What had been one mode of speech for Alcuin became the principal type of discourse for his pupil. But Hrabanus was only the first of a long line of native Frankish exegetes, and his works show only the first stage of the developing genre of Carolingian biblical commentary. The decisive form begins to manifest itself in the writings of his favorite pupil, Walafrid Strabo.[5]

The son of a poor Swabian family, Walafrid entered the monastery of Reichenau as a boy. He showed literary talent at a very early age and wrote a long poem on the death of his teacher, Wettin, before his seventeenth birthday. Two years later he was on his way to Fulda to study with the most celebrated scholar of the age, Hrabanus Maurus. Neither the climate nor the architecture of the north pleased Walafrid's gentle spirit. The poignancy of his longing for Reichenau echoes through the poem of homesickness he sent to his former master, Grimald, a poem that surely ranks as one of the loveliest and most touching personal expressions of the early Middle Ages.

But in spite of his unhappiness, Walafrid prospered at Fulda under Hrabanus's tutelage. When Louis the Pious sought a teacher for his young son Charles (823–877), offspring of a second marriage with the unpopular Empress Judith, Walafrid, then just twenty-one years old, was dispatched to fill the post. Walafrid's loyalty to the royal family was lifelong; he returned to his beloved Reichenau as abbot in 838 but always maintained contact with his former student. In fact, Walafrid met his death in an accident crossing the Loire to visit Charles, then known as Charles the Bald, King of the Franks, in 849. Hrabanus Maurus wrote his epitaph.

Even though he died at the age of forty, Walafrid left a remarkable literary legacy, including poems about his favorite subjects—friends and flowers—and a number of exegetical treatises. Ironically, the work for which Walafrid is most renowned, that standardized high-medieval crib to the Bible, the *Glossa ordinaria*, is not his. As Beryl Smalley has wistfully noted, "The myth of Walafrid Strabo's authorship [of the gloss] dies hard, since it is preserved in bibliographies and library catalogues."[6] Nevertheless, recent scholarship has demonstrated that the formation of the gloss postdates Walafrid by several centuries. It is now thought to be, at least in its final form, the product of a circle of the twelfth-century schoolmaster, Anselm of Laon (d. 1117).

Like all myths, the legend of Walafrid's authorship of the *Glossa ordinaria* can claim a kernel of truth. Walafrid made no secret of the fact that many of his commentaries were not his own compilations of patristic sources, but *adnotationes* of Hrabanus's biblical work. The Pentateuch commentaries read like ghostwritten versions of his master's more lengthy exegesis. Instead of long, rhetorical sentences, Walafrid uses short, pithy statements to make clear the meaning or meanings of each verse. This innovation must have been found useful, for it became standard practice in the second half of the century.

Evidence that Walafrid's format was a catalyst for the glossing tradition of the later schools can be seen in the complicated textual history of the *Adnotationes* on the Pentateuch. Here we find a later compilation on Genesis, perhaps written by Remigius of Auxerre, which was first joined to the rest of Walafrid's *Adnotationes* corpus in the tenth century and was widely circulated in this form. The *Adnotationes* are much shorter than Hrabanus's commentaries on the books of Moses; they also seem to have been more popular than the originals on which they were based. At least the surviving manuscripts suggest as much. While three manuscripts of Hrabanus's Leviticus commentary are extant, eighteen copies of Walafrid's *Adnotationes* survive; eight are dated pre-1000.

Modern scholars, so enamored of originality, have tended to misjudge the attitude of both Walafrid and his contemporaries to this work. In trying to gauge medieval opinion, several scholars have cited a poem which appears between the Genesis and Exodus *Adnotationes* in several manuscripts, including Reims 130, a ninth-century copy. The poem reads:

> Hunc librum exposuit Hrabanus iure sophista
> Strabus et imposuit frivolos hos titulos.
> (Hrabanus the wise man explicated this book
> And Strabo put on these frivolous titles.)

Smalley says that this is "the cream of the joke" of Walafrid's reputation, because it shows that "medieval scholars did not think highly of Strabo. His dependence on Raban was too obvious," but Alf Önnerfors has convincingly discussed the poem as an example of Walafrid's modest and gracious "Ich-Form," suggesting that he wrote it to describe his own work.[7]

Now if Walafrid himself thought that the *Adnotationes* were frivolous, we could very well wonder why he wrote them. The answer may be found in the educational purpose to which the texts were put. A shorter version of Hrabanus's Pentateuch commentaries was needed, and Walafrid produced it. Like many abridgements, it became more popular than the original. This popularity was as much a result of form as of content, for the laconic style of Walafrid's *Adnotationes*, and of his less popular commentaries on the Psalter and the Catholic Epistles, is the beginning of an exegetical tradition which finds classical expression in the *Glossa ordinaria*.

The fuss over Walafrid's authorship of the *Glossa ordinaria* is important because the gloss became a magisterial reference work of the high medieval schools, and we would naturally like to know its origin. In some ways it does begin with Walafrid. Walafrid died young, and before the middle of the century; it seems that the style of his exegetical work pointed the way for later authors. He did not change the style of his esteemed master Hrabanus, who outlived him by seven years, but the exegesis of the latter half of the ninth century increasingly resembles Walafrid's work. This is most evident in the exegesis of the school of Auxerre.

Since the fifteenth century, Haimo of Auxerre has been confused with Haimo of Halberstadt, a pupil of Alcuin; the collection of texts in *Patrologia Latina* 116–18 is under the name of this earlier Haimo.[8] This misidentification is probably the result of our paucity of information about the life of Haimo of Auxerre. We know only that he is associated with the monastery school of Saint Germain of Auxerre by the twelfth-century chronicler "Anonymous of Melk," is praised by Heiric as one of his teachers, and may have been called to the abbacy of the monastery of Sasceium, southwest of Auxerre, in the year 865. Secure manuscript traditions attribute to Haimo commentaries on the Song of Songs, Isaiah, the Pauline Epistles, and the Apocalypse, and a homiliary *De sanctis et de temporibus*. Haimo was probably the author of unpublished commentaries on Genesis and Ezekiel, which survive in very few copies, and a homily on 1 John 5:4–10 has recently been shown to be his. Commentaries on the twelve Minor Prophets may also belong to the Haimonian corpus, but more study is needed to determine which texts in this series actually belong to Haimo and which belong to other authors.

Despite the confusion surrounding Haimo, some general statements may be made about the character of his works. They are complicated pieces which weave sermons, commentaries, letters, and treatises of the Fathers into concise interpretations of the text, in a manner quite different from the *catenae* of earlier Carolingian exegetes. Haimo's method of bringing together conflicting authorities in order to find a compatible resolution to the meaning of the biblical text is a hint of the evolving Scholastic method. The importance of Haimo's work in the school tradition is further demonstrated by the fact that excerpts from his biblical teachings, combined with those of John Scotus Erigena (c. 810–c. 877), were in circulation as a set of *glossae* on the Old and New Testaments by the 860s, that is, within Haimo's own lifetime. As John Contreni has shown, these were school glosses.[9]

The schoolroom is also the best environment in which to consider Haimo's pupil, Heiric.[10] Heiric's life emerged from the shadows with Theodore von Sickel's 1861 discovery of a Melk manuscript which lists the major dates of his life. This manuscript, written at Saint Germain of Auxerre in what some think is Heiric's own hand, is the basis for all biographies of this figure. We know from this source that Heiric was born in 841, tonsured at Saint Germain in 850, ordained a subdeacon in 859, and perhaps ordained to the priesthood in 865. It has been convincingly argued that he received his earliest monastic education (to 859) at Auxerre under Haimo and studied with Lupus at Ferrières from 859 to 862 and at Saint Médard of Soissons from 862 to 865, the year in which he returned to Auxerre to replace Haimo as abbot of Saint Germain. There is no firm evidence for the date of Heiric's death, although Contreni suggests that it was possibly in the mid-880s, at which time Heiric may have been teaching at Laon.

Heiric's extant exegetical works are certainly what one would expect of a man who studied and taught in the best schools of his age. Besides being credited with the *glossae* compiled from the works of Haimo and John Scotus, he is the author of the *Collectanea*, an obvious school text drawn from classical and medieval authors, and a homiliary in the style of Haimo. Each of these deserves closer examination.

The *Collectanea* gives a fascinating glimpse of the wide-ranging sources employed in the ninth-century schoolroom. In the dedication to Hildebold, Bishop of Soissons, Heiric acknowledges that this work is a compilation of the teaching of his masters Haimo and Lupus. Included in their curriculum were the *Memorabilium dictorum vel factorum* of Valerius Maximus, Suetonius's *Lives*, two pseudonymous collections of classical writings, and the *Prognosticum futuri saeculi* of Julian of Toledo. As the prefatory poem indicates, a long section entitled the "Scolia Quaestionum" is taken from the teachings of Haimo. Heiric begins with a series of theological questions, often problems posed by conflicting passages of Scripture; the interrogatives "Quomodo," "Cur," "Quaestio est," "Quaeri potest" (How? Why? The question is; We must ask), which begin each consideration, are characteristic of the Scholastic method. Following this theological exercise are explications of difficult passages of the Bible, the prophetic books in particular but also Esther, Kings, Ezra, Job, the letters of Paul, and the Gospels.

If the *Collectanea* portrays Heiric as a mere compiler, his homiliary suggests that he was quite capable of using his broad knowledge to express his own theological insights. In the process of untangling Heiric's homiliary from that of Haimo and from the miscellaneous sermons by other authors interpolated into this tradition, Barré was struck by the "originality and doctrinal profundity" of the collection, which he called "the most remarkable of all" the Carolingian homiliaries.[11] The appreciation of medieval readers for this homiliary is evident from its complex manuscript tradition and the number of abridgements it endured. Almost immediately after they were written, many of Heiric's sermons were incorporated into a collection which included selections from Haimo's homiliary; this body of sermons had a lively transmission of its own. Barré has proposed that one of the abridged collections of Heiric's homilies may have been the work of his pupil Remigius, who even as a teacher at Paris felt justified in promoting the Auxerrois method of homiletical exegesis.

The biblical commentaries of Haimo and Heiric suggest contact with an increasingly vital urban school tradition, but it is Remigius who clearly brings Carolingian exegesis into the world which will be later known as Scholastic.[12] A pupil of Heiric at Auxerre, Remigius was called, perhaps around the year 890, to revitalize the cathedral school of Reims under the patronage of Archbishop Fulco. After Fulco's death in 900, Remigius moved on to Paris, where he taught until his death. He was highly regarded as a teacher; among his students at Paris was Odo (879–942), later abbot of Cluny and an important monastic reformer.

As one might expect, the bulk of Remigius's writings are school texts: commentaries in *glossa* form on Donatus, Priscian, Phocas, and Eutyches, the *Distichia* of Cato, Juvenal, Sedulius Rhetor, and Martianus Capella have been attributed to him. But from the evidence of the manuscripts it seems that Remigius's reputation as an exegete was every bit as extravagant. At least two different commentaries on Genesis, four on the Psalms, and two on Matthew are attributed to him, as well as interpretations of each of the remaining Old Testament historical books, the Canticles of the Old and New Testaments, the prophets Isaiah and Daniel, the Gospels of Mark and John, and the Acts of the Apostles.

Of this bounty, only one commentary on Genesis, one on the Psalms, and one on Matthew are indisputably genuine. The Deuteronomy, Mark, and John commentaries may also be shown by further study to have been written by Remigius.

Remigius's commentary on Matthew is interesting both in its procedure and in its later history. The teacher of grammar predominates in this interpretation: definitions of difficult words, sometimes a variety of definitions, are offered to the reader. It is curious that this pragmatic and technical interpretation was adapted in the eleventh century for liturgical use, first by marginal annotations, later as a series of extracts which circulated as the "Twelve Homilies" of Remigius on Matthew.

The commentary on the Psalms had a similar textual history, although it never found its way into homiletical collections, probably because the Psalms do not appear as lectionary texts. As is the case with the Matthew commentary, the original text remains unpublished, while a later redaction was printed in the *Patrologia Latina*. This commentary, extant in both a long and a short version, has a characteristically Remigian focus on grammar and definitions. It begins with a question: "It is said, what is prophecy?"; gives a definition of the term followed by a series of Old Testament examples; and then moves on to the next question: "What is a psaltery?" This close textual analysis, marked by a teacher's desire to make rough places plain, was found useful in the later Middle Ages and influenced the interpretation of Bruno of Chartreux (d. 1101) which became the basis of the *Glossa ordinaria* on the Psalms.

If Remigius's commentary on the Psalms lies at the edge of the dispute over the authorship of the *Glossa ordinaria*, the question of his interpretation of Genesis plunges us into the thick of the fray. Two quite different Genesis commentaries have been attributed to Remigius: the treatise published in the *Patrologia*, which is extensively quoted in the *Glossa*, and an unpublished text found in nine manuscripts of the tenth to the fourteenth centuries. Because the text that appears in the gloss was quoted by twelfth-century schoolmen as a work of Walafrid Strabo, modern scholarship has tended to assign it to that earlier author. There are, nevertheless, three strong reasons for a claim that Remigius wrote the published Genesis text.

In the first place, scrutiny of the manuscript tradition easily shows that the twelfth-century authors had only one reason for thinking the *Patrologia* Genesis commentary to be Walafrid's: it was joined to Walafrid's Pentateuch *Adnotationes* in an entire school of manuscript transmission. Second, in the oldest manuscript of this text, written in the late ninth century at Jumièges, this Genesis commentary follows Haimo's interpretation of the Song of Songs; both treatises are attributed here to Haimo, making a clear link to the school of Auxerre. Finally, this Genesis commentary has all the marks of the school of Auxerre: it is extremely concise, it integrates earlier Carolingian exegesis into its own synthesis, and it shows traces of the teaching of John Scotus.

The unpublished Genesis commentary also seems to be a school text in the Auxerrois tradition, showing a flair for etymological and grammatical explanations and for the resolution of inherent contradictions in the text. The oldest manuscript, which may have been written at Saint Germain of Auxerre in the tenth century, attributes the text to Remigius; indeed, only the existence of the *Patrologia* Genesis commentary makes me hesitate to do the same. Our scanty knowledge of Remigius's literary life makes it difficult to know whether he could have been the author of two commentaries on the first book of the Bible, each perhaps representative of one stage of his development. Without doubt, further study will determine whether both these Genesis commentaries can be assigned to Remigius, or whether one should be attributed to some other member of his circle.

At any rate, the presence in the *Glossa ordinaria* of a Carolingian Genesis commentary from Auxerre strengthens Smalley's claim that the high-medieval gloss tradition is a product of the region of Laon. Behind the tradition may be the innovations of Walafrid Strabo, but the exegesis of Haimo, Heiric, and Remigius suggests that the glossating of the school of Anselm of Laon may be a regional characteristic that can be traced back nearly three centuries.

With Remigius, who died in 908, we have come to the end of the ninth century. Curiously, we have also come to a hiatus in biblical study in general. As Smalley puts it, after Remigius's death "there is no important commentary, and even a dearth of compilations, for about a century and a quarter." While noting the impact of political turmoil in the tenth century, Smalley suggests that the reason for this change is the Cluniac Reform, which "emphasized the liturgy at the expense of study."[13] Insofar as this is true, it can only be considered an irony that Remigius's prize pupil, Odo of Cluny, sounded the death knell for his master's method of study. However, from the overview presented in this chapter I would like to suggest another possible interpretation of the shift away from exegesis immediately following the ninth century.

We have séen that the educational reforms of Charlemagne, which emphasized the establishment of a proper biblical text and the gathering of exegesis of the patristic age, was only the first step in the development of Carolingian exegesis. Each successive generation of scholars came closer to achieving a synthesis of this material, drawing on it in ever more complex and original ways. In the course of the ninth century, biblical interpretation became an increasingly domestic product, written by Frankish monks who had been educated in Frankish institutions. After the death of Charlemagne, the monastery schools far outstripped the palace in support of this endeavor; by the second half of the century these schools, especially in West Frankland, had well-established ties, almost of a formal nature, which allowed young scholars to study with several different masters and to investigate the holdings of several different libraries. The exegesis of Haimo, Heiric, and Remigius of Auxerre shows that a need was felt in this period to make the growing collection of biblical learning readily accessible to students on all levels. The development of the glossating techniques of that school shows the most successful method by which this was done.

In short, the paucity of biblical commentaries in the tenth century is testimony of the effectiveness of the work of Alcuin. With the exegesis of the school of Auxerre, the biblical education of the Carolingian empire was complete. Only the new set of problems posed by the Scholastic age would inspire the biblical scholarship of the twelfth-century monastic and cathedral schools.

NOTES

1. J. J. Contreni, "The Biblical Glosses of Haimo of Auxerre and John Scottus Eriugena," *Speculum* 51 (1976): 412. The largest available collection of major Christian writings of the ninth century is printed in *PL* 100–131. Most are exegetical works: commentaries, homilies, and letters in response to questions of biblical interpretation. A significant number of other exegetical texts from the period remain unedited. The only major ninth-century exegetical works in a modern edition are E. Jeauneau, ed., *Jean Scot, Homélie sur le Prologue de Jean*, SC 151 (Paris, 1969), and *Jean Scot, Commentaire sur l'Évangile de Jean*, SC 180 (Paris, 1972). An edition of the *In Matthaeum* of

Paschasius Radbertus is in preparation by B. Paulus for the Corpus Christianorum series.

2. See P. Riché, *Education and Culture in the Barbarian West, Sixth through Eighth Centuries*, trans. J. J. Contreni (Columbia, S.C., 1976), 439–46 (section entitled "The Frankish Court: A Cultural Center").

3. B. Fischer, "Bibeltext und Bibelreform unter Karl dem Grossen," in B. Bischoff, ed., *Karl der Grosse*, vol. 2, *Das geistige Leben* (Düsseldorf, 1965), 156. This lengthy essay (pp. 156–216) is the best survey of the effort toward standardization of the Bible in the ninth century. For Alcuin, see Fischer, "Bibeltext," 171–75, where he summarizes his earlier work, *Die Alkuin-Bibel* (Freiburg-im-Breisgau, 1957); F. L. Ganshof, "La révision de la bible par Alcuin," *BHR* 9 (1947): 7–20; S. Berger, *Histoire de la Vulgate pendant les premiers siècles du moyen âge* (Paris, 1893), 185–212; E. K. Rand, "A Preliminary Study of Alcuin's Bible," *HThR* 24 (1931): 323–69; and *PL* 100–101. For Theodulf, see Fischer, "Bibeltext," 175–83; Berger, *Histoire*, 145–84; and L. Delisle, "Les Bibles de Théodulf," *BECh* 40 (1879): 1–47.

4. An excellent intellectual biography of Hrabanus is given by J. McCulloh in his introduction to the *Martyrologium*, CChr.CM 44 (Turnhout, 1979), xi–xxiv. On the possibility that Hrabanus may have studied at the court school of Aachen, see D. Schaller, "Der junge 'Rabe' am Hof Karls des Grossen (Theodulf carm. 27)," in J. Autenrieth and F. Brunhöltzl, eds., *Festschrift Bernhard Bischoff* (Stuttgart, 1971), 123-41. Hrabanus's works are found in *PL* 106–12 and *MGH.Ep* 5. On his exegesis, see the work of J. B. Hablitzel, *Hrabanus Maurus: Ein Beitrag zur Geschichte der mittelalterlichen Exegese*, BSt (F) 9/3, ed. O. Bardenhewer (1906), and the source analyses by the same author in *HJ* 27 (1906): 74–85; 38 (1917): 538–52; and in *BZ* 19 (1931): 215–27. I have recently suggested that Hrabanus may have been a more "original" exegete than is generally acknowledged; see E. A. Matter, "The Lamentations Commentaries of Hrabanus Maurus and Paschasius Radbertus," *Traditio* 38 (1982): 137–63.

5. Walafrid's poetry may be found in *Monumenta Germaniae Historica, Poetae Latini Aevi Carolini* 2:301–33, with selections (including the poem to Grimald) trans. by H. Waddell, *Medieval Latin Lyrics*, 2d ed. (London, 1948), 110–17, with biographical note, 311–13. His exegesis is largely unedited, although some genuine selections appear in *PL* 113–14, the volumes largely given over to an almost useless printing of the *Glossa ordinaria* (see below). My discussion comes from study of ninth- and tenth-century manuscripts, the most important being Reims 130, Sankt Gallen 283, Einsiedeln 184 (190), Orléans 31, and München clm. 6227.

6. B. Smalley, *The Study of the Bible in the Middle Ages*, 2d ed. (Oxford, 1952; reprint, Notre Dame, 1964), 57. For a general discussion of the problems surrounding the gloss, see ibid., 46–66, which summarizes her earlier work in *RThAM* 7 (1935): 235–62; 8 (1936): 24–60; and 9 (1937): 365–400.

Smalley has continued her study of the gloss in "Les bibles de l'époque romane: glose ordinaire et gloses périmées," *CCM* 4 (1961): 15–22. Another study of note is J. de Blic, "L'oeuvre exégétique de Walafrid Strabon et la *Glossa ordinaria*," *RThAM* 16 (1949): 5–28.

7. Smalley, *Study of the Bible*, 58; A. Önnerfors, "Über Walahfrid Strabos Psalter-Kommentar," in A. Önnerfors, J. Rathofer, and F. Wagner, eds., *Literatur und Sprache im europäische Mittelalter. Festschrift für Karl Langosch zum 70. Geburtstag* (Darmstadt, 1973), 85. Haimo's works are printed in *PL* 116–18.

8. A. Wilmart first called attention to this "erreur désastreuse" of Johannes Trithemius, Abbot of Spanheim, who in 1492 assigned the Haimo collection to Haimo of Halberstadt: "Un commentaire des Psaumes restitué à Anselme de Laon," *RThAM* 8 (1936): 325–44. For Haimo, see also R. Quadri, "Aimone di Auxerre alla luce dei 'Collectanea' de Heiric di Auxerre," *IMU* 6 (1963): 1–48 (where the specter of several other Haimos is raised and disposed of); H. Barré, *Les homéliaires carolingiens de l'école d'Auxerre*, StT 224 (Vatican, 1962), and J. J. Contreni, "Haimo of Auxerre, Abbot of Sasceium (Cessy-les-Bois), and a New Sermon on 1 John V, 4–10," *RBén* 85 (1975): 303–20.

9. Printed by Contreni, "Biblical Glosses," 429–34. Contreni (pp. 428–29) believes that the glosses under the name of Haimo were notes from an early stage of Haimo's teaching career rather than extracts from his written works. He further suggests (pp. 427–28) that Heiric may have compiled this collection. For Haimo and the evolving school tradition, see E. Bertola, "Il commentario paolino di Haimon di Halberstadt odi Auxerre e gli inizi del metodo scolastico," *Pier Lombardo* 5 (1961): 29–54, and "Il precedenti storici del metodo del 'Sic et Non' di Abelardo," *RFNS* 53 (1961): 255–80. Quadri, "Aimone di Auxerre," 45, places Haimo "on the line of demarcation between the compiler of patristic extracts and the author of a commentary."

10. R. Quadri, *I Collectanea di Eirico di Auxerre*, SpicFri 11 (Fribourg, 1966), for a critical edition of Heiric's most obvious school text. For his homiliary, which is not fully published, see Barré, *Les homéliaires*, 71–93, 160–79. Quadri, "Aimone di Auxerre," 12–13, describes the Melk manuscript, which is the source of Heiric's dates.

11. Barré, *Les homéliaires*, 141–42; see pp. 91–112 and 141 for the recensions of the Haimo/Heiric/Remigius homiliary.

12. For the life and works of Remigius, see M. Manitius, *Geschichte der lateinischen Literatur des Mittelalters* (Munich, 1911), 1:504–19, although much of this is outdated. Manitius (p. 504) implies that Remigius's native tongue was a Romance, rather than a Germanic, language. Flodoard of Reims testifies to the recruitment of Remigius by Fulco of Reims; see *Historia Remensis ecclesiae*, MGH.SS 13:574. The *Vita* of Odo of Cluny, *Acta Sanctorum* 5:157, is our source for Remigius's professional activities in Paris. *PL* 131 gives some very poor editions of some of Remigius's work. In this discussion of

Remigius, I have made use of the following: Barré, *Les homéliaires*; A. E. Schönbach, *Über einige Evangelien Kommentare des Mittelalters*, Sitzungsberichte der kaiserl. Akademie der Wissenschaften 146/4 (Vienna, 1903), 174-75; C. E. Lutz, *Remigii Autissiodorensis Commentum in Martianum Capellam*, 2 vols. (Leiden, 1962-65); P. A. Vaccari, "Il genuino commento ai Salmi di Remigio di Auxerre," *Biblica* 26 (1945): 52-99; Burton Van Name Edwards, "Avranches 109 and Two Commentaries on Genesis Attributed to Remigius of Auxerre," unpublished paper; and the following manuscripts: Paris, B. N. nouv. acq. lat. 762, Einsiedeln 181 (188), Vatican lat. 646, Vatican Ottob. lat. 278. (I am indebted to Alejandro E. Planchart for a description of this last manuscript, which I have not seen.)

13. Smalley, *Study of the Bible*, 44, 45.

8

Teaching and Learning Theology in Medieval Paris

Marcia L. Colish

The Paris of the year 1100 was a small riverine fortress, confined to the walled Ile de la Cité, that was just beginning to recover its initiative after centuries of Viking devastation and the more recent efforts of the early Capetians to subdue their vassals in the Ile-de-France. As a capital, Paris was exiguous, lacking in cultural panache compared with Chartres, Laon, Rheims, Bec, or Cluny. Its chief schools were in the old abbeys of St. Germain-des-Près and Ste. Geneviève, both lying well outside the city walls and serving as the jurisdictional centers of their own largely agrarian communities. By the mid-fifteenth century, Paris was the brilliant capital of the largest, most powerful, and most centralized state in Europe, whose late Capetian and Valois monarchs had led the field in consolidating control of their national church at the expense of the papacy. The Ile de la Cité was now the administrative and ecclesiastical hub of a country dramatically enlarged following the successful conclusion of the Hundred Years' War. French institutions, French literature, French Gothic art and architecture enjoyed widespread influence in Europe at large. And the chief star in the cultural diadem of Paris was its university, where the faculty of theology held pride of place.

The development of the university of Paris as a chartered corporation with a privileged status guaranteed by pope and king went hand in hand with the emergence of Paris as the leading theological center in Europe in the High Middle Ages. Paris theologians both earned and asserted a claim to doctrinal authority in the Western church rivaling that of popes and councils alike. The changing kinds of theology they taught between about 1100 and 1450 reflect vividly the development of Parisian academic life as a whole. At the same time, the public standing of the theologians involved them in the broader controversies of the day.

For the Paris theologians, all these issues—political, ecclesiastical, and intellectual—were expressed in their academic institutions and behavior. Their theological teachings were sometimes shaped by their professional rivalries as academics. On the one hand, the Paris theologians achieved and jealously maintained a recognized group identity. On the other hand, throughout our period their teachings did not form one monolithic "Paris school" of theology but manifested themselves in a series of rival schools of thought, fiercely competitive yet coexisting within a shared Christian consensus. These successive conflicts have received traditional labels—Scholastic vs. monastic, "Augustinian" vs. "Aristotelian," realist vs. nominalist, or *via moderna* vs. *via antiqua*—that obscure as much as they reveal, for within the main chronological subdivisions of our story we will find large areas of agreement on common themes, values, questions, and methods in terms of which the comtemporary alternatives were framed, agreements integrally related to the common educational experience that united the contestants as much as their disagreements divided them.

The terms "school" and "schools of Paris" must be used loosely in the twelfth century. The major schools, for all subjects except law, spanned northern France and were not localized in Paris until late in the century. Some were cathedral schools, some monastic. Some, of both types, were lineal descendants of the Carolingian renaissance, while others owed their existence to more recent ecclesiastical and educational reform or to Capetian patronage. The intellectual excitement that a theologian could generate counted for more than the institutional setting in which he taught. Indeed, as the careers of such figures as Peter Abelard (1079–1142) and the lay theologian Manegold of Lautenbach (c. 1030–after 1103) testify, an institutional connection was not in itself a requirement; this was an age of theological entrepreneurs par excellence.

Theologians moved freely from cathedral to monastic schools and back again, just as they moved from one part of France to another and between the French and English sections of the Angevin empire. Disciples frequently criticized their masters. Staunch opponents on one issue warmly collaborated on others or were lumped together by contemporaries who objected to them as a group.

Proponents of different kinds of intellectual formation yet displayed analogous theological methods. In many ways the shifting terrain of twelfth-century theology in its northern French and Anglo-French context can be amply symbolized by Anselm of Canterbury (c. 1033–1109), monk and prelate, who addressed so many of its concerns—a style with a taste both for rigorous logic and for the language of prayer, speculation on the great questions of the incarnation, grace, and free will, and the simultaneous stress on the primacy of faith and the need to give a rational account of it to believer and nonbeliever alike.

The schools of northern France were the chief glory of the renaissance of the twelfth century that enriched, invigorated, and professionalized the teaching of all the disciplines of the traditional seven liberal arts. Theologians contributed to the disciplines themselves as well as applying their insights and methodologies to the tasks of theology proper. Antagonists such as Abelard and Bernard of Clairvaux (1090–1153), with their respective attachments to logic and rhetoric, are equally incomprehensible apart from the current educational revival. Bernard's use of antithesis as a structural device in his *De consideratione*, posing extremes and mediating between them rhetorically, can be seen as a parallel, from his preferred discipline, of the logical sifting, criticism, and synthesis of contrasting authorities typified by Abelard's *Sic et non* and by the genre of sentence commentaries represented most canonically by Peter Lombard (c. 1100–1160). Most prevalent was Augustine's view, restated and exemplified by Hugh of St. Victor (c. 1096–1141), that theology should be grounded in the Bible and informed by a broad education. "Learn everything," he urged. "You will see afterwards that nothing is superfluous. A skimpy knowledge is not a pleasing thing."[1]

A similarly broad interdisciplinary commitment can be seen in other leading theologians of the century such as Gilbert de la Porrée (1076–1154) and Peter Comestor (d. c. 1179). They, like all their contemporaries, held that theology began with biblical exegesis, although they dissociated themselves from those who said it should end there. It was, in fact, out of the enterprise of systematic Bible study and the resuscitation of the patristic and Carolingian techniques of the gloss, or continuous commentary on an entire book of the Bible, and the *quaestio*, or the analysis of particular doctrinal points in the text of Scripture, that twelfth-century theologians were alerted to one of their most fundamental insights—that revered authorities could disagree, that secular learning could shed light on the Bible, and that the disciplines could be used to resolve discrepancies in ways suited to pedagogy, learned debate, and apology.

The growing professionalization of Scripture study is reflected in the second half of the century by the production of handbooks, glossaries, and dictionaries of biblical history and by the first scheme for subdividing the books of the Bible into chapters to facilitate pedagogical and scholarly reference. These needs, coupled with the increasing availability and study of Aristotle's logic, encouraged a more dialectical approach to the biblical text and a growing preference for a literal reading, of the sort promoted by the Victorines, into which flowed a wider knowledge and more sustained use of contemporary Jewish exegesis.

This latter taste indicates a major area of concord among twelfth-century theologians despite their other disagreements. While mystical and contemplative theology and ethical theology of a purely intramural nature flourished in this period, there was an equally strong conviction that it was necessary to persuade nonbelievers and heretics. Such persons were no longer seen as abstractions or as ghosts from church history but as living realities who bulked large in the twelfth-century theological imagination. The apologetic impulse cut across vocational and scholastic lines and expressed itself in a number of genres of theological literature, from expositions of the creeds and analyses of the relations among creedal statements, biblical revelation, and the formal affirmation of newly contested doctrines, to sermons, translations, dialogues, and polemical treatises. Theologians as discordant on other matters as Bernard of Clairvaux, Abelard, Geoffrey II de Lèves, Bishop of Chartres (d. 1149), and Peter the Venerable (c. 1092–1156), Abbot of Cluny, agreed on the need to attack the Petrobrusian heresy, while Abelard and Gilbert Crispin (d. c. 1117), Abbot of Westminster, followed Anselm in stressing that debates with the Jews should be based on a common ground and employ proofs acceptable on both sides.

Apology thus joined with an expanded curriculum of secular arts and sciences and a deeper reading of the Church Fathers to promote a widespread interest in the twelfth century in defining and comparing different modes of knowledge and in situating theological knowledge and theological language in a broad philosophical context. While agreeing on the need, individual thinkers and groups disagreed on how best to meet it. While the Chartrains sought to distinguish the different sciences and to explore their aptitudes as theological tools, the Victorines were more interested in relating the discursive knowledge of science and the theological knowledge derived from revelation and contemplation, as successive epistemic states. Concepts of system also varied among thinkers who shared the view that systematic theology ought to be written. For Hugh of St. Victor the idea of sacrament, embracing all the modes of God's self-communication to humanity, supplied the framework; for Abelard systematic theology was reducible to Trinitarian theology; for Peter Lombard and his followers it embraced God, the creation, the redemption, and the means of grace available through the church. This debate was one of the few decisively won during the century as Lombard's approach outpaced its rivals.

Along with these common explorations of the scope, aim, and method of theology, certain theological themes appealed strongly to the twelfth century and likewise cut across school lines. Of high visibility was the nature of ethical acts, which also conditioned current thinking on the sacraments, Christology, and Trinitarian theology. The first two topics reflect the revolution in religious sentiment and the preoccupation with the inner life that mark twelfth-century culture, just as the latter two witness its apologetic concerns. At the same time, all these themes can be connected with twelfth-century education. The ethical predilections of the theologians parallel those of the classical authors most admired and imitated in the schools, while Christological and Trinitarian speculation was heavily influenced by the academic commentary on Boethius (c. 480–c. 524), both his logical texts and translations and his theological treatises on Trinitarian and Christological doctrine.

The debate on moral theology crystallized around Abelard's view of inner intention as the prime definition of an ethical act. Opponents on all sides agreed that Abelard had gone too far. Yet his teaching, modified to include an objective norm and the translation of sound intentions into appropriate acts, entered the mainstream of twelfth-century theology. Abelard's conception of Christ's saving work as the expression of God's love that inspires our loving response to God was also attacked. But even his staunchest critics shared his understanding of Christ's role in human and affective terms.

Trinitarian and Christological debates centered as much on Gilbert de la Porrée and Peter Lombard as on Abelard and show that one of the prime and unsolved problems for twelfth-century theologians was the lack of a common and adequate vocabulary, even among those with the greatest academic homogeneity and intellectual affinity. The thinkers whose teachings were contested all had a strongly logical bent, and all except Lombard had commented on Boethius. Their major problem was that Boethius himself had used the key terms "person" and "nature" in multiple and inconsistent ways.[2] His twelfth-century commentators understandably interpreted the same passages differently and misconstrued each other's terminology.

Abelard, himself a critic of one of Gilbert's applications of Boethian *persona* to the Trinity, frankly admitted that the philosophical language of the day made it impossible to explain precisely how a unity of substance could inhere in a diversity of persons. His own alternative position, laboring under the same difficulties, was declared heretical. At Gilbert's trial what is most striking is the disagreement of contemporary witnesses, including his own pupils and Lombard, as to what he had said, what the charges against him meant, whether he had answered them, and whether his views had been proscribed or approved. The debate over Lombard's Christology, which went through several highly publicized stages before his view was eventually vindicated at the Fourth Lateran Council in 1215, likewise turns on his use of Boethius's porous vocabulary.

These two cases were heard by church councils presided over by popes, yet the fortunes of the theologians involved were determined as much by the attack or defense of the Parisian theological establishment. This fact calls us back to academic and institutional history. By the third decade of the century a theologian who sought the title of master and the formal right to teach required a license from the bishop's chancellor or some other comparable authority. Between William of Champeaux's (c. 1070–1121) departure from the cathedral school of Notre Dame in 1108 and the beginning of Peter Lombard's teaching career there in the early 1140s, there were no Notre Dame theologians of any distinction. And until Lombard became Bishop of Paris in 1159, the incumbents of the see were distinguished more by their connections with the Ile-de-France nobility than by their capacity or desire to patronize learning. The major

Paris theologians during the intervening decades, except for the Victorines, were the independents. The latter sought and found a licensing agency in the Abbey of Ste. Geneviève.

The Abbey of Ste. Geneviève played a crucial role in the history of Paris theology for the next century and more, a role in which its moral, intellectual, and jurisdictional lassitude was just as important as its brief period of excellence. In the first half of the twelfth century, Ste. Geneviève was in a parlous state. It was a community deeply in need of reform whose main energies were consumed by the effort to evade it, from whatever quarter. The abbot possessed the right to grant licenses to teach in the precincts of his abbey. His utter disinterest in governing the activities of the theologians who taught there made his protection extremely attractive, drawing the most exciting and innovative theologians of the time and their hordes of students.

In the second half of the twelfth century, following a reform under the aegis of St. Victor, the school of Ste. Geneviève was ornamented by Simon of Tournai (c. 1130–c. 1201), a theologian whose eminence matched that of Peter of Poitiers (c. 1130–1205), Peter Comestor, Peter the Chanter (d. 1197), and Stephen Langton (d. 1228), his Notre Dame contemporaries. The fact that Ste. Geneviève and Notre Dame had eclipsed all other rivals by the end of the century was symbolized graphically by the southern enceinte of the new city walls of Philip Augustus, which sliced through the domain of St. Germain-des-Près leaving the abbey outside the city, which excluded St. Victor but which embraced Ste. Geneviève with all its lands. While no subsequent Genovefan theologian matched Simon's prominence, his career had brought his abbey to a level of academic prestige corresponding to its independence from the bishop. Parisian masters continued to invoke the option of appealing to Ste. Geneviève for their licenses even after the university had been chartered, in order to preserve or extend their liberties in relation to Notre Dame. Ste. Geneviève thus provided the academic freedom that helped Paris become the outstanding theological center of Europe in the latter part of the twelfth century.

The authority acquired by the Paris theologians by that time was one merited by their achievements. It was also enhanced by their own myth-making, which by the end of the century had concocted the legend of the three brothers, by which Peter Lombard, Peter Comestor, and Gratian (d. by 1179) were seen as siblings whose combined eminence in theology, Scripture study, and canon law guaranteed the prestige and orthodoxy of Parisian teaching. Luck enlarged that claim around 1169, when Henry II of England offered to submit his controversy with his archbishop Thomas Becket (c. 1118-1170) to the arbitration of the Paris theologians. This event never took place, and it was proposed by Henry as a ploy in the ongoing contest.[3] But it underscored the prominence and disinterestedness of the theologians and the capacity which their expertise gave them to judge and to mediate between *regnum* and *sacerdotium*. Nor were they remiss in policing their own ranks, taking the initiative in the condemnation of the views of David of Dinant (d. after 1210) and Amalric of Bena (d. c. 1207) in 1210. The fact that the critics of Lombard in the Christological debates of the twelfth century were out of the mainstream, and that his defenders were Parisians who had based their teaching on his during long and distinguished careers, is by no means an accidental feature of the outcome in 1215.

The year 1215 also marks the enactment of the first general statutes of the University of Paris, confirming privileges vis-à-vis the Bishop and Provost of Paris granted by earlier papal and royal charters. Later in the century, popes extended these liberties, guaranteeing the masters' right to advance candidates to degrees on merit against the abusive licensing practices of the chancellors. Four faculties developed within the university. The largest was arts, whose rector became the legal head of the whole corporation. Law and medicine were outstripped by theology, owing to the prestige of the subjects, its existing prominence at Paris, its utility for careerists in church and state, and the fact that Paris was the first European university with a theological faculty chartered by the pope. The university contained other subcorporations such as nations and colleges, but it was membership in a faculty that entitled a master to teach and to participate in university self-government.

The statutes of 1215 also laid down curricular norms which, as amplified over the next half-century, delineated Parisian education in theology and other fields for the remainder of the Middle Ages. A curricular revolution which accents the chief intellectual issue of the century, the reception of Aristotle and Greco-Arabic science and philosophy, occurred in the arts course and spread to theology. After a generation of dispute, the curriculum of 1255 made Aristotelian natural philosophy and metaphysics, along with the Neoplatonic *Liber de causis* ascribed to Aristotle, the largest single element in the arts course and elevated logic over grammar and rhetoric as the basic preparatory discipline.

Theologians continued to argue over how much, and how, this new learning should be applied to theology, some embracing it warmly but critically, contributing to its study and incorporating it in their work, and others treating it gingerly. But no theologian, however squeamish, could avoid this material, owing to the education and professional techniques he shared with his colleagues. Because theologians had to achieve a degree in arts and to teach in the arts faculty for at least two years before beginning their graduate work, they acquired a common terminology and understanding of the range of contemporary philosophical options. Whatever their own later opinions, what and how they learned and taught in arts made their approach analytical, speculative, and polemical. This not only was a function of their intellectual formation and their pedagogical conviction that alternative views should always be brought to bear on all questions, but also points to a sharp escalation of the apologetic imperative.

The thorniest heresies of the day were wholesale counter-theologies which had to be attacked systematically. Judaism and Islam were now confronted as competitors bolstered by a sophisticated scientific and philosophical culture. University theologians also competed with each other for the handful of chairs in their faculty and for the students on whose numbers their income as well as their prestige depended. Wherever a theologian stood on the big question of synthesizing Greek philosophy with Christian doctrine, he absorbed and used a good deal of philosophy as a consequence of the curricular and pedagogical mandates of the university which were prerequisites for his academic survival. Rival schools of thought all used the Aristotelian vocabulary of being, essence, substance, and accidents to describe God, humanity, and the presence of Christ in the sacraments, as well as natural phenomena.

The model of science, with its given first principles used as criteria of what can be deduced logically from them, was widely applied to theology. Aristotle's psychology and biology revised the conception of Christian ethics, and his metaphysical upgrading of the natural world informed the century's approach to ethics and to sacramental theology alike.

The theologian's training also involved a two-part course following the arts degree, lasting at least eight years and deferring his theological license to his thirty-fifth year at the earliest—an education more grueling and protracted than that of any other learned professional. First came four years of Bible study. Thirteenth-century exegetes sought to emend the text and to study biblical thought as an organized whole, reflecting the wish to systematize and to use the Bible more accurately in theological construction and apologetic debate. Myriad strategies were proposed for studying Scripture and its major subdivisions in some definite moral or pedagogical order that placed each book in its wider context logically and theologically.

Scripture scholars seconded their twelfth-century predecessors in their generous use of previous commentators, the liberal arts, and philosophy to elucidate the text and in preferring the Psalms and the Pauline Epistles to other biblical books. The latter taste stemmed partly from the accepted view that the Psalms were the prime guide to the Christian life and that Paul was the model theologian, and partly from the fact that each of these units of Scripture contained problems of style, chronology, and the relation of parts to the whole on which exegetes could exercise their analytical skill. While the Parisians worked essentially in Latin, they were attuned to textual questions, comparing the Septuagint, Greek readings found in patristic translations, and liturgical quotations with the Vulgate, and sometimes preferring them to it. Handbooks, commentaries, and biblical *quaestiones* proliferated and were added to the curriculum of biblical study.

On completion of his biblical course, the young theologian taught Scripture for two years, alternating lectures on Old Testament and New Testament books. The central role of the Bible in theology and the ongoing conception of the theologian as "master of the sacred page" are visible in the work of the leading theologians of all schools across the thirteenth century.

Next came a two-year course in systematic theology based on the *Sentences* of Peter Lombard, already the model for this type of instruction in the late twelfth century. By now Lombard was accoutered with his own authoritative glosses, which were likewise included as subjects of study. Lombard had discussed creation as well as God, the redemption, and the sacraments. While the opinions he assembled were largely patristic, his open-ended format and comparative methodology made it easy for thirteenth-century sentence commentators to include the new science and metaphysics. The study of Lombard thus flowed smoothly into the *summa*, a characteristic genre of theological literature which, while including all the topics treated by Lombard in the same order, could express an individual theologian's emphasis and the extent and type of philosophy he wished to use.

After his course on the *Sentences*, the candidate taught them for two years. Then came three or four more years as a regular participant in theological disputation and preaching, his final oral examination, the award of the doctorate, and his admission to the theological faculty as a licensed master. He proceeded to deliver an inaugural lecture and taught for at least two years at that level. Whether or not he acquired a coveted chair, he often moved on with startling rapidity to ecclesiastical preferment or administrative work in a religious order; theologians rarely grew old in the schools.

The form and substance of a thirteenth-century theological education often inspired doctrinal debates and developments. Some of the theological concerns of the century stemmed directly from the theologians' philosophical training. A case in point is their pervasive and otherwise inexplicable fascination with angelology, despite the marginal role of angels in the divine economy and the heretics' lack of interest in them. The real challenge was the attempt to reconceptualize angels in terms of Neoplatonic or Aristotelian metaphysics, retaining their pure spiritual nature, their inferiority to the Creator, and their free will, without fudging either the philosophy or the biblical account. Previous Jewish and Muslim thinkers had wrestled with the same problem. Neither they nor their thirteenth-century Christian successors could find a generally acceptable way of resolving it.

Contrasting philosophical convictions also informed the disputes over God's instrumental causation, although this topic might hinge as well on patristic or devotional predilections and had far wider theological ramifications than did angelology. Bonaventure (1221–1274) combined Neoplatonic emanationism, Augustinian illuminationism, and the Franciscan mystic's sense of God's abiding presence in nature. His critics charged him with an immanentalism that made God responsible for sin and evil. Most Christian Aristotelians saw God as governing the world through autonomous secondary causes. Their critics taxed them with annulling divine providence and with reducing God to a mere first cause. Thomas Aquinas (c. 1225–1274) tried to mediate with the Avicennan idea (Avicenna, Arabian Muslim philosopher, 980–1037) that God, as a metaphysical efficient cause, remained the ground of being sustaining secondary causes. No consensus was reached, yet the contestants agreed that the attributes chiefly manifested by God and mirrored in the creation were his rationality and benevolence.

Academic infighting, both intrafaculty and interfaculty, also precipitated doctrinal controversy. The two chief instances, which intersected between the 1250s and 1270s, were the contests between the secular and mendicant theologians and the struggle between the theologians as a group and the arts faculty over who should control the teaching of philosophical ideas that had theological implications.

When the Dominican and Franciscan friars arrived on the scene they were brilliant and innovative theologians, profound exegetes, and broad-gauged philosophers at a time when their secular counterparts were mediocrities. The claim that the friars' lack of Parisian licenses and loyalties should debar them from the theological faculty was thus shot through with professional and personal jealousies. As the scholarship gap between the two groups widened in the third quarter of the century, William of St. Amour (c. 1200–1272) led the seculars in a doctrinal attack on the mendicant vocation itself. He did not shrink from exploiting the current split between Franciscan moderates and rigorists, a split which left the rebuttal mainly to the Dominicans, who asserted not merely the legitimacy of mendicant orders but the superiority of monastic vows over priestly ordination as the highest Christian calling. Once the dust had settled, the Dominican view was absorbed into the consensus and flowed into later ethical and ecclesiological discussions.

In the concurrent wrangle between arts and theology, theologians who objected to broad syntheses of philosophy and theology and to the Averroistic interpretation (Averroes, Spanish Muslim philosopher, 1126–1198) of Aristotle taught by some arts masters broke ranks from their other allegiances, formed a self-named "Augustinian" party, and succeeded in associating Thomistic Aristotelianism with the Averroism it rejected. The doctrinal lines were deliberately confused in the interest of academic politics. The Bishop of Hippo would have had difficulty recognizing his progeny in the faction that flaunted his name as a code word for orthodoxy. Franciscans who used a good deal of Aristotle themselves and who joined Aquinas in attacking Averroism allied with the "Augustinians."

The upshot was the intervention of the Bishop of Paris in 1270 and 1277 with condemnations of the objectionable teachings, both Averroistic theses that did lead to heterodoxy and Aristotelian and Thomistic ones that did not. Paradoxically, these condemnations were welcomed by most Paris theologians even though their corporate identity was predicated on their right and capacity to police themselves. The bishop clearly exceeded his brief; and further, the theses he listed were so garbled that it would have been hard to find a Paris master at the time who taught them as stated.

The condemnations of the 1270s have often been read as having banished philosophy from the theological enterprise. What they did accomplish was both to encourage Averroists to move elsewhere and to put Paris theologians in control of teaching in the areas of philosophy that had caused the trouble. The condemnations did not succeed in destroying Thomism. Chiefly responsible for its comparative decline in the late Middle Ages were the Dominicans themselves. Instead of reconsidering the doctrines at issue, which signaled points where Aquinas's Aristotelianism and Christianity failed to cohere, they taught them defensively, locking themselves into a position that grew increasingly uninteresting to their contemporaries.

Other regroupings were occasioned by the emergence of new religious orders and secular figures, like the Augustinian eremites and Henry of Ghent (d. 1293), who made their own eclectic theological choices. It was the Franciscans' urge to renovate their own theology in the persons of Duns Scotus (c. 1264–1308) and William of Ockham (c. 1300–c. 1349) that produced the decisive reshuffle in Parisian theology between the 1280s and 1340s. Ockham, especially, dominated the *via moderna*, and his new formulations and concerns influenced most theologians for the rest of the Middle Ages whether they agreed with him on all points or not. Both Scotus and Ockham were Oxonians, although Scotus taught at Paris for two years. Both had Parisian followers and critics but show that the creative impulse was now coming increasingly from outside Paris.

Ockham drew a sharp distinction between the knowledge accessible to reason and the knowledge of faith. The acceptability of this distinction to his contemporaries reflects both their narrowing of the theologians' mandate and their notion of the capacities of reason itself. In contrast with their predecessors from Anselm to Aquinas, fourteenth- and fifteenth-century theologians abandoned apology and made no effort to render their faith comprehensible to Jews, Muslims, or philosophically motivated nonbelievers, echoing by this default the sense of their age that the most effective policy toward intellectual heterogeneity was persecution, ghettoization, or massacre.

At the same time, the terminist logic now taught in the Parisian arts course, and the epistemology associated with it, had grown increasingly post-Aristotelian, reversing the efforts of the thirteenth-century friars and proponents of modistic logic to teach a logic that could structure the data of extra-mental reality as well as governing the modalities of concepts. While agreeing that concepts stand for things outside the mind at the initial stage of signification, the terminists were far more interested in how terms signify in the context of propositions, thus making the analysis of truth claims primarily a function of the logical and semantic cogency of propositions themselves.[4]

Attached to an epistemology that confined certitude to the knowledge of individual things subject to empirical verification, this logic restricted the perceived scope of human reason and encouraged theologians to think that reason, so defined, had little or nothing to contribute to their work. One plausible response would have been to abandon theological speculation altogether and not just the *summa* form, limiting themselves to Bible study. Our lack of a systematic study of exegesis in the fourteenth and fifteenth centuries makes impossible any generalizations about their actual approach to the sacred page or how they used Scripture in their theology. One thing certain is that the taste for speculation and the habit of logic died hard, to the point where the *moderni* were criticized from within and without the academy for their dialectical gamesmanship.

Within the range of views on specifics encompassed by the *via moderna* there was strong agreement that the attribute of God most in need of defense was his utter transcendence over his creation. This concern inspired the rejection of Augustinian illuminationism, Neoplatonic emanationism, and Aristotelian naturalism in many quarters, all seen as binding God, and humanity as well, to necessitarian laws of nature. Once that binding was broken, the appeal of any kind of natural theology collapsed, a trend reflected in the abbreviation or omission of comment on creation in the study of the *Sentences*. Yet natural law was not abandoned as a meaningful concept in ethics or in publicistic writing. Theologians continued to apply the laws of human logic to God, transferring necessitarianism from nature to supernature.

This shift underlies many of the keenest debates of the age. It was widely held that divine grace and predestination annihilated the human being's free response. Even those theologians mislabeled "Pelagians" by their critics, who deemed a human response possible at all, thought that it received merit purely at God's good pleasure. Here the non-Euclidian processes of justification and sanctification were subjected to a zero-sum analysis. Together stressing the omnipotence of God, they hotly debated his knowledge of future contingents, his ability to alter the past, and his power to act outside of or against the order of nature and grace that he had created—questions whose very formulation imposed logical and chronological strictures on God's activities. Those theologians who went furthest in asserting God's absolute freedom from any natural or supernatural law still circumscribed him by the logical law of contradiction.

Parisian theologians contributed to these developments, although they rarely initiated them. The main field where they remained at the frontiers of their disciplines was ecclesiology, a fact mirroring the catalytic role of the French kings in the contemporary ecclesiastical crisis and their emergence as the chief patrons and taskmasters of the university theologians.

At the start of the fourteenth century the lines were crisply drawn by the policy of Philip IV toward Pope Boniface VIII (pope 1294–1303) and the Knights Templars. Philip demanded and received adherence to the royal party line as the condition of teaching theology at Paris. The deepening of the crisis in the Great Schism and conciliar movement and the perceived compatibility of conciliarism with Gallicanism made the conciliar theory virtually the house ecclesiology at Paris, in the hands of such major thinkers and activists as Henry of Langenstein (c. 1330–1397), Pierre d'Ailly (1350–1420), and Jean Gerson (1363–1429). While locating jurisdictional sovereignty in the church in the general council, Parisian theologians continued to locate doctrinal sovereignty in their own teaching authority, a position they asserted both at the Council of Basel (1431–1449)[5] and on home ground in a new attack on the mendicants, ejecting the Dominicans from the faculty for two decades for refusing to treat the Immaculate Conception as an article of faith.

These sweeping magisterial claims, however, were made at a time when political and other developments and the theologians' own response to them reduced both the ecumenicity of the university and the theologians' own credibility. Faced with the economic depression of the period, Paris, like other universities, aristocratized its student body, accepting candidates who could pay their own way. Such persons expected academic as well as social deference, leading to the dilution of standards for degrees and the delegation of the masters' teaching obligations to their students. The diplomatic polarizations abetted by the Avignonese papacy and the Schism, coupled with the Hundred Years' War, the refusal of the French kings to grant benefices in their church to foreign clerics, and the chartering of universities elsewhere, Gallicized the population of the University of Paris and made it easier for the kings to expand their control over a group composed of their own subjects.

At the same time, the theologians were put under greater pressure to lend their support to partisan national causes, thereby undercutting their ability to speak with general authority. Paris theologians, especially in the Hundred Years' War era, were co-opted by a shifting series of powers that be. Theologians arbitrated repeatedly between rebels and the government, sometimes being guided more by the winds of fortune than by their judgment of the rights of the parties. John Petit's tyrannicide theory was dismissed as the vaporings of a political hack because he had written it to defend the Burgundian assassination of the Duke of Orléans. Most damaging of all, the Paris theologians, with the sole exception of Gerson, collaborated in the condemnation of Joan of Arc (1412–1431). Her swift rehabilitation after the French won the war redounded to the theologians' intense discredit, at the very time when the conciliar movement, in which they had figured so prominently, fell apart. The French kings wasted no time in picking up the pieces, and in a series of acts between 1446 and 1499 they deprived the university of its legal independence and firmly subordinated it to royal authority.

In some respects theology in medieval Paris can be understood most easily as the history of a medieval guild, winning its autonomy so as to exercise a profession whose norms its practitioners are best qualified to judge, letting the defense of its status transcend the purposes for which it existed, succumbing to politicization, and being absorbed into a larger and more powerful political unit by the end of the period. In the late fifteenth century the University of Paris still retained enough control over educational policy to permit the importation and growth of Renaissance humanism there. But the fields most deeply affected by these new stirrings were philology, rhetoric, philosophy, and law, rather than theology. The impact of late Scholasticism and of humanism on both Catholic and Protestant theological renewals in the sixteenth century would be felt most tellingly in other lands and schools.

BIBLIOGRAPHICAL ESSAY

While theology and education in high medieval Paris have received lavish attention, the literature reveals some striking omissions and imbalances. The pedagogical and institutional setting has been outlined superbly by G. Paré, A. Brunet, and P. Tremblay, *La renaissance du XIIe siècle: Les écoles d'enseignement* (Paris, 1933), and G. Leff, *Paris and Oxford Universities in the Thirteenth and Fourteenth Centuries: An Institutional and Intellectual History* (New York, 1968), chaps. 1, 3-4. The corporate status of the university and its theologians in the wider institutional context that affected it is described brilliantly, for the beginning and end of our period, by two volumes in the *Nouvelle histoire de Paris* series: J. Boussard, *De la fin du siège de 885-886 à la mort de Philippe Augustus* (Paris, 1976), and J. Favier, *Paris au XVe siècle: 1380-1500* (Paris, 1974). Two excellent works on exegesis in the twelfth and thirteenth centuries are C. Spicq, *Esquisse d'une histoire de l'éxègese latin au moyen âge* (Paris, 1944), and B. Smalley, *The Study of the Bible in the Middle Ages*, 2d ed. (Oxford, 1952; reprint Notre Dame, 1964), the former stressing exegetical methods and genres and the latter relating Bible study more closely to modes of education and philosophical currents.

For the twelfth century the two best surveys remain J. de Ghellinck, *Le mouvement théologique du XIIe siècle*, 2d ed. (Bruges, 1948), and M.-D. Chenu, *La théologie au douzième siècle* (Paris, 1957; English trans. in part by J. Taylor and L. K. Little [Chicago, 1968]), the former chronological and the latter thematic in approach. The newest scholarship has been digested ably by G. R. Evans in two books, *Anselm and a New Generation* (Oxford, 1980) and *Old Arts and New Theology: The Beginnings of Theology as an Academic Discipline* (Oxford, 1980), and by D. E. Luscombe, *The School of Peter Abelard: The Influence of Abelard's Thought in the Early Scholastic Period* (Cambridge, 1969). An important paper showing the impact of the learned disciplines on theological debate is N. Häring, "The Case of Gilbert de la Porrée, Bishop of Poitiers (1142-1154)," *Mediaeval Studies* 13 (1951): 1-40.

For the thirteenth century, P. Glorieux, *Répertoire des maîtres en théologie de Paris au XIIIe siècle*, 2 vols. (Paris, 1933-34), remains the guide to the contemporary cast of characters and their writings. M.-D. Chenu, *Toward Understanding St. Thomas*, trans. A. M. Landry and B. Hughes (Chicago, 1964), Part 1, provides a useful introduction to the genres of theological literature, its techniques and terminology. His *La théologie comme science au XIIIe siècle*, 3d rev. ed., Bibliothèque thomiste 33 (Paris, 1957), remains required reading. Confessional or intraconfessional interests, or the reaction against them, have led scholars to focus preclusively on the friars in the second half of the century and to study them one-sidedly. E. Gilson, *History of Christian Philosophy in the Middle Ages* (New York, 1955), and F. Van Steenberghen, *La Philosophie au XIIIe siècle* (Louvain, 1966), while they are rival authorities, agree in reading theologians as if they were philosophers, while J. Pelikan, *The Growth of Medieval Theology (600–1300)*, vol. 3 of *The Christian Tradition* (Chicago, 1978), chap. 3, tends to isolate theology from philosophy. A more balanced approach to both the figures studied and the aspects of their thought considered can be found in such analyses of central themes as J.-M. Parent, "La notion de dogme au XIIIe siècle," *Études d'histoire littéraire et doctrinale du XIIIe siècle*, ser. 1, Publications de l'Institut d'Études Médiévales d'Ottawa 1 (Paris, 1932), 141–64, and W. H. Principe, *The Theology of the Hypostatic Union in the Early Thirteenth Century*, 4 vols., Pontifical Institute of Mediaeval Studies, Studies and Texts 7, 12, 19, 32 (Toronto, 1963–75).

Surveys of Paris theology in the fourteenth and fifteenth centuries are sparser, reflecting both the frontier character of the scholarship on that period and the diminished centrality of Paris at the time. Three able recent studies including Parisians as well as non-Parisians, when read together, give an excellent sense of the current state of the question. F. Oakley, *The Western Church in the Later Middle Ages* (Ithaca, N.Y., 1979), sees the concerns of theologians as related organically with their past and as conditioned primarily by the contemporary crisis in the church. G. Leff, *The Dissolution of the Medieval Outlook: An Essay on Intellectual and Spiritual Change in the Fourteenth Century* (New York, 1976), stresses the features that differentiate fourteenth-century theologians from the previous period and emphasizes their philosophy. S. Ozment, *The Age of Reform: 1250–1550: An Intellectual and Religious History of Late Medieval and Reformation Europe* (New Haven, 1980), chaps. 1–4, highlights the theological issues that relate the later Middle Ages to the Reformation.

NOTES

1. Hugh of St. Victor, *Didascalicon* 6.3, trans. J. Taylor (New York, 1961), 137.

2. For the ambiguities of Boethius on *persona*, see M. Nédoncelle, "Les variations de Boèce sur la personne," *RevSR* 29 (1955): 201–38; for his ambiguities on *natura*, see K. Bruder, *Die philosophischen Elemente in den Opuscula sacra des Boethius: Ein Beitrag zur Quellengeschichte der Philosophie der Scholastik* (Leipzig, 1928), 64–80.

3. For a detailed account of this ploy in Henry's overall strategy, see B.

Smalley, *The Becket Controversy and the Schools: A Study of Intellectuals in Politics* (Totowa, N.J., 1973), 165–66 and passim.

4. E. A. Moody, "The Medieval Contribution to Logic," in *Studies in Medieval Philosophy, Science, and Logic: Collected Papers, 1933–1969* (Berkeley and Los Angeles, 1975), 371–92, gives a masterly summary of this important topic.

5. A. Black, "The Universities and the Council of Basle: Collegium and Concilium," in J. Ijsewijn and J. Paquet, eds., *The Universities in the Late Middle Ages* (Louvain, 1978), 511–23, provides an excellent treatment of the role of Paris theologians as conciliar theorists and politicians.

9

Theology and Learning in
Early America

Melvin B. Endy, Jr.

The school of theology known as Consistent Calvinism or the New Divinity, which based itself on and developed the thought of Jonathan Edwards (1703–1758), was the first systematic and self-conscious theological movement to arise on American soil. Its members developed the first distinctive American form of graduate theological education. Although both the New Divinity's theology and its parsonage seminaries have been given scholarly attention, the relationship between them has not received close scrutiny. I propose to discuss the light that the parsonage seminaries shed on the mind of the New Divinity, the way in which their theology shaped their approach to theological education, and the significance of this theological school in the history of American theological education.[1]

Before the Great Awakening of the early 1740s, the undergraduate curricula at Harvard and Yale constituted the heart of the professional training of Congregational ministers educated in the colonies. Modeled after the English universities, and particularly the Puritan stronghold Cambridge, Harvard and Yale had similar curricula designed primarily to provide future clergy with a classical education in grammar, logic, natural philosophy, mathematics, rhetoric, metaphysics, ethics, and theology. In addition to the biblical materials used in grammar and logic courses and to the natural theology included in the study of natural philosophy, metaphysics, and ethics, students studied theology two days a week for four years and mastered at least the Westminster Confession and Cathechism, William Ames's *Medulla Theologiae* (1627) and *De Con-*

scientia (1632), and Johannes Wollebius's *Christianae Theologiae Compendium* (1626).[2]

The majority of the graduates—particularly those planning to enter the ministry—completed the requirements for a master of arts, but this involved no lengthy or prescribed course of study. Most pursued their lives and studies away from the college after graduation. Returning to college shortly before the third commencement since their graduation, they presented written synopses in logic, natural philosophy, or metaphysics, submitted a "commonplace" or sermon, and answered formally a few questions. Since acquiring the bachelor's degree, they might have continued to study theology on their own or with the assistance of a clergyman, but neither ministerial associations nor congregations had any developed views on graduate ministerial education that constituted normative standards.

In both England and America in the seventeenth and early eighteenth centuries, clergy of a Puritan persuasion provided guidance in theology to those who sought them out, and some apparently allowed candidates to live with them and to serve a kind of apprenticeship. We do not know precisely how extensive the practice was. The occasional and somewhat accidental references to such arrangements indicate that it was informal and far from normative. A small minority of college graduates in the colonies stayed at college to study for the master's degree, but most of these studied part-time while employed as tutors. Harvard in 1721 and Yale in 1754 provided professors of divinity, in part to assist graduate theological students, but this did not increase the popularity of graduate study in residence.

Of Jonathan Edwards, Frank Hugh Foster has written:

> A figure so unique as his, and one of so great eminence as a practical worker, could not fail to attract attention and . . . draw pupils for longer or shorter instruction in the ministerial calling. It was in this way that he gained for the new principles which he was presenting two adherents who were to prove during his lifetime efficient colaborers with him in his practical efforts, and after his death successors and leaders in his school. These were Bellamy and Hopkins.[3]

From Edwards's associations with Bellamy and Hopkins there developed both a distinctive theological tradition and an educational vehicle by which it was spread among ministerial candidates and handed down for several generations. Like Edwards, Samuel

Hopkins (1721–1803) and Joseph Bellamy (1719–1790) were both publishing systematic theologians and theological instructors of
ministers; Hopkins was the more prominent as a spokesman for
what was often called "Hopkinsianism," and Bellamy was "probably the most influential of all the theological mentors."[4]

From the middle of the eighteenth century until the 1820s, when
most Congregational ministerial candidates began attending such
newly formed seminaries as those at Andover, Yale, and Harvard,
probably a majority of the Congregational ministerial candidates
supplemented their college education by living and studying in a
parsonage seminary under the guidance of a minister with an
established reputation as an instructor. Since this development was
sparked by the candidates rather than by the instructors, and was
not made a formal educational requirement by denominational
agencies, we have no official list of such seminaries and their
instructors.

Probably many ministers of all theological persuasions engaged
in the practice at one time or another, but the roughly twenty-five
or so instructors we hear of as most prominent in the movement
were virtually all representatives of Consistent Calvinism, and the
inner circle of those who trained the greatest numbers and
achieved the largest reputations were closely interrelated by theology and friendship as New Divinity leaders. They included, in
addition to Bellamy and Hopkins, John Smalley at New Britain
(ministry dates: 1757–1820), Levi Hart at Preston (1761–1808),
Stephen West at Stockbridge (1756–1819), Charles Backus at Somers
(1773–1803), Asa Burton at Thetford, Vermont (1777–1836), and
Nathaniel Emmons at Franklin (1769–1840), each of whom trained
over fifty ministers, and Nathan Perkins at West Hartford (1771–
1838), Alvan Hyde at Lee (1790–1833), and Asahel Hooker at
Goshen (1790–1813), who prepared thirty to forty each.[5]

Any attempt to account for the rise of the parsonage seminaries
must consider first the increasingly secular tone of Harvard and
Yale in the middle of the eighteenth century. The series of scientific
discoveries from Kepler to Newton had created a new intellectual
climate that increasingly made metaphysics, theology, and ethics
less central in the colleges and of less interest to most students,
even though the stated objectives of the colleges had not altered.
At the same time, the cultural climate was changing. The challenge
of the political arena, the opportunities of the economic scene, and
the fascination of the social and recreational world pushed prepara-

tion for the ministry well into the background for most undergraduates. The decreasing numbers of students who saw their undergraduate training as a preparation for the ministry or who might look on the colleges as centers for graduate preparation had good reason to seek graduate training elsewhere.

The two major studies of American theological education in the seventeenth and eighteenth centuries have discussed the development of the New Divinity seminaries primarily in the context of the Great Awakening. According to Alice Gambrell, the "revivalistic zeal" of the Awakening called for "a new type of theological education." William Shewmaker writes that the supporters of the Awakening saw the need "of raising up, and the perpetuation, of a type of ministry different from that which had hitherto prevailed in America."[6] Foster's remarks about the response to Edwards point in the same direction by reminding us of the "star" aura that the Awakening gave to certain ministers by casting a spotlight on their charisma and persuasive powers and by making them the direct cause of religious renewal for many.

The parsonage seminaries had elements of an apprenticeship experience in which the instructor became, as Heman Humphrey observed in connection with Asahel Hooker, "the model to all the young men who pursued their theological studies under his care."[7] Living with an experienced minister for anywhere from several months to a year or more, the students could discuss their religious experience and observe their instructor in preparation and action as a minister in his daily round of activities. Tryon Edwards, in his "Memoir" of Bellamy for the latter's *Works*, wrote that Bellamy conversed with each pupil about his personal experience as a Christian.[8] Moreover, students had to write sermons as part of their education and usually were given the opportunity to deliver one or more sermons in some corner of the parish under the critical eye of their mentors.

But it would be misleading to allow the remarks of Gambrell and Shewmaker about the new type of theological education and of ministry, along with the apprenticeship aspects of the seminaries, to lead us to the New Divinity for the beginnings of the conception of the ministry that came to the fore in nineteenth-century evangelical Protestantism. According to this revivalistic conception, the essential prerequisites of a minister are a personal conversion experience and the kind of skill in preaching and counseling that awakens the sleeping and brings the scrupulous to the breaking point and that ultimately renders theology irrelevant. In the words of Charles Grandison Finney, "If a minister knows how to win souls, the more learning he has the better. But if he has any other kind of learning and not *this*, he will infallibly fail. . . . Those are the *best educated ministers* who win the most souls."[9] The students and instructors in the New Divinity theological schools believed emphatically that the goal of their education was indeed what was later called "winning souls," but where the revivalists came increasingly to believe that theology was essentially irrelevant to the process, the Consistent Calvinists believed that theology was the key to vital religion. The memoirs invariably describe the students not as serving an apprenticeship but as studying theology, and the mentors "superintended the theological studies" of their charges.[10]

Clearly both the students and their instructors saw themselves not as creating a new kind of clergy but as carrying forward the Puritan conception of the ministry, in which theological education was focused primarily on mastery of doctrine for the purpose of expounding revealed truth. Like their Puritan predecessors, who believed that sermons and lectureships were at the heart of vital religion and that the minister had to be well trained in Reformed theology in order to wrest the "doctrine" from his text and expound it before applying it, the New Divinity instructors believed that "right conceptions of God lay the best and only foundation for religious knowledge and right sentiments in general."[11]

What a former pupil, David Thurston, said of Asa Burton could be applied to all the Consistent Calvinist theological instructors: "He placed a great value upon truth. Few minds have ever been more strongly or solemnly impressed with the importance of correct views of all subjects, especially of religion." John Smalley believed that everyone needed to "obtain a doctrinal knowledge of the truth, in some good measure, before they can have repentance unto life, or believe to the saving of the soul," and that all Christians throughout their lives needed constant instruction in "the doctrines of religion."[12] The instructors were themselves described as "intellectual" or "doctrinal" or "argumentative" preachers who demanded of their parishioners careful listening and close reasoning.[13] It was natural that they should place the study of theology at the center of their professional lives and that they should make it the heart of the ministerial education of those who came to study with them.

The Consistent Calvinists diverged from the major approach of their Puritan forebears to the ministry and to ministerial education in two respects that place them at an even greater distance than the Puritans from romantic evangelical Protestantism. The Puritans had placed Reformed systematic theology at the heart of theological education and had taught that ministers had to learn how to explain for listeners the connections among the *loci* of their systems. Candidates studied the basic outlines of Reformed theology as found, for example, in Ames's *Medulla*, but within that outline a would-be minister was free to develop his own thought in light of his experience and intellectual propensities. There was room for both those who placed greater emphasis on religion of the heart and those who took a more intellectualistic or conceptual approach to religious conviction, for both preparationists and those who verged on antinomianism.

The instructors in the parsonage seminaries went about their task differently. The traditional understanding of the Great Awakening as the refractory process in which most of the previously unified New England Congregationalist ministers were propelled into one of three newly formed theological schools, namely, the New or Consistent Calvinists, the Old Calvinists, and the liberals or Arminians, is an oversimplification. Neither the so-called Old Calvinists nor the Arminians formed a self-conscious school of thought, and many ministers resisted being labeled.[14] But the New Divinity instructors did see themselves primarily as developers and defenders of an important theological appproach that stood in opposition to the theology of those who would either chip at the edges of true Calvinism as they understood it or toss it aside in favor of Arminianism. Their primary task was to enable their students to master the true system of doctrine and the polemical theology necessary to defend it against its detractors.

The Consistent Calvinists believed that Edwards's theology was the only appropriate theological tradition for their time. Although some of them found imperfections in the Edwards corpus and endeavored, with Emmons, to improve on the master and even to "add some pittance to the common stock of theological knowledge," they essentially saw themselves as passing on to an ever-growing number of pulpits ministers who had learned the only true system of doctrine. Students commonly described them as teaching in the manner of oracles specially chosen to pass on a tradition of thought from on high.[15] Although the impetus for the tradition of living and studying with a prominent minister originally lay with the students, and although some of the most prominent instructors claim to have responded reluctantly to such requests, few seem to have had any doubt that their relationship to their students was that of master to disciples. What Enoch Pond said of Emmons was typical: "He had the faculty of imbuing them with his own peculiar sentiments, and of working out of them everything of an opposing tendency. Of all young men whom he instructed in theology, very few left him without becoming pretty thorough Hopkinsians." In the discussions that were regularly held in the parsonages and in their critical responses to assigned essays, the New Divines expounded and defended their view for their disciples. "Impatient of contradiction and resistance," they "could not, with much patience, hear any of them even questioned."[16]

The focus of reading and discussion in the seminaries was the Edwardsean system of divinity approached in a set order, beginning with the doctrine of God. Questions were posed on particular *loci* for students to read, think, and write about. The assigned or suggested reading usually centered on Edwards or a treatise of Hopkins or Bellamy, although many teachers relied on their own lectures or manuscripts as well. Theology was approached polemically, with the focus on eighteenth-century arguments between Calvinists and their—usually Arminian—opponents. There seems to have been relatively little concern for learning the history of doctrines or of schools of Christian theology or for setting the traditional struggles between orthodoxy and heresy over such doctrines as the Trinity, Christology, or original sin in their historical context. Most of the instructors were unable to assign extensive reading in the history of theology and in the theological traditions of Europe since the Reformation; their rural parish libraries were spotty at best in all but, in some cases, contemporary debates.

Although the instructors differed in their intellectual propensities, most made few pretensions to wide reading or intellectual attainments. What mental acuteness they had was not that of searching, expansive minds or great scholars. Timothy Woodbridge said of Stephen West that his mind was marked by

> extreme acuteness, rather than comprehensiveness or versatility. He would survey and analyze a subject in some of its more difficult and complex relations, with amazing sharpness and accuracy. He had not that extraordinary expansion of mind which is requisite to survey a great subject in all its bearings—his path in inquiry was narrow, but it was as clear as a ray of light.

Even those more intellectually inclined were limited in their perspectives. Nathaniel Emmons, who thought it incumbent on his students to become theologians in their own right, hoped to continue to study and debate theological issues when he got to heaven, but those theologians he mentions as the most desired discussants include, in addition to some Old Testament worthies, Paul, Luther, and some minor eighteenth-century figures.[17] Speaking at the semicentennial of the founding of Andover Seminary, Leonard Bacon said of the thinking of the parsonage seminary instructors that it was "logical, acute, discriminative" but "not characteristically learned, and therefore it had necessarily somewhat of a provincial tone. It was not in full communion either with the theology of the ages long ago, or with the contemporaneous theology of other countries and of other evangelical communions."[18]

But no matter. The point of the instruction was not to expand the perspective of the student or to provide an exciting adventure of the mind. It was to learn well the doctrines that were the keys to the whole Consistent Calvinist system—what Emmons called "the nerves and sinews of the gospel."[19] The doctrine of God, or more precisely, of the perfections and providence of God, was most often seen as the essential doctrine of the New Divinity. Hopkins wrote:

> All who agree in their sentiments respecting the divine character will also agree in the same system of religious truth; and the origin of the differences and opposition of opinion that have taken place among professing Christians, respecting the doctrines of Christianity, is their different and opposing notions of the character and perfections of God.

According to Emmons, every system has some fundamental principle without which it cannot exist, whether it be the Newtonian philosophy, with its principle that all motion has an external cause, or civil government, with its principle that all humanity has rights that each is to enjoy so far as is consistent with the general good. The fundamental principle of Christianity is that "God had decreed all things from eternity. The doctrine of divine decrees is the light, strength, and glory of the whole gospel." In his more expansive moments, Emmons listed the following as the particular doctrines that ministers should dwell much on: God's purpose in creation, the place of evil in God's best of all possible plans, the all-determining sovereignty and the decrees of God, the fall and moral corruption of humankind, the grace of God in salvation, and the irresistible agency of God in the renovation of the sinner.[20]

The Consistent Calvinists diverged from the mainstream of Puritan thought on the ministry and on theological education not simply in their narrower, more polemical way of theologizing but also in their whole approach to theology as it relates to the ministerial enterprise. For the Puritans, theology was at the center of ministerial education not because the minister was primarily a theologian but because theology was closely related to the minister's pastoral duties. If exposition of doctrine was central in the sermon, so also were "application" of it to the lives of the parishioners and the homiletical skills needed to bring that application home to the heart. Application was also required in catechizing, pastoral visiting, counseling, and enforcing ecclesiastical discipline. The Puritans knew that the kind of theology that enabled them to speak powerfully to individuals in their sermonizing and catechizing and in their counseling and disciplining was an experiential theology. With such a theology, they could teach parishioners that God was speaking to their individual situations through Scripture, the history of their times, and their personal history.

By the study of history, particularly church history, one learned the pattern of God's general providence and of his manner of dealing with his peculiar people. The careful study of "cases of conscience" taught one how to see God's hand in the struggles and joys of personal experience. The unique guide for interpreting both history and personal experience was Scripture. It was of the utmost importance that the minister have at his command the necessary linguistic, grammatical, logical, and rhetorical knowledge for understanding the word of God in Scripture and for applying it to individual lives and to the times. For these reasons Puritan treatises on ministerial education such as Richard Baxter's *The Reformed Pastor* (1655) and Cotton Mather's *Manductio ad Ministerium* (1726) stressed the importance in theological education of the linguistic and historical tools for proper exegesis, of church history, and of ethics.[21]

The New Divines were in some ways a product of this approach to theology and to the ministerial calling, and they probably intended no major changes in it. Although riveted on a particular theology, determined to inculcate it, and highly doctrinal in their preaching, many of them managed to keep their more abstruse metaphysical views out of the pulpit and to emphasize the "practical bearings" of their doctrines.[22] At the same time, the basic thrust of their approach was more deductive and conceptual and less experiential than that of their predecessors, and as a result their conception of the ministry and of theological education was more narrowly focused on theology.

To the Consistent Calvinists, theology was not so much the interpreter of the dialogue between Scripture and historical and personal experience as it was a self-contained system of thought that captures the human understanding by its self-evident appeal and its logical coherence. They had great confidence that the key to a person's heart was the understanding. As Emmons put it,

> The understanding is the inlet to the other powers of the mind, no objects or truths can impress the mind, unless they are first perceived by the understanding. The wise preacher, therefore, will address the understanding before the conscience; and the conscience before the heart.

Only so can he make "the deepest impression on the human mind."[23] Nor were they discouraged by the differing mental abilities and training of their hearers or by the fact that throughout most of history the vast majority of humankind had been impervious to appeals to the understanding. In eighteenth-century America, these theologians believed, one found large and growing mental capacities, so that even the lowliest could understand the essential aspects of God's ways with humanity. Indeed, according to Emmons, it was impossible for anyone to understand the gospel and still disbelieve it. "If ministers, therefore, would universally preach so, as to make their people really understand the gospel, there would not be a single person who could become an infidel."[24]

Impressing the minds of hearers or readers, moreover, did not require starting anew to explain each doctrine, because of the deductive approach appropriate to theology. One simply explained the fundamental principle, namely, the doctrine of God's perfections and sovereignty, and showed how all else flowed from this. A Puritan theologian might have explained the apparently contradictory statements of Scripture about the sovereignty and grace of God on the one hand, and the freedom and exertions of humankind on the other hand, by referring to the paradoxes of experience and their practical resolution. The New Divines deduced the proper understanding of human freedom from their doctrine of God, insisted that the two beliefs had to be understood as part of an internally consistent system of thought, and interpreted experience in light of the fundamental principle.

Hopkins claimed to have provided the proper understanding of the benevolence and sovereignty of God and, beginning with these, to have taken from the contradictory statements of the Calvinist standards those beliefs not in accord with the proper understanding of God and to have reduced the rest to an internally consistent and logically connected scheme. Hence the "consistency" of this Calvinism.[25] Of Emmons, Edwards A. Park wrote:

> After establishing a few general principles, he aimed to develop their connection with all the doctrines of Theology and the consequent inter-dependence of these doctrines upon one another. He thus deduced inference from inference in a lengthened chain of logical sequences, and derived a whole system of Theology from a few fundamental principles.[26]

The teachers taught their students not only that it was important to learn the system in its interconnections for their own theological command, but also that they should preach in such a manner as to make clear how each doctrine follows from the rest. Preaching "one great, comprehensive, and perfectly connected scheme" will make them more consistent in their preaching, enable their hearers to see the clear difference between their thought and that of Arminians and other heretics, and enable them to gain most knowledge of the gospel. "For no subject in divinity can be said to be really known, without being known in its various connections with the other branches of divinity and with the general scheme of divine grace."[27]

Because they believed theological understanding to be the one essential for vital piety, and because they approached theology deductively rather than experientially, the Consistent Calvinist instructors virtually limited their teaching to systematic theology. The parsonage seminaries provided ideal settings for apprenticeships, but few seem to have functioned as such. Preaching was obviously important to the New England theologians, and their charges were asked to prepare sermons. But in their own ministries the teachers spent relatively little effort "applying" the sermon or developing a rhetoric and a style that would move listeners. Some, such as Bellamy and Backus, were affecting preachers by virtue of personality and delivery, but of most it was said that they were "grave" preachers who in a "highly doctrinal" manner did not hesitate "to declare all the counsel of God, whether the people would hear or whether they would forebear [*sic*]."[28] Their approach to rhetoric was: "First, have something to say; second, say it."[29] Intent on clear, logical, unanswerable argumentation, they customarily read their sermons—sometimes with unattractive nasality—to congregations that found it hard to remain attentive. Chester Dewey's description of Ephraim Judson's preaching is typical; Judson's sermons "contained a large amount of well digested, well arranged thought, without any attempt at elegance of style; and his manner seldom rose to much earnestness."[30] Because of their approach to preaching, they spent little time with their students on homiletics.

Nor did the seminary instructors concern themselves much with their students' approach to applying the gospel in their other ministerial functions. Although they varied in their approaches to the ministry, and some, such as Alvan Hyde, spent much time in visitation and other parish responsibilities, most devoted the better part of their time to their studies and were not known for either zeal or carefully developed approaches to their pastoral duties. Concerned above all with the theological understanding of their parishioners, and viewing theology as a self-contained deductive system, they developed no considered views on the ways in which theology can inform the other ministerial functions. We hear no complaints from parishioners that their ministers were subjecting them to experiential learning schemes in which students applied their learning in the parish, nor do we hear that the ministers' own propensity for study was inducing them to rely unduly on apprentices in their daily rounds.

Indeed, what is noteworthy is how little their activities as teachers intruded on the lives of their parishes or even into their own round of activities. Their pedagogical activity receives relatively little attention in the brief biographies and memoirs in Sprague's *Annals of the American Pulpit* and elsewhere. Although Benjamin Trumbull (1735–1820) was not as prominent and probably not as zealous an instructor as Bellamy and Emmons, Payson Williston's remarks on Trumbull's approach to teaching and on its typicality are instructive:

> As a theological instructor, he was of course abundantly competent, though I cannot say that he manifested his accustomed ardour in that part of his duty. Nearly all that he did for us was to hear our recitations to Vincent's *Catechism*, to direct us in regard to our reading, and occasionally to criticise our arguments and compositions; but that was the fashion of the day, and was not to be imputed to him as indicating any particular delinquency.[31]

Even more illuminating in regard to the theology of the New Divines was the fact that they virtually restricted the curriculum to systematic theology. They included little, if any, work in church history, "cases of conscience," or the linguistic or historical tools necessary for careful exegesis. They could assume that their students had received undergraduate training in Ames's *Cases of Conscience*, church history, and especially languages, but they also knew that this had been increasingly perfunctory as the eighteenth century progressed and that Hebrew had virtually disappeared from the curriculum. Since theology was in no significant sense conceived by them as "a search for God in time and memory," the study of theology was not a bridge to or foundation for the understanding of history or personal experience. At least, such experience was in no significant sense a source for theology.[32]

More surprising is the lack of concern for the historical and linguistic foundations for exegesis. Bellamy spoke for all when he said, "The Bible is the only test by which we try doctrines, to discover whether they be divine truths." Bellamy saw himself as a guide to Scripture for his students and considered it an important function to help with difficult passages.[33] But the approach to theology taken by the school made the members less and less searching in their uses of Scripture, which became primarily a source of corroboration for the doctrines that followed deductively from their self-evident understanding of God. Because they were good Protestants, and especially because they had a conceptual or highly propositional view of religion, the New Divines assumed that Scripture is "sufficiently plain and intelligible to every capacity." "The Bible is the Word of God; he gave it to be a rule of faith to all; he knew the characteristics, the circumstances, and the capacities of all; it must, therefore, be plain and intelligible to all."[34]

But this faith in the foresight of a reasonable God receded in practice. According to Emmons, since many passages of Scripture seem to contradict others or the central meaning of the gospel, one needs an acknowledged and infallible standard by which the true meaning of difficult passages may be discerned. "No man, I believe, has ever formed, or ever can form, a consistent scheme or system of divinity from the Bible alone, without the aid of some systematical writer, or instructor."[35] Consistent Calvinism was the "consistent scheme" by which Scripture was in fact interpreted, and the instructors saw themselves as guides enabling their students to make Scripture as consistent as their theology. Thus Hopkins explained to his students that when Scripture says God repented of having made humankind or grieved because of the sin introduced into the world, it does not mean what it appears to mean, since such an idea conflicts with the central principle of the theological scheme.[36]

Since most of the teachers were not especially proficient in Hebrew and Greek or in command of the history of exegesis or of the historical tools necessary for understanding Scripture in context, it is not surprising that they did not emphasize exegesis in their schools. But even had they been learned exegetes, their approach to theology meant that proper training in systematic theology, rather than linguistic or rhetorical or historical knowledge, was the key to the interpretation of the Bible. On this issue, as on many, Emmons said openly what appeared merely as the tendency of the thought of others when he admitted that knowledge of the customs of the people of Scripture and of biblical philology was not essential. When Scripture is approached in proper doctrinal fashion, "every scriptural doctrine of importance may be discovered, understood, and maintained without much critical learning."[37]

As followers of Jonathan Edwards, the Consistent Calvinists have most often been understood primarily as apologists for the Great Awakening or as the theologians of the first great Amerian revival. Because of their emphasis on the majesty and sovereignty of God, the fallenness and helplessness of humanity, and the irresistible grace of God, they are portrayed as the champions of the Calvinist/Puritan insistence on humanity's need for conversion by the overwhelming grace of God over against Arminian rationalism's confidence in the mental and moral powers by which humanity understands and becomes acceptable to God. As such they are the link between Edwards, the theologian of the Great Awakening, and Nathaniel William Taylor (1786–1858), the theologian of the evangelical revivalism of the first half of the nineteenth century. Although Taylor accepted elements of Arminianism and was opposed by the remaining Consistent Calvinists, all were members of what Foster has called the "New England school of theology" and were grouped as exponents of a Calvinist theology of regeneration.

Given this historiographical perspective, it has often been difficult to understand why the Consistent Calvinists were not more successful as an engine of revivalism. Although seasons of renewal producing both new members and increased vitality for old members took place in many congregations in the eighteenth century, experiences of regeneration strong and widespread enough to be a significant cultural influence did not occur. Since the parsonage seminaries were responsible for increasing the number of Consistent Calvinists in Connecticut and Western Massachusetts parishes until they constituted a majority by 1800, this is difficult to understand. Most often it is attributed to the reigning rationalism and/or to the political and military preoccupations of the times. A look at the mind of the New Divines in the context of their approach to the ministry and hence to theological education provides another reason. They were so much affected by the rationalism of their time that they were more ambivalent about affective religion than we—and probably even they—have realized. At least, their conception of regeneration was sufficiently rationalistic to be self-defeating.

The Consistent Calvinists' reliance on the appeal to the understanding of their listeners did not, in itself, distinguish them from their Puritan predecessors, whose religion was of the head as well as of the heart. But the extent of their confidence in human reasoning powers and in the rationality of Christianity surely did distinguish them, as did their suspicion of any appeal to the emotions. These theologians were children of the Enlightenment to a degree that has not always been realized by students of the movement. As Calvinists stressing the sovereignty and glory of God and the fallenness of humanity, they opposed the Arminians' tendency to elevate the moral character of humankind, but they were fully caught up in the enthusiasm for the rational powers of humanity that followed from the scientific developments that led to the Newtonian view of the universe. Indeed, the belief that theology should be a "consistent" or law-abiding system deducible from the central principle of the all-determining sovereignty of God was seen as parallel to the Newtonian systems being deducible from the principle of motion. Even the New Science's mathematical or quantitative approach to understanding the universe provided a model for theology.

Starting with the premise of the sovereignty of God and a form of Christianity that seemed to many of their contemporaries to make God an arbitrary tyrant, the New Divines argued that God's ways are not humanity's and that God, who had created the world for his own glory, was beyond the full comprehension of finite and fallen creatures. Humanity's understanding of God's ways is limited, according to Bellamy, and we should remember that "all the hard thoughts of the divine conduct, which are to be found in the hearts of mankind, through a fallen, depraved, guilty world, arise entirely from our partial views and bad taste." Even when our heart is renewed there may be some doctrines, such as that of three persons in one God, that we may have to accept simply because they are revealed.[38]

But the New Divinity seems at the same time to have been caught up in the myth of progress given impetus by the scientific developments, particularly as the myth related to human understanding. Bellamy tends to use developmental language when referring to human understanding, and he gives the distinct impression that humanity can understand much more about God than it yet has. We do not fully understand the divine plan because

> we came into existence, as it were, but yesterday; we are just emerging out of nonentity; we still border on non-existence; we are but half awake, if so much. When we enter into the eternal world, if this short period is well spent, we may hope to have our intellectual powers quite awake.

Hence the appropriate response to "hard thoughts of the divine conduct" is not only to seek a renewed heart but "to endeavor to enlarge our views of God's universal plan, and search into the nature of the divine government, and the glorious designs and noble ends which infinite wisdom has in view, and will at last accomplish."[39] Emmons also believed in "the large and noble capacities of the human mind" and in its constant progress:

> And, as all the powers and faculties of the mind brighten and expand by exercise; so a man's capacity for improvement increases, as the means and thirst for improvements increase. Accordingly the path of knowledge, has resembled the path of the just, which shineth more and more unto the perfect day. One generation have been improving upon another, from age to age. And the improvements and discoveries of the last and present century are truly surprising.

They justify the expectations of greater understanding in divinity and metaphysics as well as in the physical sciences.[40]

The conviction of the Consistent Calvinists was that their major calling was to enable humanity to understand better the ways of God. God's plan had appeared "hard" not because of some qualitative difference between the infinite Creator and the finite creature but because of humanity's mental infancy. "The truth is," wrote Emmons, "rationality is the same for all intelligent beings. Reason is the same in God, in angels, and in men." "Hence we are not to suppose, that the nature of the Supreme Being differs from the nature of other intelligent beings, merely because he is incomprehensibly great." Emmons reveals a quantitative mind set in arguing that God's "incomprehensibility" stems not from his being different from rational creatures but from being greater in those mental qualities we recognize as admirable. Although we cannot always see the whole of a mountain as clearly as a hill, he reasoned, we can see the visible portion of the mountain as clearly as the hill. The case is similar with regard to spiritual matters.

> Can we not as clearly perceive reason in a man, as in a child? In a philosopher, as in a peasant? In a Newton or a Bacon, as in those of much meaner capacities? Why then should we not as clearly perceive power, wisdom, goodness, justice, or any other natural and moral excellency in the fountain as in the streams? In God as in the creature? Where there is the most power, the most wisdom, and the most goodness, there these excellencies are the most easily seen.[41]

Although Emmons may have been more rationalistic than other New Divines, they had all learned from Hopkins himself that God's ways and humanity's, at least in the world of reason and ideas, do not differ. The holiness of God is not a distinct characteristic but merely "the goodness of his moral character in general." God has "absolute, uncontrollable sovereignty," but if you conceive of this sovereignty as consisting in God's "doing what he will, merely because he will, and without any possible reason why he wills thus," you misunderstand the matter. God had reasons for all that he did, and those reasons were evident to the mind that would search diligently.[42]

The New Divinity believed, then, that humanity could understand God's ways and that Christianity was an eminently reasonable religion. In the view of Emmons, "It is the reasonableness of this revealed religion that has convinced ninety-nine in a hundred, if not nine hundred ninety-nine in a thousand, of those who in all ages have embraced it, either in speculation or in practice."[43] These theologians had as much confidence as any of their contemporaries that the being and character of God were manifest in the benevolent design and orderliness of the natural world.[44] Their use of the "external" or historical arguments for the truth of the revelations of Christianity, such as the arguments from historical success, miracles, and prophecy, were equally typical. The manner in which the Scriptures were given to the world, the character of the writers, the miracles that confirmed what they wrote, the biblical predictions or prophecies, and Christianity's spread and triumph all provided overwhelming appeals to the understanding.[45]

But the peculiar form of apologetics and the *raison d'être* of all Consistent Calvinism was its attempt to prove to contemporaries that, contrary to common opinion, the sovereignty of God, the sinfulness of humanity, Adam's role in our fall, and all the other doctrines of orthodox Calvinism not only were compatible with but also proved the benevolence or "amiableness" of God. Since God and humanity share the same reason, it was their job to show that God exercised sovereignty in ways that we could find reasonable, and they were convinced that only a God who had humanity's interest at heart could be considered reasonable. Only what appears to us to proceed from benevolence can be considered a moral perfection in God, given the structure of the human mind. The "absolute, uncontrollable sovereignty" of God is in fact "benevolence, clothed with omnipotence, or doing what it pleases."

> Infinite greatness, understanding, and power, without any rectitude, wisdom, and goodness of heart, if this were possible, would not be desireable and amiable, but worse than nothing, and infinitely dreadful. Therefore, they who do not understand the true moral character of God, and discern the excellence and glory of it, have not the knowledge of God; his real amiableness and glory are hid from them.[46]

The world has been created for the glory and enjoyment of God, as Calvinists had always believed, but now it was to be understood that God's enjoyment and glory are dependent on the well-being of at least a goodly portion of his creatures: "So that," says Hopkins, "it is not strictly true, that creatures add nothing to the enjoyment or happiness of God, even his essential happiness, and that he would have been as completely blessed forever, as he really is, had there been no creatures." According to Smalley, if God can be said to have created all things for himself as his "chief" end, the happiness of his creatures was his "ultimate" end.[47]

The Consistent Calvinists expended most of their theological energy attempting to justify the ways of God to their listeners and readers by demonstrating that God's creation and providence were designed precisely to produce the greatest possible human happiness. They believed that if one properly understood God and the benevolence of his plan for the world, one would clearly see the glory and beauty of God—and especially his benevolence—and would be irresistibly drawn to worship and service. Emmons wrote:

> Only draw the character of the Supreme Being and describe his power, wisdom, goodness, justice, and mercy, before the most ignorant and uncultivated savage; and, as soon as he understands the character of God he will feel that he ought, that he is morally obligated to love and obey the great Parent of all.[48]

Because God was the all-determining sovereign, and because all humankind have sinned and deserve damnation, and because only some will be saved by the grace of God, the burden on the theologians was to justify God in the face of the pervasive evil in the world. Since God foreknew and foreordained all that comes to pass, they had to demonstrate that it was better for God to create than not to create, and that "all the sin and sufferings which have taken place, or ever will, are necessary for the greatest good of the universe, and to answer the wisest and best ends, and therefore must be included in the best, most wise, and perfect plan."[49]

It is neither necessary nor possible to discuss here the various ways in which the New Divinity attempted to accomplish this task. Suffice it to indicate that they argued, in broad outline, that God's plan was the one best suited to show God's perfections—including God's justice and mercy—in all their glory, to show us our hearts and our absolute dependence on a loving God, and to advance the moral system.[50] What is most noteworthy for our purposes is that they applied what ethicists call the "principle of proportion" in a utilitarian manner to show that the plan chosen by God was calculated to produce at least enough happiness to outweigh the evil and that this principle was applied in a mathematical or quantitative manner. Although the burden of their form of argumentation tended to make them minimize the number of the damned, they were perfectly willing to allow that the damned might outnumber the saved without damaging the "greatest happiness" argument. It does not follow, said Hopkins, that there is less good in the universe than would otherwise be the case simply because a great number are made eternally miserable by sin, since the amount of happiness produced in the saved—an amount which might even include their knowledge of the state of the damned—could outweigh the suffering of the damned even if their number does not.[51]

The quantitative view of happiness is "graphically" depicted by Bellamy:[52]

> Suppose the number of angels to be three; and all remaining innocent to have one degree of holiness and happiness apiece; the sum total would be three degrees of holiness and happiness. But if one falls, and the other two increased in holiness and happiness a hundred fold, then the sum total of holiness and happiness will be two hundred degrees. But if the misery of the damned is augmented in the same proportion as the happiness of the blessed, then the misery of one lost angel will be one hundred degrees; besides the happiness he lost, which was supposed to be one degree. Now, therefore, subtract one hundred and one from two hundred, and the remainder will be ninety-nine; that is, there will be ninety-nine degrees of happiness left. And if this will be the case, were the number of the angels supposed to be three, it will also, proportionably, in any given number. So that, if there are but half so many good angels, as there are now supposed to be of mankind inhabiting the earth, yet the clear gain will be above ninety-six hundred millions of degrees of happiness more than if all had stood, as will appear from the following table.

If all had stood		On the present plan	
Number of angels supposed	Proportionable degrees of happiness	Number of angels supposed	Proportionable degrees of happiness
3	3	3	99
30	30	30	990
300	300	300	9900
300,000,000	300,000,000	300,000,000	9,900,000,000
		From	9,900,000,000
		Subtract	300,000,000
		Remainder	9,600,000,000 clear gain

Jonathan Edwards, founder of the New Divinity, accompanied his appeal to the head with one to the heart, as the *Treatise on Religious Affections* makes clear. But among his supposed followers the emphasis on the reasonableness of religion was accompanied by a strong suspicion of the role of the emotions in religion. In theory they were still preaching for revivals. Emmons's statement on the primary importance of appealing to the understanding goes on to allow that, once the understanding and conscience have been addressed, "then the affections may be raised as high as possible." But we are told that he spoke little of the affections and counseled his students that their voice, looks, gestures, and whole deportment should be directed toward the mind.[53]

Discussions of the religious affections are not prominent in the works of any of these theologians, and they appear to have been suspicious of emotion in their own ministries. Charles Backus was one of the more "affecting" among them, but he was said to be wary of heated emotions in religion and constantly on guard against "enthusiasm, wild-fire, and every species of disorder."[54] The note that rings through most of the descriptions of their approach to preaching is captured in the observation of Royal Robbins concerning Smalley, that he valued a "sober, chastened form of religious feelings, based on knowledge and directed by rigid principle." Robbins continues in a manner that describes well the whole contingent of New Divines:

> On the whole, he appears to me as a specimen of the sober, staid, reasoning, and conservative class of Divines, essentially sound in the faith, who appeared on the stage subsequently to the great religious awakenings about the middle of the last century, and who, by a natural reaction caused by the irregularities of that period, were rendered, perhaps, too cautious of excitement and over-action in the concerns of the spiritual life.[55]

The New Divines apparently believed that they were working for revivals. The reason they largely failed is that they worked at "having the distinguishing doctrines of the Bible clearly and fully stated and enforced, to produce a genuine revival of religion."[56] Theirs was too enlightened an approach to foster renewals of the character of the Great Awakening, and the men they sent to the pulpits of Western Massachusetts and Connecticut did as they had been taught.

This analysis of the Consistent Calvinists and their parsonage seminaries leads to the conclusion that they left a mixed heritage in regard to teaching and learning the Christian tradition. Equating systematic and apologetic theology, they believed in the absolute centrality of theological reflection to the life of the church and to ministerial training. Ministerial education was for equipping future clergy with the ability to convince unbelievers and to enable Christians to give reasons for the faith they held by relating that faith to the intellectual and cultural assumptions of their day. Contrary to what one might expect of the theologians growing out of the Great Awakening, they did not contribute to the revivalistic conception of the ministry that came to the fore in nineteenth-century America.

The main service of the Consistent Calvinists appears to have been to make Calvinism acceptable to some Americans of the Revolutionary and early National eras, thereby making the transition to Arminian evangelical Protestantism more gradual. To the extent that they were successful in appealing to the minds of their hearers and influencing their students to do likewise, they made the Calvinist God acceptable in the era of the American Enlightenment, thereby reducing the number of New Englanders susceptible to the arguments of the Unitarians and increasing the number of those able to harmonize their religion with the Enlightened political principles that played so large a role in their lives.[57]

Keeping religious experience from determining the theological agenda and from eventually replacing theology is one thing; virtually excluding it from the theological enterprise is another. The New Divines were so committed to their own kind of apologetic theology, and so rationalistic in their approach to theology, that they may have contributed to the anti-intellectual and anti-theological strain in American religion by rendering theology irrelevant once their age had passed. Conceiving of religion as preeminently an affair of the understanding, and conceiving of theology as a deductive system, they appear to have given theology no intrinsic connection to the non-apologetic functions of the ministry. They were so insistent about justifying the ways of the God of Calvinism to their parishioners that they seem not to have been able to give them a heartfelt conviction of their sinfulness or to speak to their concerns in counseling and disciplining.

Even more consequential for their approach to ministerial education, they saw no intrinsic connection between their theology and a rigorous education in exegesis, the history of doctrine, church history, and ethics. Since they did not conceive of theology as an activity requiring searching reflection on personal and historical experience as it is illuminated by the God of history revealed in Scripture, they focused their education exclusively on contemporary systematic apologetic theology.

Despite its belief in progress, eighteenth-century rationalism was remarkably confident of the adequacy of its grasp on reality. The New Divines were, as Calvin Chapin said of John Smalley, "perfectly satisfied" with their theological views. Emmons, it was said, was not known to have grown dissatisfied with a single sentence he had written in the course of his long career.[58] Since religion for them was a propositional affair, and since the basic propositions were self-evident in Scripture and to reason and the source of all other propositions, "There is the same safety and consistency in owning and subscribing an orthodox creed, as in owning and subscribing the Bible itself."[59]

Possessing such theological self-confidence, the Consistent Calvinists brought experience and Scripture within the bounds of their theology rather than searching Scripture, personal experience, and history for indications of God's ways with humanity. Their complacency was thus reinforced. Pursuing their theological and educational vocation in dialogue primarily with the disputants of the eighteenth century and largely without the exegetical and theological dialogue of the ages, they provided a truncated theological education and inculcated in their students a theology that lacked the means of responding when Romanticism began to make inroads on Enlightenment rationalism. As a result, the seminary movement that, beginning with the founding of Andover in 1808, rapidly overtook the parsonage seminaries by the 1820s and 1830s was in certain respects a repudiation of the provincialism and narrowness of the Consistent Calvinists. At the same time, remembering the later history of American revivalism, with its disregard for theology, and noting the meager theological equipment of much of the American clergy, we can be instructed by this first American school of theology and by its approach to seminary education. Its theological rigor and its attempt to provide theological answers to the intellectual challenges of its era are still worthy of emulation.

NOTES

1. On the parsonage seminaries and American theological education before the nineteenth century, see A. Gambrell, *Ministerial Training in Eighteenth-century New England* (New York, 1937); W. O. Shewmaker, *The Training of the Protestant Ministry in the United States of America, before the Establishment of Theological Seminaries* (New York and London, 1921); and N. A. Naylor, "Raising a Learned Ministry: The American Education Society, 1815–1860" (Ph.D. diss., Columbia University, 1971). The most comprehen-

sive exposition of the theology of the school is found in F. H. Foster, *A Genetic History of New England Theology* (Chicago, 1907). Another useful discussion is by J. Haroutunian, *Piety versus Moralism: The Passing of the New England Theology* (New York, 1932 [1970]). Haroutunian's judgment of the "moralism" of the school is disputed by J. A. Conforti, *Samuel Hopkins and the New Divinity Movement: Calvinism, the Congregational Ministry, and Reform in New England between the Great Awakenings* (Grand Rapids, 1981).

2. R. Warch, *School of the Prophets: Yale College, 1701–1740* (New Haven and London, 1973), chaps. 8 and 9; S. E. Morison, *Three Centuries of Harvard, 1636–1936* (Cambridge, Mass., 1936), chaps. 2, 4, 5, 6.

3. Foster, *Genetic History*, 107.

4. Gambrell, *Ministerial Training*, 105. Bellamy was pastor at Bethlehem from 1740 to 1790. Hopkins was at Sheffield (named Great Barrington in 1761) at the Second Parish from 1743 to 1769, and at the First Congregational Church of Newport, Rhode Island, from 1770 to his death in 1803.

5. See W. B. Sprague, *Annals of the American Pulpit*, vols. 1 and 2 (New York, 1857), articles on the subjects mentioned; L. Bacon, "Commemorative Discourse," *A Memorial of the Semi-centennial Celebration of the Founding of the Theological Seminary at Andover* (Andover, 1859), 75–80; Gambrell, *Ministerial Training*, 110–30; and Shewmaker, *Training*, 150–55. Gambrell and Shewmaker are the main guides to the larger list of roughly twenty-five instructors.

6. Gambrell, *Ministerial Training*, 102–3; Shewmaker, *Training*, 145.

7. Sprague, *Annals* 2:320.

8. Tryon Edwards, "A Memoir of His Life and Character," in *The Works of Joseph Bellamy, D.D.*, 2 vols. (Boston, 1853), 1:lix.

9. C. G. Finney, *Lectures on Revivals of Religion* (1835), ed. W. McLoughlin (Cambridge, Mass., 1960), 186.

10. See the relevant articles in Sprague, *Annals*. On Hopkins's shift from seeking out Edwards to gain "the spiritual and practical benefit of Mr. Edwards' example" to a focus on studying his theology, see Bacon, "Commemorative Discourse," 76, 79.

11. S. Hopkins, *System of Doctrines*, in *The Works of Samuel Hopkins, D.D.*, 3 vols. (Boston, 1854), 1:37. On the Puritan approach to the ministry, see W. Hudson, "The Ministry in the Puritan Age," in H. R. Niebuhr and D. D. Williams, *The Ministry in Historical Perspective* (New York, 1956), 180–206; and Gambrell, *Ministerial Training*, chap. 1. For Edwards's doctrinal definition of clerical education, see *The True Excellency of a Gospel Minister*, vol. 8 of *Works* (Worcester, 1808–9), 362–63. S. Mead describes the later evangelical Protestant conception of the ministry in "The Rise of an Evangelical Conception of the Ministry in America (1607–1850)," in Niebuhr and Williams, *Ministry*, 207–49.

12. "Asa Burton," in Sprague, *Annals* 2:147; J. Smalley, *Sermons on Various Subjects, Doctrinal and Practical* (Middletown, 1814), 321–22.

13. See, e.g., the articles on William Robinson of Southington, Asa

Burton, Nathan Perkins, Alvan Hyde, Levi Hart, Stephen West, and Charles Backus in Sprague, *Annals* 1 and 2.

14. See D. Harlan, *The Clergy and the Great Awakening in New England* (Ann Arbor, 1979–80).

15. See, e.g., "Levi Hart," in Sprague, *Annals* 1:594; and Gambrell's remarks on Bellamy, *Ministerial Training*, 106.

16. The Pond quotation is in E. A. Park, "Memoir of Nathaniel Emmons," *Works of Nathaniel Emmons* (Boston, 1861), 1:220–21. "Joseph Bellamy" and "John Smalley," in Sprague, *Annals* 1:408, 561.

17. "Stephen West" and "Nathaniel Emmons," in Sprague, *Annals* 2:554; 1:706. On the libraries and intellectual attainments of the New Divinity instructors, see Gambrell, *Ministerial Training*, chaps. 5, 6. See also "John Smalley," in Sprague, *Annals* 1:561; and "Memoir of Asa Burton, Thetford, Vermont," *American Quarterly Review* 10 (1838): 333.

18. Bacon, "Commemorative Discourse," 105.

19. N. Emmons, *A Collection of Sermons . . . on Various Subjects* (Boston, 1813), 132–33.

20. Hopkins, *System of Doctrines*, in vol. 1 of *Works*, 37; Emmons, *Systematic Theology*, in vol. 2 of *Works* (Boston, 1860), 335, 340; and *Sermons*, 132–33.

21. See Hudson, "Ministry in the Puritan Age," 189–203; Gambrell, *Ministerial Training*, chap. 1; J. W. T. Youngs, Jr., *God's Messengers: Religious Leadership in Colonial New England, 1700–1750* (Baltimore and London, 1976), chaps. 2, 3; and D. D. Hall, *The Faithful Shepherd* (Chapel Hill, N.C., 1972), chap. 1.

22. "Nathan Perkins," in Sprague, *Annals* 2:4. See also "Alvan Hyde" and "Levi Hart," in ibid., 2:304–5; 1:593.

23. Emmons, *Sermons*, 202–3.

24. Ibid., 283–84. On Emmons's confidence in the ability of even the lowliest to understand theology, see *Sermons*, 24. In discussing whether understanding compels active belief, Emmons sometimes admitted that the heart may determine one's response to the gospel, but once convinced, one will at least know and be convicted by the truth, whether one lives by it or not. Presumably the minister can do no more at that point. Emmons, *Systematic Theology*, 124. See also Smalley, *Sermons on a Number of Connected Subjects* (Hartford, 1803), 54.

25. Park, "Memoir," in Emmons, *Works* 1:182.

26. "Nathaniel Emmons," in Sprague, *Annals* 1:699. Trying to "harmonize all truth in one system, which he believed to be Calvinistic," was "the favorite peculiarity of Dr. Emmons as a theologian" (p. 703).

27. Emmons, *Sermons*, 140.

28. "Alvan Hyde," in Sprague, *Annals* 2:303.

29. "Nathaniel Emmons," in Sprague, *Annals* 1:707.

30. Sprague, *Annals* 2:21. See "John Smalley" and "Levi Hart," in ibid., 1:562, 593–94. Of Jonathan Edwards, Jr. (see ibid., 1:659–60), who also served on occasion as an instructor, it was said that "in the pulpit, he was

too profound to be interesting, or always intelligible to ordinary minds" and that his nasal twang was difficult to listen to.

31. Sprague, *Annals* 1:590.

32. The phrase in quotation marks is the title of a book by John Dunne (New York, 1969).

33. Bellamy, *A Letter to Scripturista*, in *Works* 1:599; Sprague, *Annals* 1:411.

34. Emmons, *Sermons*, 41, 43.

35. Emmons, *Systematic Knowledge of the Gospel*, in *Works* 1:317–18, 325.

36. Hopkins, *System of Doctrines*, 57.

37. Emmons, *Systematic Knowledge of the Gospel*, 328.

38. Bellamy, *The Wisdom of God in the Permission of Sin*, in *Works* 2:39–40. The remark on the Trinity is by Hopkins, *System of Doctrines*, 66.

39. Bellamy, *The Wisdom of God in the Permission of Sin*, 35, 39–40.

40. Emmons, *Sermons*, 13–14, 23–24.

41. Ibid., 22, 181–82.

42. Hopkins, *System of Doctrines*, 41–42, 55.

43. Emmons, *Systematic Theology*, 124.

44. See, e.g., Smalley, *Sermons* (1803), 43.

45. See, e.g., Hopkins, *The Reason of the Christian's Hope*, in *Works* 3:700. Hopkins here preaches that the resurrection took place in such a manner as to give "incontestable evidence" "to a sufficient number of chosen, competent witnesses, who could not be deceived."

46. Hopkins, *System of Doctrines*, 55, 41.

47. Ibid., 56; Smalley, *Sermons* (1803), 48.

48. Emmons, *Sermons*, 18–19. See also Smalley, *Sermons* (1803), 55–56; and Bellamy, *True Religion Delineated*, in *Works* 1:15.

49. Hopkins, *System of Doctrines*, 91.

50. Bellamy, *True Religion Delineated*, 30–31.

51. Hopkins, *Sin Through Divine Interposition an Advantage to the Universe*, in *Works* 2:528.

52. Bellamy, *The Wisdom of God in the Permission of Sin*, 55.

53. Emmons, *Sermons*, 202–3, 207.

54. Sprague, *Annals* 2:63. The younger Edwards (1:658–59) was said to be strongly opposed to "that blustering declamation in the pulpit, which gratifies, without instructing, the vulgar portion of the community."

55. Sprague, *Annals* 1:564–65.

56. "Asa Burton," in Sprague, *Annals* 2:147.

57. This perspective enables us to understand why they emphasized so strongly a specific theological tradition even though, as recent scholarship has made clear, the lines between the so-called Old Calvinists and the New Divinity were more fluid than has often appeared. See, e.g., Harlan, *Clergy and Great Awakening*. To the extent that the Old Calvinists constituted a theological school, the two schools could unite against the liberals because, despite their differing approaches to theology, theirs was not a struggle between rabid revivalists and their opponents but between different

approaches to Calvinism by ministers who all believed, in theory at least, in a very chastened, reasonable form of religious renewal. In this regard it is worth noting that S. Mead, *Nathaniel William Taylor, 1786–1858: A Connecticut Liberal* (Chicago, 1942), argues that Taylor is more in the tradition of the Old Calvinists than of the New Divinity.

58. Sprague, *Annals* 1:561, 700.
59. Emmons, *Sermons*, 117.

10

The Idea of Theological Education at the University of Berlin: From Schleiermacher to Harnack

John M. Stroup

Ein stiller Geist ist jahrelang geschäftig,
Die Zeit nur macht die feine Gärung kräftig.
(A quiet spirit is active long,
Time just makes the fine brew strong.)
—Goethe

According to Adolf von Harnack (1851–1930), scientific scholarship (*Wissenschaft*) is "the knowledge of the real for purposeful action."[1] In the case of history, this scholarship has the purpose of fitting us "to intervene in the course of history" by rejecting "the past when it reaches into the present as a hindrance," by doing "the right thing in the present," and by preparing "prudently for the future." That is, Harnack's historian decides "what of the past shall continue to be efficacious and what must be done away with or transformed."[2] In Harnack's terms, then, the question for us is this: what in nineteenth-century German Protestantism can (and ought to) be of enduring significance and usefulness?

Western history from 1815 to 1914 may be seen as an attempt to come to terms with the Enlightenment, the French Revolution, and the revolutionary imperialism carried out by Napoleon. If we leave out of consideration the advocates of the continued search for radical upheaval without limits, our nineteenth-century story becomes a tale of varying attempts to arrange matters after the recently survived earthquake in order to ensure that future shocks would do minimal damage. Virtually all these efforts mixed concessions to the Enlightenment cataclysm with attempts to insulate certain items from the catastrophe of modern times.

Such a story can be written about European politics and society as a whole. It can also be written about European ecclesiastical and theological activity. The religious proposals, like those in politics, sort themselves out into two kinds of methods for restoring order. Some wished to admit as few concessions as possible to emancipation and rationalization. Others instead made a virtue of necessity and acknowledged in their theology the just claims of reason to be freed from control by the institutional church. This emancipated approach has rightly been called liberal theology. In choosing this theology as my topic, I am judging the liberal tradition of cooperation with modern culture to constitute German Protestantism's enduring legacy to the church in an age of pluralism.

The liberal stream in German Protestantism is distinguished by the refusal to allow the course of modern history to assign Christianity to barbarism, and scientific scholarship to unbelief—a refusal enunciated by F. D. E. Schleiermacher in 1829, and by Harnack in 1923 during the controversy with Karl Barth.[3] Indeed, Schleiermacher (1768–1834) contended that the Reformation itself had concluded an "eternal treaty" between living Christian faith and independent scientific research.[4] On the basis of this treaty, Schleiermacher tried to keep Christianity and culture in contact, refusing to separate them. This distinctive refusal led Schleiermacher, in his sketch of theological study published for use in his Berlin lectures, to put forward a philosophical theology vitally concerned with determining the essence of Christianity on historical-critical principles.[5]

The same distinctive refusal marks the career of Harnack at Berlin. He embraced modern scholarship so as to commit himself to a program of historical-critical searching for the essence of Christianity. Harnack's program eventuated in the conclusion that with Luther "the *history of dogma*, which had its beginnings in the age of the Apologists, nay, of the Apostolic Fathers, *was brought to an end*."[6] For with Luther's reform, "the inviolable system of doctrine established by the Holy Spirit" was "abolished." Thus for Luther (1483–1546) and for all Protestants who let "Luther be Luther," the faith resulting from the Reformation can in no way be constrained by reverence for human dogmatic formulas. Luther's criticism of Catholic dogma led to a Protestant religious faith which "rises superior, not merely to this or that particular dogma, *but to dogmatic Chris-*

tianity in its entirety."[7] Harnack went so far as to maintain that, in the Reformation view,

> Christianity is something else than a sum of traditional doctrines. Christianity is not Biblical Theology, nor is it the doctrine of the Councils, but it is the *spirit* which the Father of Jesus Christ awakens in hearts through the Gospel. All authorities which support dogma are abolished; how then can dogma maintain itself as infallible *doctrine*; but what, again, is a dogma without infallibility? Christian doctrine establishes its rights only for faith; what share, then, can philosophy still have in it? but what, again, are dogma and dogmatic Christianity without philosophy?[8]

On this account, Harnack could recognize no "history of dogma in Protestantism" after Luther's "great Reformation writings." Instead, Harnack could only point to the continuing Protestant criticism of all doctrinal formulae, a criticism which embodied a continuing struggle for a "right understanding of the Gospel" within modern civilization. The enterprise of Protestantism becomes then a critical search for the essence of Christianity. This search leads directly to the Enlightenment's radical breach with confessional rigor—a breach which, Harnack asserts, "can be described by no one as a breach with the Reformation."[9]

An openness to modern culture, joined to willingness to criticize finite expressions of the Christian tradition regarded as absolute, can be taken as characteristic of the German liberal Protestant tradition. This trait was most strikingly evident in university theology, and it was nowhere more manifest than in the idea of theological education upheld in the University of Berlin in the century from Schleiermacher to Harnack.[10]

The fundamental statement of the liberal Protestant idea of theological education is Schleiermacher's 1811 outline of theological study, revised in 1830. The outline connects the theological disciplines with the purpose of leadership in the church. Schleiermacher makes plain that the goal to which the church must be directed is that of striving "ever more purely to present the idea of Christianity."[11] Here as well is the notion of a free and open application of philosophy and historical research in Christian theology so as to serve the church.

These ideas received institutional codification in the statutes of the Berlin theological faculty.[12] Although not promulgated until 1838 (long after Schleiermacher's independence of spirit had caused him to fall from favor during the era of reaction), the statutes still in many ways hark back to Schleiermacher.[13] He, together with Wilhelm von Humboldt (1767–1835), must rank among the chief founders of the University of Berlin (c. 1810).

The statutes of the Berlin theological faculty recall the original impulses active in the plans for setting up the university put forward by Schleiermacher and Humboldt. Particularly important is the first paragraph of the statutes:

> The theological faculty has the vocation of proceeding according to the doctrine of the evangelical church so as not only to propagate the theological sciences in general, but also especially to make competent by means of lectures and other academic exercises the young men who dedicate themselves to the service of the church.[14]

The weight accorded here to the advancement of theological scholarship is striking. Anyone familiar with the regulations and organization of the Berlin theological faculty will realize that here was an institution so set up as to encourage not simply the practice of theological scholarship by the faculty, but as well the recruitment of new scholars and teachers—and the training of pastors actively supportive of the liberal and critical approach. That even the reaction after the close of the Napoleonic period did not permanently impair the ability of Berlin to function in this way can be attributed to the enduring power of the ideas about education and scientific scholarship put forward by the founders of the University of Berlin.

These ideas ultimately derive from the single idea of scientific scholarship as a process brought about by the free, inner drive to know for its own sake. One of the most important statements of this idea was made by Schleiermacher in 1808.[15] The same idea animates Humboldt's memorandum of 1809–1810 on the organization of higher scientific institutions in Berlin. During the difficult period of the Napoleonic Wars, Humboldt characteristically avoided any search for immediate utility, arguing instead that scientific scholarship was to be freely pursued for its own sake, driven by an impulse emerging from the depths of the human spirit; it was not to serve any immediate practical purpose,[16] but to seek an answer to problems which are never to be regarded as fully solved. As one recent historian of the University of Berlin has put it in this same connection:

> Scientific knowledge [*Wissenschaft*] is something incomplete. It depends on seeking and finding new truths—that is, upon research;

and even in transmitting truth the point is not handing on something given, but rather a spontaneous reflection upon principles.[17]

Such an idea of *Wissenschaft* could appeal to the pioneers of Idealism and Neohumanism for many reasons—not least of which was the way it could be used in opposition to the narrowly utilitarian pedagogical notions of cameralist social engineers in the service of the absolutist state.[18] For the proponents of the all-encompassing Idealist concept of knowledge did not oppose purposeful action as an educational goal; the careers of Schleiermacher and Humboldt abundantly demonstrate that they favored such action. They did, however, criticize the view that education should be dissolved into processes of technical training in which each discipline would be pursued in virtual isolation from all others according to norms of immediate social and economic utility.

The reception of Idealism at Berlin and elsewhere meant, as Walter P. Metzger has pointed out, that "the search for truth" was seen as being "not an occupation, but a calling—a transcendent necessity."[19] As a result,

the very notion of *Wissenschaft* had overtones of meaning utterly missing in its English counterpart, *science*. The German term signified a dedicated, sanctified pursuit. It signified not merely the study of the "exact sciences," but of everything taught by the university; not the study of things for their immediate utilities, but the morally imperative study of things for themselves and for their ultimate meanings.[20]

The unified concept of scientific knowledge in German Idealism encompassed what we now separate into natural sciences and humanities. They were held together by use of the speculative philosophy of nature; in consequence, it seemed possible, as Thomas Nipperdey puts it, for the founders of the University of Berlin to regard *Wissenschaft* as "a whole; philosophical reflection upon the totality of the world and upon meaning is proper to each discipline."[21]

As it was institutionalized at Berlin, the idea of a search for total knowledge was one that could be seen to have three corollaries. First, because the new view of science in Idealist transcendental philosophy implied "a universal and coherent . . . system of the unity and universality of man's total knowledge,"[22] the then-current proposals to dissolve universities into separate specialized technical academies had to be rejected—even though they were favored by the French example. The professors and students in a university, rather than being forever isolated within the confines of glorified technical schools lacking mutual ties, ought instead to "represent the totality of knowledge." In other words, the inculcation of a drive for true knowledge and the development of a mind capable of living and creative scholarship depend on initial and recurrent exposure to what Martin Redeker sums up as "the scientific spirit as expressed in philosophy."[23] Schleiermacher's statement of this point links the notion of a totality of knowledge with the realization that one's own branch of learning can be fully appropriated as a way of life only when studied in connection with the basic philosophical curriculum: "The totality of knowledge should be shown by perceiving the principles as well as the outline of all learning in such a way that one develops the ability to pursue each sphere of knowledge on his own."[24]

Thus knowledge is to be sought without having the direction of investigation chiefly determined by considerations of immediate utility; each branch of knowledge gains its true significance only when questions of meaning and issues of relation to the totality of the world are taken into account. Therefore, within the university, students are expected to begin their studies in the philosophical faculty before proceeding to specialization; furthermore, professors in the faculties of theology, law, and medicine are expected on occasion to teach some part of pure scholarship.[25]

The second corollary of the search for total knowledge was the linking of research and teaching: professors at the university should also when possible be active in the academy of sciences. (Schleiermacher was permanent secretary to the philosophical division in the Berlin Academy of Sciences.)[26] Humboldt argued that an academy of sciences should be independent of the university (which had its own program of research), yet in part composed of university professors. Such an arrangement would be profitable for the academy and would stimulate the productivity of university professors and students in all disciplines.[27] Thus students would be caught up in the spirit of search and research, and those who went on to specialized study would not limit themselves to the narrowly technical or the dogmatically prescribed.[28]

Next came the third corollary claim: the state should permit freedom in teaching and research so as to help create within the framework of the state what Redeker, echoing contemporary terminology, describes as a "community of justice and culture."[29] In general, this meant that professors should concentrate on research and that students should think first of study rather than of issues of career.[30] In practical terms this signified that, though the state "drew up the [university] budgets, created new chairs, appointed professors, and framed the general scheme of instruction," still the universities were granted a certain autonomy: the faculty ordinarily controlled "the election of academic officials, the appointment of lecturers . . . , and the nomination of professors."[31] Since the advancement of research and the training of researchers or professionals serving in institutions sympathetic to the ideal of research in their field was a basic aim, students were free to study what they liked wherever they wished. Moreover, the professor was "free to examine bodies of evidence and to repeat his findings in lecture or published form." In Metzger's elegant phrase, academic freedom was regarded as "the atmosphere of consent that surrounded the whole process of research and instruction."[32]

The double purpose of the Berlin theological faculty was that of propagating and advancing the theological disciplines while training pastors able to carry out the tasks required of them. Clearly the concept of *Wissenschaft* held by the founders of the University of Berlin is one important presupposition for the existence of the theological statutes of 1838. Merely to list the other presuppositions threatens to require a socioeconomic history of nineteenth-century Germany.

The Berlin attempt to institutionalize Schleiermacher's and Humboldt's ideal of research and teaching was the product of a remarkable coincidence of circumstances. The Evangelical church and the university theological faculty were distinct from each other. The church carried out its own program of selecting candidates for ordination;[33] the task was not abandoned to the university. Hence the possibility of fostering an ideal of theological scholarship was enhanced: education for ministry could take place in a setting not under the direct control of the church and to some degree potentially insulated from the direct effects of those periodic waves of irrationalism commonly legitimated in ecclesiastical circles by invocation of the claims of faith.

Other circumstances tended to create the ideal of theological education as a search. A well-established German Evangelical tradition maintained the necessity of massive amounts of learning for leaders in the church.[34] Furthermore, in Protestant Germany the territorial churches—though they were bound to the symbolical documents—lacked any one organ whose interpretation of doctrine could reasonably be asserted as correct and valid for all the Evangelical churches.[35]

Moreover, a network of humanistic *Gymnasien* in the nineteenth century made it feasible to expect a certain level of linguistic proficiency in university students. Though traditional Christianity was out of vogue with many of the educated at the opening of the century, the concept of a theology influenced by a nonecclesiastical *Christentum* could readily be joined to the ideology of Idealism and Neohumanism to produce a theological version of *Bildung* (cultivation of the person by education). Updated Christianity played a significant part in the ideology of the classically educated, morally and aesthetically formed, and totally rounded personality. By means of this ideology of *Bildung,* the non-noble educated sought to advance their social claims in a society still dominated considerably by the nobility. Liberal *Christentum* could be used as part of this set of ideas, and such ideas required that theology be pursued in a university setting.[36]

Behind all these presuppositions was the circumstance that Prussia as an artificial creation was a state resting on an ethos of bureaucratic rationalization and an ethos of duty and diligence. As Hegel put it, the Prussian state was built on intelligence.[37] Within this setting, theological education could not avoid taking on at times a scientific (or at least a scholarly) shape rarely seen in modern times outside Northern Europe.

Schleiermacher as one of the founders of the University of Berlin tried to find a form for the idea of theological education corresponding to the aims behind the new university. Already in 1808, in an influential book on the general task of the university, Schleiermacher contended that the theological faculty had arisen in order to preserve for the church its heritage, to separate truth from error, and to furnish for "the further elaboration of doctrine and the church an historical basis, a sure and determinate direction, and a common spirit."[38] Here he foreshadows the bold reorganization of theological study that he was to put forward in 1811 and 1830.

Schleiermacher's presentation of the system of theological study is organized around the relation of the theological disciplines to the task of providing guidance and leadership to the church.[39] Yet, as Wolfhart Pannenberg has shown, the unity of theology for Schleiermacher derives from the inner principle according to which the components of theology are connected to the "essence" of Christianity.[40] And Schleiermacher's view of most of theology is shaped by attention to historical problems. Philosophical theology has the task of determining the "idea" or "essence" of Christianity by applying philosophical principles to empirical data. Historical theology is described as "verification" of philosophical theology: it "presents each moment in its true relation to the idea of Christianity."[41] "Historical theology" encompasses exegetical theology, the study of postcanonical data concerning doctrine and institutions, and the present state of doctrine and ecclesiastical organization. As such, "historical theology" is for Schleiermacher the "foundation" of practical theology: it constitutes the indispensable precondition for exercising good judgment about how we ought to try to influence the future unfolding of Christianity.[42] Practical theology, then, studies the technical aspects of guiding the current church toward a purer expression of the essence of Christianity in the future.[43]

The Statutes of 1838 not only give guidelines for advanced study, but above all set forth the major disciplines to be studied by future pastors.[44] Enumerated in this connection are encyclopaedia[45] and methodology of theology; introduction to the Old and New Testaments; biblical criticism and hermeneutics; history of the Old Testament with biblical archaeology; exegesis of the Old and New Testaments; church history and history of dogma; dogmatics, ethics, and symbolics; and practical theology.

The period of political and ecclesiastical reaction between the Carlsbad Decrees of 1819 and the middle of the century had grave consequences for theological education. The result, as Max Lenz puts it, was that by the 1840s "to a growing degree . . . the Berlin theology withdrew from the totality of scientific life in the university" in favor of training shepherds of congregations devoted to edification in a traditionalistic sense.[46] Corresponding to this development was the eclipse of the speculative philosophy of nature, which at the start had held together the humanities and the natural sciences. The eventual result would be the rise of positivism in the natural sciences, a positivism which seemed to condemn theology to life in isolation.[47] The theological faculty, which had included not only Schleiermacher but also those of Hegelian persuasion, registered these pressures toward isolation. Particularly significant was the publication of David Friedrich Strauss's *Life of Jesus* in 1835, an event which the Hegelian Philipp Konrad Marheineke himself admitted was a blow from which Hegelian theology could scarcely recover. Strauss's conclusions seemed to confirm the inevitability of a narrowly ecclesiastical trend in theology.[48]

Reaction and narrowness of focus resulted as well from pressure to limit academic freedom. This pressure, coming from both governmental and Neo-Pietist Junker circles, was a serious factor in the nineteenth-century "overcoming" of theological Enlightenment. Already in 1817 an honorary theological doctorate was conferred at Berlin on grounds of the candidate's personal piety in the service of religious awakening.[49] In the unrest of 1819, W. M. L. De Wette was dismissed from Berlin (even as Bruno Bauer was to be transferred from Berlin to Bonn in 1839).[50] By 1822 Schleiermacher himself was in danger of dismissal on account of his opposition to censorship and the secret police (a danger averted by the responsible government minister).[51] In 1817 a Neo-Pietist seminary had been established by the government at Wittenberg;[52] this was, however, but the prelude. Neo-Pietist reaction continued to grow, especially with the increasing influence of the unstable crown prince Friedrich Wilhelm, who well before his accession in 1840 saw to it that anti-Enlightenment religion came into fashion.[53]

Especially important here was Schleiermacher's opponent Ernst Wilhelm Hengstenberg, an exegete who taught at Berlin from 1828 until his death in 1869. He is remembered not only for his political acumen and his bouts of depression but also for his success in seeing to it that only men of the properly ecclesiastical temper proceeded to habilitation. Particularly favored in the Prussian universities during this era were academic studies defending the Mosaic origin of Deuteronomy, the Johannine authenticity of the Fourth Gospel, and the historicity of the canonical accounts of Balaam's ass and Joshua's address to the sun.[54] Moreover, from 1852 on, the church officials regularly had something to say about new appointments to the theological faculty.[55]

These developments challenged Schleiermacher's idea of theological education. The political overcoming of theological Enlightenment doubtless contributed to the decline in the number of students of theology at Berlin from 641 in 1830 to 214 in 1847.[56] Yet the ideal set forth in the statutes under Schleiermacher's general influence was not dead.

To begin with, the second half of the nineteenth century saw a gradual easing of pressure on the university. Metzger observes that this "more permissive attitude" was built into the Prussian Constitution of 1850, with its specification that "science and its teaching

shall be free." Indeed, by 1891 the American psychologist and edu-
cator G. Stanley Hall could proclaim, "The German University is
to-day the freest spot on earth."[57]

Hall's claim ought not to be taken to mean that ecclesiastical and
governmental pressures had ceased. Recurrent serious incidents
affecting academic freedom illustrate how pressure continued—for
example, the celebrated controversy about the Apostles' Creed.[58]
Harnack's difficulties with the ecclesiastics continued for much of
his career. Though Harnack was selected by the Berlin faculty as its
first choice,[59] his appointment to Berlin was opposed by the
ecclesiastical bureaucracy because of his views on the New Testament canon, miracles, and the dominical institution of baptism.[60]

The instances of ecclesiastical narrow-mindedness (or confessional rigor, as one will) did not end with Harnack's call to Berlin
after a session of the ministers presided over by Bismarck himself.[61]
Still, the second half of the century saw a less traditionalistic attitude in Berlin; so great was the change that, for example, a Neo-
Pietist attempt to cast doubt on the Copernican cosmology aroused
only ridicule.[62] The closing years of the nineteenth century witnessed a rebirth of freedom in teaching and research. The research
carried out under Harnack and the work at Berlin of the Hegelian
Otto Pfleiderer (1839–1908) attest to this rebirth.[63] Responsible for it
was not only the fact that the government and its bureaucracy were
now determined to promote solid theological scholarship, but also
the willingness of the government to buy off the reactionaries by
creating for them a *Gegenprofessur* in systematics filled by Adolf
Schlatter (1852–1938) and then by Reinhold Seeberg (1859–1935).[64]

The climate at the end of the century allowed a certain return to
the grand, universal ideal of theological education. As Max Lenz
notes, the later nineteenth century was not lacking in efforts to use
the concept of development as a way of reasserting the unity of natural and humane studies that had been shattered by the turn from
speculative philosophy and by the emphasis on specialized
research.[65] Corresponding to this in theology was the growing
importance of the school of Albrecht Ritschl (1822–1889). His
approach laid great stress on the historical character of revelation,
and thus held it to be obligatory for the church to encourage rigorous scholarship.[66]

The embodiment of this vision of theological education was Adolf
von Harnack. He and his pupils constituted a mighty reassertion
in practice of an idea of theological education that took seriously a

universal concept of scientific research put at the service of the church.[67] This fact can readily be forgotten if we concentrate only on Harnack's repeated difficulties with the institutional church, or if we regard him simply as a product of influences from positivism, Kant (1724–1804), Goethe (1749–1832), and Ritschl. Though all these points are well taken, a close reading of Harnack shows that he advocated a reworking of the grand and universal idea of theological study put forward by Schleiermacher.

Fundamental here is Harnack's universal concept of scientific investigation.[68] The universality of his concept of *Wissenschaft* was perhaps best stated only a few months before his death in 1930, when he asserted that "natural science and the sciences of the spirit and culture should work together; neither may be pursued at the expense of the other, for both are equally required for the knowledge of the universe."[69] Harnack's dependence on the classic Idealist concept of *Wissenschaft* and education can be seen in his simultaneous demands for connected pursuit of teaching and research and for what at the close of his career he termed a "universal philosophical overview."[70]

Harnack's reliance on what Ernst Troeltsch calls "the great idealistic-historical method,"[71] with its insistence on the unitary character of the historical method, meant that church history acquired a key place in theology.[72] This well-known reliance also furnished the presupposition for Harnack's specific views on theological education, views that have attracted relatively little attention. An examination of Harnack's ideas in this connection shows first that Schleiermacher (and the whole tradition of liberal Protestantism) was in Harnack's mind when he wrote on this topic, and second that—even in the twentieth century—Harnack was determined to uphold the Berlin tradition of a unitary concept of *Wissenschaft* broad enough to encompass theology as a rigorous discipline put at the service of the church.

Evidence for these two points occurs in abundance if one examines writings stretching from the turn of the century to Harnack's death in 1930, a time when consensus on theological education was becoming more difficult to achieve. As a result of the decay of consensus, Harnack found himself reasserting the tradition of Schleiermacher in the face of attacks from more than one front. It was in these years that Harnack felt called upon to stress the significance of Schleiermacher for the University of Berlin.[73] In the same period, Harnack brought out the importance of Schleiermacher's historical approach for theological study, reasserting that all investigation of church history must aim at "comprehending the essence of the Christian religion." This task was carried out by all the great theologians; here Harnack named Ritschl, Origen, Augustine—and Schleiermacher.[74]

Harnack put forward his version of the implications of his unitary notion of *Wissenschaft* for theology as an ecclesiastical discipline in the course of at least three debates. The first took place in 1901 and concerned the relation of theology to comparative religion.[75] The second occurred immediately after the close of the First World War and dealt with the place of theological education and the church in national life during the time of reorganization.[76] The third took the shape of an argument with Harnack's student Karl Barth (1886–1968), a debate symbolized by Harnack's famous "Fünfzehn Fragen an die Verächter der wissenschaftlichen Theologie unter den Theologen" ("Fifteen Questions to Those Among the Theologians Who Are Contemptuous of the Scientific Theology") of 1923.[77]

In an article written in 1901, Harnack argued against proposals for transforming theological faculties into agencies for the study of comparative religion, that is, faculties in which Christianity might not necessarily occupy the central place.[78] In the same article, Harnack criticized ecclesiastical constraints on theological work, for they were contrary to his ideal of a truly scientific theology put at the service of the church.[79] Throughout the article, Harnack presupposed a unitary method in scholarship leading to the "reine Erkenntnis des Objekts," the pure knowledge of the object of investigation.[80] Yet Harnack insisted that the exactness and honesty of the rigorous historical method is truly conservative in its "respect for the facts."[81] Furthermore, Harnack dared to suppose that the Protestant church actually wants professors and pastors who, in their "respect for the facts" driving them toward a pure knowledge of the object, can be trusted to use that knowledge for the good of the church.[82]

Central to the views in Harnack's article of 1901 is the late-eighteenth-century concept of *Wissenschaft* as being "not completed doctrine, but research that is always to be subjected to investigation" so that *Wissenschaft* "is bound only to critically-ordered experience."[83] Such a concept of *Wissenschaft* could be expected to function for the benefit of the church only if it was held that Christianity rested on some factual source and experience capable of being investigated. In this connection Harnack could call on a tradition going back to Schleiermacher and the Pietists. For Harnack, the "self-witness" of Jesus has produced "an inner fact [Tat-bestand]," an experience of salvation that—transmitted through the centuries—constitutes "an ongoing fact."[84] The temporal results of this religion and its claim are the object of historical investigation, so that theological science can have the task of preserving the "purity" of this spiritual property in the effort to achieve "ever clearer knowledge" of its "historically recognizable traits."[85] The similarity here to Schleiermacher's view is striking, for Schleier-macher had held that a philosophical theology based on historical theology could benefit the church leadership by helping to give "an authentic representation of the essence of Christianity" that could serve to identify "diseased deviations" in the Christian commu-nity" as a precondition for their removal.[86]

Clearly Harnack's idea of theology and theological education in many ways represents a reworking of Schleiermacher's. For Har-nack, exegetical, historical, and systematic data are all to be inves-tigated by the unitary method of historical science;[87] here he differs from certain of the theologians after Schleiermacher, some of whom had hoped to confine historical criticism to areas safely enough insulated to prevent damage to canonical and dogmatic material. Harnack could allow this freedom for ecclesiastical theol-ogy only because he (like Schleiermacher) was convinced that through such rigorous historical investigation the essence of Chris-tianity could be so liberated as to assist in the derivation of norms for the practical guidance of the church. Given this view, Harnack could on different occasions be equally emphatic in insisting that the Berlin faculty must train both scholars and pastors, for only the pastor with a rigorous theological training could be expected to be equal to the task of perceiving the appropriate norms for present and future practical leadership in the church. A steady supply of both academic and parish theologians was demanded by Harnack's view of how theological and religious life determined by the gospel must function.[88]

The First World War and the ensuing collapse signified an end to institutional and theological presuppositions for many of Harnack's readers. Faced with an uncertain future, Harnack reasserted the Berlin tradition. In an article printed in the *Preussische Jahrbücher* for March of 1919, Harnack rejects the demand for abolition of the theo-logical faculties voiced after the World War.[89] Harnack draws upon Schleiermacher's view of theological study in order to explain what he is now defending.[90]

As Harnack saw matters in 1919, the "object" treated by theological faculties is "the Christian religion."[91] Their "task" consists in investigating the Christian religion.[92] Harnack repeats the familiar claim that theology is concerned with religion, in particular "with the greatest historical experience which humanity has undergone, with Jesus Christ and the effects that have proceeded from him."[93] It is this heritage which theological faculties are to protect and put into living effect in all areas of life—particularly by training pastors and teachers.[94]

As for the work of the theological faculty in detail, for Harnack it pursues the investigation in historical sequence of Scripture, the Catholic church, and "Evangelical faith and Evangelical piety" in their connection with intellectual history for a double reason. It does this

> not only in order to provide ever more scholarly light on them, but also in order to derive from this [knowledge] the right norms for the guidance of souls and the leadership of the church; for, like all sciences, the theological has a double goal—deepening of knowledge and equipping for practical action.[95]

The possibility of such norm derivation in a theology conceived as historical scholarship is given in Harnack's very concept of the humanities as *Geisteswissenschaften*, for according to Harnack they are, in contrast to the natural sciences, disciplines concerned with norms as well as with description and analysis.[96]

In considering these matters, Harnack as it were points to the double task assigned by the theological statutes of the Berlin faculty. In so doing, he shows by his use of the concepts *Seelenführung* and *Kirchenleitung*[97] that he stands in the tradition represented by Schleiermacher's introduction to theology, with its stress on how theological scholarship can assist in the direction of souls and the leadership of the church.

Further, in good Schleiermacherean fashion, Harnack in his article of 1919 defends the retention of systematic and practical theology in the university against critics who called for their removal. In so doing he invokes Schleiermacher.[98] For Harnack, the study of systematic theology is intended to show "how evangelical Christianity is to be presented and taught" and as well to help elaborate a Christian philosophy of religion. That Harnack is here restating and reworking parts of Schleiermacher's outline of theological study is evident. Likewise Harnack's defense of practical theology depends on Schleiermacher. For Harnack, practical theology must provide the "history and theory of ecclesiastical functions" so as to furnish "norms for ecclesiastical activity."[99] Understood in this way, practical theology is the "crown of the theological disciplines, and to eliminate it" would signify "the dissolution of theology."[100] Here we find in Harnack an echo of Schleiermacher's claim that practical theology is the "crown of theological study" and a powerful restatement of Schleiermacher's insistence that theological skills and data, considered apart from their connection with guiding the church, cease to be theological and revert to that nontheological discipline to which their content pertains.[101]

Harnack's general position on theological method and education was thus clearly marked off from several alternatives. Rejected in 1901 was the proposal to move toward turning Christian theological faculties into agencies for the study of comparative religion. Rejected in 1919 was the possibility of replacing theological faculties with denominational seminaries (or their functional equivalent, allowing the institutional church in practice to dictate to existing faculties the extent to which historical criticism could be applied and as well to pronounce on the fitness of candidates for university chairs).[102] Indeed, in 1919 Harnack made plain his opposition to abolition of university theological faculties precisely because he feared the resultant influence of narrow ecclesiasticism on future clergy, who would be subjected to church-controlled training in the name of separation of church and state.

Harnack in 1919 already anticipated a widespread rebirth of theology in the strictly ecclesiastical sense as a discipline ultimately cut off from cultural life as a whole—that is, he anticipated the rise of what was to become the Dialectical Theology. He rejected it in 1919 with a clear call for taking "practical theology" in the broad Schleiermacherean sense rather than as a simple guide to preaching.[103] At the same time, Harnack cautioned that the call for dissolving university theological faculties reflected a tendency that threatened to ruin a German Idealism rooted in the Reformation while depriving the state of any possibility of encouraging a fruitful cooperation of scientific education with religious education.[104] For Harnack this threat raised the possibility of a clergy exercising popular influence of a one-sidedly ecclesiastical variety, for pastors trained only in church seminaries would be isolated from the movement of culture as a whole.[105]

Yet, to reiterate, these points do not mean that Harnack wished to reduce pastoral activity and personal piety to historical scholarship. Rather is it the case that both of the former can flow from it readily, for Harnack believed that "in the Christian religion a major item is the knowledge of God as the Absolute Spirit."[106] Since, according to Harnack, "religion is a determination of feeling and willing, grounded in inner and historical experiences,"[107] and "all history is *Geistesgeschichte*,"[108] therefore: "*You are yourself* everything that has happened . . . in history, and it only depends of your appropriating it with consciousness."[109] In short, Harnack finds God in inner experience within time and in the historical records that give us access to such experiences. For him, the only meaning of the Christian religion is "eternal life in the midst of time, by the strength and under the eyes of God."[110] Quite correctly has Peter Berger argued that, in the Harnackian continuation of Schleiermacher, systematic theology became "a primarily historical discipline," one which—taking its cue from Schleiermacher—"traced back" religion by means of "historical and phenomenological operations" to the original, the "core experience of God" with which each tradition began.[111]

For Harnack, canonical texts are not protected from critical inquiry; there can be ultimately for all branches of study "only *one* scientific method" and "only *one* scientific *task* —the pure knowledge" of the object.[112] Indeed, as Harnack came to hold during the debate with Barth, "the task of theology is one with the tasks of science in general."[113] All this can be accepted readily because, for Harnack, a witness to Christ proceeds directly from an investigation of how eternal life has been made manifest in the midst of time.[114]

Harnack's idea of theological education thus restates Schleiermacher's ideal of the unity of scholarly theology and training for ministry in such a way that the work of the historian (and of the pastor as historical theologian) gives a highly significant answer to the issue of Christian speech about God. Indeed, it would not be amiss to follow G. Wayne Glick here and to observe that, for Harnack, the ultimate human duty is to overcome the world by knowing God—a duty that can be fulfilled only by "knowing history" so as to overcome it.[115] The vocation of the historian begins to merge with the calling of the believer.

This approach was to be repudiated by one of Harnack's pupils, Karl Barth.[116] Barth would identify the task of theology with the task of preaching in such a way as to reduce historical work to the status of a mere auxiliary discipline serving the needs of exegesis, dogmatics, and practical theology.[117] Barth's demotion was a logical one for him, since he denied that "so-called church history" gave any independent answer to the question of Christian speech about God. In this denial Barth was not at all far removed from the view of Harnack's critic Franz Overbeck (1837–1905), who warned that the study of church history was the best school for learning to doubt the existence of a God.[118]

Moreover, though Barth did hold that theology was a *Wissenschaft*, the early Barth insisted so strongly on the way theology is determined by the special character of its object that this theological *Wissenschaft* threatened to move into total isolation from all other forms of *Wissenschaft*. In the controversy with Barth, Harnack sharply warned that "each age possesses only one science," that Barth wished to "transform the theological professor's chair into a pulpit," and that the contempt for reason and science represented by Barth's method threatened to deliver the church over to "occultism" and "revival preachers, who freely create their understanding of the Bible and who set up their own dominance."[119] While Harnack's fears were certainly exaggerated, Barth himself wrote that by calling theology a *Wissenschaft* he intended to make a "protest" against the "confessedly 'pagan' general concept of *Wissenschaft*."[120] Here—despite Barth's great debt to Harnack—was a negative judgment on the theological method taught at Berlin and a denial of the validity of Harnack's effort at using a unitary concept of *Wissenschaft* in theology.[121]

Another of Harnack's students judged the teacher's historical approach more positively than Barth's premises would seem to allow. In 1930 the twenty-four-year-old Dietrich Bonhoeffer (1906-1945) spoke to those who mourned Harnack's passing. He said:

> At this moment, thousands of young theologians look back with me at their great teacher. . . .
>
> We saw in him the champion of the free expression of a truth once recognised, who formed his free judgment afresh time and time again, and went on to express it clearly despite the fear-ridden restraint of the majority. . . .
>
> But Adolf von Harnack—and for us this was the most important thing—was a theologian, a conscious theologian, and we believed that this was the only standpoint from which it was possible to understand him completely. Therefore it should be stated clearly once again in this context too. He was a theologian. That does not mean in the first place that he wrote a *History of Dogma*. Theology means speaking of God.

The work of any theologian is never concerned with anything less. In Harnack, the theologian we saw contained the unity of the world of his spirit; here truth and freedom found their true connection without becoming arbitrariness. . . . He thought that in the holy spirit of Christianity the spirit of every age found its destiny, and that the message of God the Father and the human child had eternal validity and therefore validity for us also.[122]

In these words Bonhoeffer pays tribute to the enduring importance of the idea of theological education at Berlin.

NOTES

1. A. von Harnack, *RuA* 5:178. On the whole, translations from Harnack are my own unless otherwise noted, though on occasion I have consulted the translation in G. W. Glick, *The Reality of Christianity: A Study of Adolf von Harnack as Historian and Theologian* (New York, 1967); see Glick, 91, 60, 62. My essay is heavily indebted to the reflections in two works: W. Pannenberg, *Wissenschaftstheorie und Theologie* (Frankfurt a.M., 1973), chaps. 4, 5, 6; and W. Sundberg, "The Development of Dogma as an Ecumenical Problem: Roman Catholic–Protestant Conflict over the Authority and Historicity of Dogmatic Statements" (Ph.D. diss., Princeton Theological Seminary, 1981).

2. Harnack, *RuA* 6:7–8, following the trans. in Glick, *Reality of Christianity,* 97–98; see also ibid., 60, 108. Italics in original text removed by me.

3. F. D. E. Schleiermacher, *Sämmtliche Werke* 1/2 (Berlin, 1836): 614, 617–18; Harnack, *RuA* 7:51–54, esp. questions 8 and 15; see also H. M. Rumscheidt, *Revelation and Theology,* Monograph Supplements to *SJTh* (Cambridge, 1972).

4. Schleiermacher, *Sämmtliche Werke,* 1/2:617–18.

5. Schleiermacher, *KD* (1830), §§ 24, 27, 32, 34, 35–37, 65. For an English version (not used in the preparation of this chapter unless so noted), see Schleiermacher, *Brief Outline on the Study of Theology,* trans. T. N. Tice (Richmond, 1970).

6. Harnack, *HD* 7:228.

7. Ibid., 227, 268, 267.

8. Ibid., 267–68.

9. Ibid., 268–70; cf. Sundberg, "Development of Dogma," 73–77; also Pannenberg, *Wissenschaftstheorie und Theologie,* 379, citing T. Rendtorff, *Theorie des Christentums* (1972), 41ff. The same distinctive refusal to separate theology from the development of modern culture characterized the work of Paul Tillich (1886–1965), who taught at Berlin from 1918 to 1924.

10. For the background in Semler (1725–1791), see H.-E. Hess, "Theologie

und Religion bei Johann Salomo Semler" (Theol. dissertation, Kirchliche Hochschule Berlin, 1974), with extensive bibliography.

11. Schleiermacher, *KD* (1811), 7, § 28; cf. 2, § 5.

12. Harnack, *RuA* 6:199–217, esp. 203–4; *RuA* 2:159–87; *RuA* 4:153–64; E. Horn, "Berlin, Universität," *RGG*¹ 1: cols. 1041–54, esp. 1045–46; M. Hertz, "Schulze, Johannes Karl Hartwig," *Allgemeine Deutsche Biographie* (1891; reprint, Berlin, 1971): 33:5–18; Daude, *Die Königl. Friedrich-Wilhelms-Universität zu Berlin. Systematische Zusammenstellung der . . . Bestimmungen* (Berlin, 1887); L. Zscharnack, "Das erste Jahrhundert der theologischen Fakultät Berlin," *CCW* 20 (1910): 469–73, 484–85, 492–98; Zscharnack, "Berlin, Universität," *RGG*² 1: cols. 915–19; J. G. Fichte, *Sämmtliche Werke*, ed. J. Fichte (Berlin, 1846), 8 (= 3/3): 95–219; Harnack, *GAW* 2.

13. Schleiermacher, *Gelegentliche Gedanken über Universitäten im deutschen Sinn. Nebst einem Anhang über eine neu zu errichtende* (Berlin, 1808); M. Redeker, *Schleiermacher: Life and Thought*, trans. J. Wallhausser (Philadelphia, 1973), 94–100, 185–86; Harnack, *RuA* 6:203–4.

14. "Die Statuten der theologischen Fakultät v. 29. Januar 1838," in Daude, *Die Königl. F.-W. Universität*, 46.

15. Lenz, 1:125; Schleiermacher, *Gelegentliche Gedanken*.

16. W. von Humboldt, "Über die innere und äussere Organisation der höheren wissenschaftlichen Anstalten in Berlin," Harnack, *GAW*, 2:361–67.

17. T. Nipperdey, "Die Idee von der wahren, zweckfreien Wissenschaft: Der preussische Militär- und Verwaltungsstaat und die moderne Universität," *Frankfurter Allgemeine Zeitung*, November 21, 1981, sect. "Bilder und Zeiten." Cf. G. Lessing, *Lessing's Theological Writings*, trans. H. Chadwick (Stanford, 1957) (= Lachmann-Muncker 13:23–24): "The worth of a man does not consist in the truth he possesses, or thinks he possesses, but in the pains he has taken to attain that truth. In this alone his ever-growing perfection consists."

18. See J. Stroup, "Protestant Churchmen in the German Enlightenment—Mere Tools of Temporal Government?" *Lessing Yearbook* 10 (1978): 149–89.

19. R. Hofstadter and W. P. Metzger, *The Development of Academic Freedom in the United States* (New York, 1955), 372.

20. Ibid., 373.

21. Nipperdey, "Die Idee von der wahren, zweckfreien Wissenschaft." On the speculative philosophy of nature, see E. Spranger, *Berliner Geist* (Tübingen, 1966), 210.

22. Redeker, *Schleiermacher*, 96.

23. For all this see ibid.

24. Schleiermacher, *Sämmtliche Werke*, 3/1:558, as translated in Redeker, *Schleiermacher*, 96.

25. Schleiermacher, *Gelegentliche Gedanken*, 80, 78; see also Nipperdey, "Die Idee von der wahren, zweckfreien Wissenschaft."

26. Redeker, *Schleiermacher*, 185, citing Harnack, *GAW* 1/2:848, 626.

27. Humboldt in Harnack, *GAW* 2:361–67; see also Harnack, *RuA* 6:204–6 and 2:189–215.

28. Hofstadter and Metzger, *Development of Academic Freedom*, 373–74.

29. Redeker, *Schleiermacher*, 97.

30. Nipperdey, "Die Idee von der wahren, zweckfreien Wissenschaft."

31. Hofstadter and Metzger, 385.

32. Ibid., 386–87.

33. Zscharnack, "Das erste Jahrhundert"; R. M. Bigler, *The Politics of German Protestantism* (Berkeley, 1972); G. Pariset, *L'État et les Églises en Prusse Sous Frédéric Guillaume Ier (1713–1740)* (Thèse, Paris, 1896); E. Foerster, *Die Entstehung der Preussischen Landeskirche*, 2 vols. (Tübingen, 1905); G. Heinrich, "Amtsträgerschaft und Geistlichkeit," in G. Franz, ed., *Beamtentum und Pfarrerstand 1400–1800*, Deutsche Führungsschichten in der Neuzeit 5 (Limburg/Lahn, 1972), 179–238; H. Brunschwig, *Enlightenment and Romanticism*, trans. F. Jellinek (Chicago, 1974), 24.

34. J. Wallmann, *Der Theologiebegriff bei Johann Gerhard und Georg Calixt*, BHTh 30 (Tübingen 1961); J. L. von Mosheim, *Kurze Anweisung, die Gottesgelahrtheit vernünftig zu erlernen*, ed. C. E. von Windheim (Helmstedt, 1756); J. L. von Mosheim, *Pastoral-Theologie*, 2d ed. (Leipzig and Ansbach, 1763).

35. E. Spranger, "Das Wesen der deutschen Universität," in M. Doeberl et al., eds., *Das akademische Deutschland* (Berlin, 1930): 3:1–38, esp. 9.

36. See R. Vierhaus, "Bildung," and T. Rendtorff, "Christentum," *GG* 1:508–51, 772–814.

37. Hegel, cited in R. Koselleck, *Preussen zwischen Reform und Revolution*, Industrielle Welt 7 (Stuttgart, 1967), 399, n. 7.

38. Schleiermacher, *Gelegentliche Gedanken*, 73.

39. Schleiermacher, *KD* (1830), § 3.

40. Pannenberg, *Wissenschaftstheorie und Theologie*, 430.

41. Schleiermacher, *KD* (1830), § 27; cf. § 24. See also Harnack, *RuA* 4:61, on church history as a means of illuminating the essence of Christianity.

42. Schleiermacher, *KD* (1830), § 27; *KD* (1811), 2d part, Einleitung, § 3 = 24–25; see also C. Welch, *Protestant Thought in the Nineteenth Century* (New Haven, 1972), 1:69–70.

43. Schleiermacher, *KD* (1811), 7, § 28; 8, §§ 29–31 = Einleitung.

44. Statutes of 1838 in Daude, *De Königl. F.-W. Universität*, 72–82, §§ 87–118; 56–57, § 39.

45. On the notion of systematic theological encyclopedia, see C. F. G. Heinrici, *Theologische Encyklopädie*, GThW 1/1 (Freiburg i.B. and Leipzig, 1893); Heinrici, "Encyklopädie, theologische," *RE* 5:351–64.

46. Lenz, 2/2:112.

47. Spranger, *Berliner Geist*, 210.

48. Bigler, *Politics*, 117, citing P. K. Marheineke, *Zur Kritik der Schelling' schen Offenbarungs-Philosophie* (Berlin, 1845).

49. Bigler, *Politics*, 130.

50. Ibid., 44, 178.

51. Ibid., 161.

52. Ibid., 65.

53. Ibid., 137–38; *ODCC* (1958 ed.), 621.

54. Bigler, *Politics*, 92; Lenz, 2/2:280f. and n. 2; 379.

55. Zscharnack, "Das erste Jahrhundert," 493.

56. Bigler, *Politics*, 122. Halle had a larger enrollment of theological students than did Berlin. For figures, see F. Eulenburg, *Die Frequenz der deutschen Universitäten*, ASGW.PH 24/2 (Leipzig, 1904).

57. Hofstadter and Metzger, *Development of Academic Freedom*, 385, 392.

58. Schiele, "Apostolikumstreit," *RGG*[1] 1: cols. 601–8; AZH[1], 193–214.

59. AZH[1], 156.

60. Ibid., 161. Since 1855 the Evangelischer Oberkirchenrat had been entitled to lodge such objections. Here Harnack's chief opponent was the court pastor Rudolf Kögel (1829–1896). Kögel had formerly been secretary to the Pietist Halle theologian F. A. G. Tholuck (1799–1877), a man noteworthy for his mental instability, his opposition to the ideas of Semler, Herder, and Humboldt, and his grammatical errors in exegesis. See AZH[1], 158; Stephan, "Kögel," *RGG*[1] 3: cols. 1550f.; Bigler, *Politics*, 87; Lenz, 2/1:324; W. Schrader, *Geschichte der Friedrichs-Universität zu Halle* (Berlin, 1894).

61. AZH[1], 171; J. Pelikan, *Historical Theology* (New York, 1971), 129, 141; Zscharnack, "Das erste Jahrhundert," 496; "Lisco, Heinrich," *RGG*[1] 3: col. 2172.

62. "Knak, Gustav," *RGG*[1] 3: col. 1538.

63. E. Hirsch, *Geschichte der neuern evangelischen Theologie* (Gütersloh, 1949–54), 5:562–70 (on Pfleiderer).

64. Zscharnack, "Das erste Jahrhundert," 496.

65. Lenz, 2/2:377.

66. Heinrici, *RE* 5:359.

67. See Glick, *Reality of Christianity*, 62, 211.

68. See Ernst Troeltsch in W. Pauck, *Harnack and Troeltsch* (New York, 1968), 97; Pannenberg, *Wissenschaftstheorie und Theologie*, 377, n. 704; also nn. 69–70 below; Harnack, *RuA* 8:177–80; Glick, *Reality of Christianity*, 87–93. For the general relation of Harnack's view of religion to Schleiermacher's, see P. L. Berger, *The Heretical Imperative* (Garden City, N.Y., 1980), 116–28, and n. 41 above. See also Harnack, *RuA* 4:56. For background, see the useful but inadequate study by H. Wagenhammer, *Das Wesen des Christentums*, Tübinger Theologische Studien 2 (Mainz, 1973).

69. Quoted in Dietrich Gerhard, "Adolf v. Harnacks letzte Monate als Präsident der Kaiser-Wilhelm-Gesellschaft," *Jahrbuch der Max-Planck-Gesellschaft zur Förderung der Wissenschaften e.V.*, Jahrgang 1970: 142.

70. For Harnack's requirement of *Forschung und Lehre* and a *universale philosophische Zusammenschau*, see ibid., 142–44.

71. See Troeltsch in Pauck, *Harnack and Troeltsch*, 99.

72. Ibid., 36 and n. 58, 97, 102; Harnack, *RuA* 2:165f.

73. See the references to Schleiermacher in the volumes of Harnack, *RuA*; e.g., "Die Aufgabe der theologischen Fakultäten und die allgemeine Religionsgeschichte. Nebst einem Nachwort," *RuA* 2:159–87, esp. 161, 163, 170, 177; the standpoint of this article should be compared with that of Schleiermacher, *KD* (1830), §§ 79–80; "Die Königlich Preussische Akademie der Wissenschaften," *RuA* 2:205–6; "Die Bedeutung der theologischen Fakultäten," *RuA* 8:113–31, esp. 117, 127 = *RuA* 6:199–217. I realize that in the present chapter one-sided emphasis is given to the significance of Schleiermacher for Harnack. A larger study would need to take account of how Harnack came to terms with the entire Protestant heritage from the nineteenth century and would have to give due place to Humboldt and others in the shaping of the ideal of *Wissenschaft*.

74. See Troeltsch in Pauck, *Harnack and Troeltsch*, 102, and Harnack on the great theologians in his "In memoriam: Albrecht Ritschl," *RuA* 6:335–36.

75. See n. 73 above, citing "Die Aufgabe"; see also C. Colpe, "Bemerkungen zu Adolf von Harnacks Einschätzung der Disziplin 'Allgemeine Religionsgeschichte,'"*Neue Zeitschrift für systematische Theologie und Religionsgeschichte* 6 (1964): 51–69.

76. See n. 73 above, citing "Die Bedeutung" (Harnack, *RuA* 6:199–217 = *RuA* 8:113–31). Attacks on the status of university theological faculties were nothing new. At the time of Schleiermacher, the French in Napoleonic Germany suggested that faculties of Christian theology be abolished, though this suggestion was not made everywhere and was certainly not carried out. For the nature of the proposals, see J. Stroup, *The Struggle for Identity in the Clerical Estate*, Studies in the History of Christian Thought 33 (Leiden, 1984), Appendix I. On Harnack's opposition to the demand of 1919 for abolishing theological faculties, see his *RuA* 6:208–9, 199, 205–6.

77. Harnack, *RuA* 8:132–4 (English title after K. R. Crim; see n. 112 below).

78. Harnack, *RuA* 2: 180; see also Pannenberg, *Wissenschaftstheorie und Theologie*, 362–63, for the situation around 1901.

79. Harnack, *RuA* 2:175.

80. Ibid., 166, 176, 180.

81. Ibid., 166.

82. Ibid., 176.

83. Ibid., 174f.

84. Ibid., 173.

85. Ibid., 174.

86. Schleiermacher, *KD* (1830), § 40; cf. § 65. The translation here is that of Tice (n. 5 above), 31–32. See also *KD* (1830), § 258, for an effort to require "ecclesial interest" and "scientific spirit" for those engaging in practical theology (Tice, 81).

87. Cf. P. Meinhold, *Geschichte der kirchlichen Historiographie*, OA 3/5

(Freiburg, 1967); 2:278; Harnack, *RuA* 2:165: "Eine besondere Methode, aber, nach welcher die christliche Religion zu studieren ist im Unterschied von den anderen, kennen wir nicht."

88. See, e.g., Harnack, *RuA* 2:174–76, as well as many other passages. On axiology in Harnack's work, see Glick, *Reality of Christianity,* 161–76. See also K. H. Neufeld, *Adolf von Harnack: Theologie als Suche nach der Kirche,* KKTS 41 (Paderborn, 1977), 22: "Harnacks Grundliebe ist die *Kirche,* nicht nur in ihren geschichtlichen Gestalten, sondern in erster Linie als Aufgabe der eigenen Zeit."

89. Harnack, *RuA* 8:113–31 = 6:199–217.

90. Ibid., 8:127.

91. Ibid., 121–22.

92. Ibid., 122.

93. Ibid., 130.

94. Ibid.

95. Ibid., 122.

96. Ibid., 124–25.

97. Ibid., 6:208, 211, 213. For the slightly different terminology for these ideas in Schleiermacher, see *KD* (1811), 7–8, §§ 28–30; *KD* (1830), §§ 25–26 (*Kirchenleitung*), § 263 (*Seelenleitung*); *KD* (1811), 81, § 21; *KD* (1830), § 6. The echoes of these secs. of *KD* in Harnack deserve attention; see Harnack, *RuA* 6:208–13; cf. Glick, *Reality of Christianity,* 7, 29, 43, 71, 74, 77, 79, 116, 126, 130, 164, 176, 207, 291–93, 332, 343; Harnack, *HD* 7:272; *RuA* 4:159; *RuA* 2:177.

98. Harnack, *RuA* 6:213.

99. Ibid.

100. Ibid., terming practical theology the "Krone der theologischen Disziplinen." Cf. Schleiermacher, *KD* (1811), 8, § 31: "Die praktische Theologie ist die Krone des theologischen Studiums."

101. Harnack, *RuA* 6:213; cf. Schleiermacher, *KD* (1830), § 6.

102. Harnack, *RuA* 2:159–87; 6:199–217, esp. 206.

103. Ibid., 8:127. = 6:213.

104. Ibid., 130. = 6:216–17.

105. Ibid., 119f. = 6:205–6.

106. Ibid., 4:55.

107. Ibid., 56.

108. Ibid., 6:187; cf. Glick, *Reality of Christianity,* 107–8.

109. Harnack, *RuA* 6:187, here echoing yet altering the translation in Glick, 108.

110. Harnack, *What Is Christianity?* trans. T. B. Saunders (New York, 1957), 8.

111. Berger, 120, 121, 123, 125–26. For Hegelianism and Harnack, see Pauck, *Harnack and Troeltsch,* 97ff.

112. Harnack in K. Barth, *Theologische Fragen und Antworten* (Zollikon, 1957), 31. Here in the main I follow the translation of K. R. Crim in J. M.

Robinson, ed., *The Beginnings of Dialectic Theology* (Richmond, 1968), 186, rather than that in Rumscheidt, *Revelation and Theology*, 53. See also Glick, *Reality of Christianity*, 223–25.

113. Harnack in Barth, *Fragen*, 14, following the translation of Rumscheidt, *Revelation and Theology*, 36, and Crim and Robinson, *Beginnings of Dialectic Theology*, 171.

114. Additional investigation might suggest that Harnack's differences with Barth are in some ways linked to differences in the conception of what is historically significant and factual in the events and experiences connected with Jesus Christ. It would be interesting to inquire whether and how such differences could be related to differing positions on the strategy to be adopted so as to guard against the corrosive effects of historical criticism and relativism. Worthy of attention in this connection is Harnack, *Die Entstehung der christlichen Theologie und des kirchlichen Dogmas. Sechs Vorlesungen* (Gotha, 1927; reprint, Darmstadt, 1967 = Libelli 239).

115. Glick, *Reality of Christianity*, esp. 10, 312; Harnack in AZH², 130–31. See also Glick, *Reality of Christianity*, 209 and 101.

116. E. Busch, *Karl Barth*, trans. J. Bowden, (Philadelphia, 1976), 39, 147; Barth, *Fragen*, 7–31.

117. Barth, *Fragen*, 10; idem, *Kirchliche Dogmatik* (Zürich, 1947), 1/1: 3. See also Rumscheidt, *Revelation and Theology*, 188ff.

118. On Barth, see n. 117 above; F. Overbeck, *Christentum und Kultur*, (Basel, 1919), 265–66. See also H. Schindler, *Barth und Overbeck* (Gotha, 1936).

119. Harnack to Barth, trans. K. R. Crim in Crim and Robinson, *Beginnings of Dialectic Theology*, 1:171, 174 = Harnack in Barth, *Fragen*, 13–17; also Rumscheidt, *Revelation and Theology*, 35–39; see also the comments of Jaroslav Pelikan in Glick, *Reality of Christianity*, xiii; see also Pannenberg's account of the controversy between H. Scholz and Barth in 1930–1936 in Pannenberg, *Wissenschaftstheologie und Theologie*, 273 (citing Scholz in ZZ 9 [1931]:48).

120. Barth, *Kirchliche Dogmatik* 1/1:9.

121. On Harnack, cf. *RuA* 2:165: "Aber weiter, nur nach einer und derselben Methode können die Religionen studiert werden, nämlich der geschichtlichen, und diese läßt sich nicht willkürlich beschränken." See also *RuA* 4:44–45.

122. D. Bonhoeffer, trans. E. H. Robertson and J. Bowden, *No Rusty Swords: Letters, Lectures, and Notes 1928–1936*, vol. 1 of *Collected Works* (New York, 1965), 29–31. See also G. Krause, "Bonhoeffer, Dietrich," *TRE* 7:55–66, esp. 55 (Bonhoeffer's "Gedenkrede auf Harnack ist ein Bekenntnis zur Wahrheitssuche der Liberalen Theologie") and 58 (influence of the Berlin faculty's liberal theology on Bonhoeffer's criticism of the Dialectical Theology).

APPENDIX

Selected Bibliography of the Works of Jaroslav Pelikan

prepared by Jane R. Baun

Professor Jaroslav Pelikan's published works are organized here into seven categories:

1. Books
2. Works and series edited or translated
3. Essays in books
4. Articles in journals
5. Forewords to works of others
6. Articles and addresses of general interest
7. Encyclopedia articles

Book reviews, sermons, and other occasional pieces have not been included. Within each category, items are arranged chronologically.

1
BOOKS—AUTHOR

"The Bible of Kralice." B.D. thesis, Concordia Theological Seminary, 1946.

"Luther and the *Confessio Bohemica*." Ph.D. diss., The University of Chicago, 1946.

From Luther to Kierkegaard: A Study in the History of Theology. Saint Louis: Concordia Publishing House, 1950. 2d ed. with preface (paperback). Saint Louis: Concordia Publishing House, 1963. Japanese translation: Tokyo: Seibunsha, 1967.

With Richard R. Caemmerer. *The Cross for Every Day: Sermons and Meditations for Lent.* Parts II and IV. Saint Louis: Concordia Publishing House, 1952. Pp. 47–88, 99–113.

Fools for Christ. Philadelphia: Fortress Press, 1955. British edition: *Human Culture and the Holy: Essays on the True, the Good, and the Beautiful.* London: SCM Press, 1959.

Luther the Expositor: Introduction to the Reformer's Exegetical Writings. Companion volume to *Luther's Works*, American Edition, edited by Jaroslav Pelikan. Saint Louis: Concordia Publishing House, 1959. Japanese translation: Toyko: Seibunsha, 1959.

The Riddle of Roman Catholicism. Nashville: Abingdon Press, 1959. Paperback edition: Nashville: Abingdon Press, Apex Books, 1959; London: Hodder & Stoughton, 1960.

The Shape of Death: Life, Death, and Immortality in the Early Fathers. Nashville: Abingdon Press, 1961. Paperback edition: Nashville: Abingdon Press, Apex Books, 1961; London: Macmillan & Co., 1962; Westport, Conn.: Greenwood Press, 1978.

The Light of the World: A Basic Image in Early Christian Thought. New York: Harper & Brothers, 1962.

Obedient Rebels: Catholic Substance and Protestant Principle in Luther's Reformation. New York: Harper & Row, 1964; London: SCM Press, 1964.

The Christian Intellectual. Religious Perspectives Series, edited by Ruth Nanda Anshen, vol. 14. New York: Harper & Row, 1965; London: William Collins Sons, 1966.

The Finality of Jesus Christ in an Age of Universal History: A Dilemma of the Third Century. Ecumenical Studies in History, vol. 3. London: Lutterworth Press, 1965; Richmond: John Knox Press, 1966.

Spirit versus Structure: Luther and the Institutions of the Church. New York: Harper & Row, 1968; London: William Collins Sons, 1968.

Development of Christian Doctrine: Some Historical Prolegomena. New Haven: Yale University Press, 1969.

The Emergence of the Catholic Tradition (100–600). Vol. 1 of *The Christian Tradition: A History of the Development of Doctrine.* Chicago: University of Chicago Press, 1971.

Historical Theology: Continuity and Change in Christian Doctrine. Theological Resources. New York: Corpus and Philadelphia: Westminster with London: Hutchinson, 1971.

The Spirit of Eastern Christendom (600–1700). Vol. 2 of *The Christian Tradition: A History of the Development of Doctrine.* Chicago: University of Chicago Press, 1974.

The Growth of Medieval Theology (600–1300). Vol. 3 of *The Christian Tradition: A History of the Development of Doctrine.* Chicago: University of Chicago Press, 1978.

Scholarship and Its Survival. Princeton: Carnegie Foundation for the Advancement of Teaching, 1983.

Reformation of Church and Dogma (1300–1700). Vol. 4 of *The Christian Tradition: A History of the Development of Doctrine.* Chicago: University of Chicago Press, 1984.

The Vindication of Tradition: The Jefferson Lecture in the Humanities for 1983. New Haven: Yale University Press, 1984.

2
WORKS AND SERIES EDITED
OR TRANSLATED

Luther's Works. American Edition. Vols. 1–30. Vols. 12, 14, 21, 26, and 27 translated in whole or in part. Saint Louis: Concordia Publishing House, 1958–69.

"Apology of the Augsburg Confession." Edited and translated. In *The Book of Concord: The Confessions of the Evangelical Lutheran Church,* edited by Theodore G. Tappert, 97–285. Philadelphia: Fortress [Muhlenberg] Press, 1959.

Makers of Modern Theology. With individual introductions. 5 vols. New York: Harper & Row, 1966–68.

The Preaching of Chrysostom: Homilies on the Sermon on the Mount. With an introduction. Philadelphia: Fortress Press, 1967.

Interpreters of Luther: Essays in Honor of Wilhelm Pauck. Philadelphia: Fortress Press, 1968.

Twentieth Century Theology in the Making. With introductions. 3 vols. London: William Collins Sons, 1969–70. New York: Harper & Row, 1971.

The Preaching of Augustine: "Our Lord's Sermon on the Mount." With an introduction. Translated by Francine Cardman. Philadelphia: Fortress Press, 1973.

3
ESSAYS IN BOOKS

"Form and Tradition in Worship: A Theological Interpretation." In *First Liturgical Institute, Valparaiso University,* 11–27. Valparaiso, Ind.: Valparaiso University Press, 1950.

"Practical Politics." In *The Christian in Politics: Proceedings of the Institute of Politics,* edited by Alfred Looman and Albert Wehling, 9–34. Valparaiso, Ind.: Valparaiso University Press, 1950.

"Theology and Missions in Lutheran History." In *Proceedings of the Thirtieth Convention of the Atlantic District of the Lutheran Church—Missouri Synod,* 33–38. Saint Louis: Concordia Publishing House, 1951.

"Luther's Doctrine of the Lord's Supper." In *Proceedings of the Thirtieth Convention of the English District of the Lutheran Church—Missouri Synod,* 12–33. Saint Louis: Concordia Publishing House, 1957.

"Dogma" and "Dogmatics." In *A Handbook of Christian Theology: Definition Essays on Concepts and Movements of Thought in Contemporary Protestantism,* 80–85. New York: Meridian Books, 1958.

"Die Kirche nach Luthers Genesisvorlesung." In *Lutherforschung Heute.* Referate und Berichte des 1. Internationalen Lutherforschungskongresses, edited by Vilmos Vajta, 102–10. Berlin: Lutherisches Verlagshaus, 1958.

"Luther and the Liturgy." In *More About Luther.* Martin Luther Lectures, vol. 2, pp. 3–62. Decorah, Iowa: Luther College Press, 1958.

"Ein deutscher lutherischer Theologe in Amerika: Paul Tillich und die dogmatische Tradition." In *Gott ist am Werk: Festschrift für Landesbischof D. Hanns Lilje zum sechzigsten Geburtstag*, 27–36. Hamburg: Furch-Verlag, 1959.

"Totalitarianism and Democracy: A Religious Analysis." In *God and Caesar: A Christian Approach to Social Ethics*, edited by Warren A. Quanbeck, 99–114. Minneapolis: Augsburg Publishing House, 1959.

"Creation and Causality in the History of Christian Thought." In *Issues in Evolution*, vol. 3 of *Evolution after Darwin*, edited by Sol Tax and Charles Callender, 29–40. Chicago: University of Chicago Press, 1960.

"Luther's Attitude toward Church and Councils." In *The Papal Council and the Gospel: Protestant Theologians Evaluate the Coming Vatican Council*, edited by Kristen E. Skydsgaard, 37–60. Minneapolis: Augsburg Publishing House, 1961. German translation: "Luthers Stellung zu den Kirchenkonzilien," in *Konzil und Evangelium*, edited by Kristen E. Skydsgaard, 40–62. Göttingen: Vandenhoeck & Ruprecht, 1962.

"Overcoming History by History." In *The Old and the New in the Church: Studies in Ministry and Worship of the World Council of Churches*, edited by G. W. H. Lampe and David M. Paton, 36–42. London: SCM Press, 1961; Minneapolis: Augsburg Publishing House, 1961.

"Bergson among the Theologians." In *The Bergsonian Heritage*, edited by Thomas Hanna, 54–73. New York: Columbia University Press, 1962.

"The Early Answer to the Question concerning Jesus Christ: Bonhoeffer's *Christologie* of 1933." In *The Place of Bonhoeffer: Problems and Possibilities in His Thought*, edited by Martin E. Marty, 145–65. New York: Association Press, 1962; Korean translation by Han Kook Bai: Seoul, 1966.

"Issues That Divide Us: Protestant." In *Christians in Conversation*, Papers from a colloquium at Saint John's Abbey, Collegeville, Minnesota, 3–19. Westminster, Md.: Newman Press, 1962.

"The Protestant Concept of the Church: An Ecumenical Consensus." In *Proceedings of the Seventeenth Annual Convention* (Catholic Theological Society of America), 131–37. Yonkers, N.Y., 1962.

"Religious Responsibility for the Social Order—A Protestant View." In *Religious Responsibility for the Social Order, a Symposium by Three Theologians*, by Jaroslav Pelikan, Gustave Weigel, and Emil L. Fackenheim. New York: National Conference of Christians and Jews, 1962.

"The Functions of Theology." In *Theology in the Life of the Church*, edited by Robert Bertram, 3–21. Philadelphia: Fortress Press, 1963.

"The Vocation of the Christian Apologist: A Study of Schleiermacher's *Reden*." In *Christianity and World Revolution*, edited by Edwin H. Rian, 173–89. New York: Harper & Row, 1963.

"American Lutheranism: Denomination or Confession." In *What's Ahead for the Churches*, edited by Kyle Haselden and Martin Marty, 187–95. New York: Sheed & Ward, 1964.

"In Defense of Research in Religious Studies at the Secular University."

In *Religion and the University*, 1–19. York University Gerstein Lectures. Toronto: University of Toronto Press, 1964.

"Methodism's Contribution to America." In *History of American Methodism*, edited by Emory Stevens Bucke, vol. 3, pp. 596–614. Nashville: Abingdon Press, 1964.

"The Mortality of God and the Immortality of Man in Gregory of Nyssa." In *The Scope of Grace: Essays in Honor of Joseph Sittler*, edited by Philip J. Hefner, 79–97. Philadelphia: Fortress Press, 1964.

"*Justitia* as Justice and *Justitia* as Righteousness." In *Law and Theology: Essays on "The Professional Responsibility of the Christian Lawyer,"* edited by Andrew J. Buehner, 87–98. Saint Louis: Concordia Publishing House, 1965.

"Constitution on the Sacred Liturgy—A Response." In *The Documents of Vatican II*, edited by Walter M. Abbott, 179–82. New York: America Press, 1966.

"Relevance: The Preoccupations of Theology." In *Jesus Christ Reforms His Church*, Proceedings of the Twenty-sixth North American Liturgical Week, 30–38. Washington, D.C.: Liturgical Conference, 1966.

"Tradition, Reformation, and Development." In *Frontline Theology*, edited by Dean Peerman, 101–7. Richmond: John Knox Press, 1966.

"Continuity and Order in Luther's View of Church and Ministry." In *Kirche, Mystik, Heiligung und das Natürliche bei Luther*, Vorträge des Dritten Internationalen Kongresses für Lutherforschung, edited by Ivar Asheim, 143–55. Göttingen: Vandenhoeck & Ruprecht, 1967.

"Luther's Defense of Infant Baptism." In *Luther for an Ecumenical Age*, edited by Carl S. Meyer, 200–218. Saint Louis: Concordia Publishing House, 1967.

"The Past of Belief: Reflections of a Historian of Doctrine." In *The Future of Belief Debate*, edited by Gregory Baum, 29–36. New York: Herder & Herder, 1967.

"The Theology of the Means of Grace." In *Accents in Luther's Theology*, edited by Heino O. Kadai, 124–47. Saint Louis: Concordia Publishing House, 1967.

"*Verius Servamus Canones*: Church Law and Divine Law in the Apology of the Augsburg Confession." In *Studia Gratiana* 11 (1967), *Collectanea Stephan Kuttner*, edited by Alphons Stickler, vol. 1, pp. 367–88. Bonn, 1967.

"Adolf von Harnack on Luther" and "Wilhelm Pauck: A Tribute." In *Interpreters of Luther: Essays in Honor of Wilhelm Pauck*, edited by Jaroslav Pelikan, 253–74, 1–8. Philadelphia: Fortress Press, 1968.

"Jozef Miloslav Hurban: A Study in Historicism." In *The Impact of the Church upon Its Culture: Essays in Divinity*, edited by Jerald C. Brauer, vol. 2, pp. 333–52. Chicago: University of Chicago Press, 1968.

"Renewal of Structure versus Renewal by the Spirit." In *Theology of Renewal*, Proceedings of the Congress on the Theology of the Renewal of the Church, Centenary of Canada, 1867–1967, edited by L. K. Shook, vol.

2, pp. 21–41. Montreal: Palm Publishers, 1968. French edition: "L'Esprit et les structures selon Luther, étude sur 'La Captivité babylonienne de l'Église'" In *La Théologie du Renouveau*, edited by Laurence K. Shook and Guy-M. Bertrand, vol. 1, pp. 357–74. Montreal: Éditions Fides, 1968.

"The Christian Religions." In *East Central Europe: A Guide to Basic Publications*, edited by Paul L. Horecky, 329–33. Chicago: University of Chicago Press, 1969.

"Theology and Change." In *Theology in the City of Man*, Saint Louis University Sesquicentennial Symposium, 375–84. New York: Cross Currents Corporation, 1969, 1970.

"De-Judaization and Hellenization: The Ambiguities of Christian Identity." In *The Dynamic in Christian Thought*, edited by Joseph Papin, 81–124. Villanova, Pa.: Villanova University Press, 1970.

"*Didakhe* and *Diadokhe*: A Personal Tribute to Johannes Quasten." In *Kyriakon*, Festschrift Johannes Quasten, edited by Patrick Granfield and Josef A. Jungmann, vol. 2, pp. 917–20. Münster: Verlag Aschendorf, 1970.

"'Council or Father or Scripture': The Concept of Authority in the Theology of Maximus Confessor" and "*Puti Russkogo Bogoslova*: When Orthodoxy Comes West." In *The Heritage of the Early Church: Essays in Honor of the Very Reverend Georges Vasilievich Florovsky*, edited by David Neiman and Margaret Schatkin, 277–88, 11–16. Orientalia Christiana Analecta, no. 195. Rome: Pontificale Institutum Studiorum Orientalium, 1973.

"The Doctrine of Filioque in Thomas Aquinas and Its Patristic Antecedents: An Analysis of *Summa Theologiae*, Part I, Question 36." In *Saint Thomas Aquinas 1274–1974: Commemorative Studies*, edited by Armand A. Maurer, vol. 1, pp. 315–36. Toronto: Pontifical Institute of Mediaeval Studies, 1974.

"Luther Comes to the New World." In *Luther and the Dawn of the Modern Era*, Papers for the Fourth International Congress for Luther Research, edited by Heiko A. Oberman, 1–10. Leiden: E. J. Brill, 1974.

"The Ukrainian Catholic Church and Eastern Spirituality." In *The Ukrainian Catholic Church 1945–1975*, edited by Miroslav Labunka and Leonid Rudnytzky, 114–27. Philadelphia: St. Sophia Religious Association of Ukrainian Catholics, 1976.

"We Hold These Truths to Be Self-evident: Reformation, Revolution, and Reason." In *The Historical Context and Dynamic Future of Lutheran Higher Education*, edited by J. Victor Hahn, 8–17. Washington, D.C.: Lutheran Educational Conference of North America, 1976.

"Christianity," by H. H. Walsh, revised by Jaroslav Pelikan. In *A Reader's Guide to the Great Religions*, 2d rev. ed., edited by Charles J. Adams, 345–406. New York: Macmillan Company and The Free Press, 1977.

"Historical Reflections on the Fortieth Anniversary of Saint Vladimir's Seminary." Crestwood, N.Y.: Saint Vladimir's Seminary Press, 1978.

"*Imago Dei*: An Explication of *Summa Theologiae*, Part I, Question 93." In

Calgary Aquinas Studies, edited by Anthony Parel, 27–48. Toronto: Pontifical Institute of Mediaeval Studies, 1978.

"A First-generation Anselmian, Guibert of Nogent." In *Continuity and Discontinuity in Church History*, essays presented to George Huntston Williams, edited by F. Forrester Church and Timothy George, 71–82. Studies in the History of Christian Thought, edited by Heiko A. Oberman, vol. 19. Leiden: E. J. Brill, 1979.

"Voices of the Church." In *Proceedings of the Thirty-third Annual Convention* (Catholic Theological Society of America), edited by Luke Salm, 1–12. The Bronx, N.Y., 1979.

"The Wisdom of Prospero." In *Minutes of the Ninety-fourth Meeting* (Association of Research Libraries), 67–72. Washington, D.C., 1979.

"The Two Sees of Peter." In *The Shaping of Christianity in the Second and Third Centuries*, vol. 1 of *Jewish and Christian Self-Definition*, edited by E. P. Sanders, 57–73. Philadelphia: Fortress Press; London: SCM Press, 1980.

"The 'Spiritual Sense' of Scripture: The Exegetical Basis for Saint Basil's Doctrine of the Holy Spirit." In *Basil of Caesarea: Christian, Humanist, Ascetic*, edited by Paul Jonathan Fedwick, vol. 1, pp. 337–60. Toronto: Pontifical Institute of Mediaeval Studies, 1981.

"The Doctrine of the Image of God." In *The Common Christian Roots of the European Nations: An International Colloquium in the Vatican*, vol. 1, pp. 53–62. Florence: Le Monnier, 1982.

"The Place of Maximus Confessor in the History of Christian Thought." In *Maximus Confessor*, Actes du Symposium sur Maxime le Confesseur Fribourg, edited by Felix Heinze and Christoph Schoenborn, 387–404. Paradosis: Études de littérature et de théologie ancienne, no. 27. Fribourg: Éditions Universitaires Fribourg Suisse, 1982.

4
ARTICLES IN JOURNALS

(NOTE: *CTM* = *Concordia Theological Monthly*)

"Natural Theology in David Hollaz." *CTM* 18 (1947): 253–63.

"The Structure of Luther's Piety." *Una Sancta* 7 (1947): 12–20.

"Luther's Attitude toward John Hus." *CTM* 19 (1948): 747–63.

"Luther's Endorsement of the *Confessio Bohemica*." *CTM* 20 (1949): 829–43.

"The Doctrine of Man in the Lutheran Confessions." *The Lutheran Quarterly* 2 (1950): 34–44.

"The Origins of the Object-Subject Antithesis in Lutheran Dogmatics." *CTM* 21 (1950): 94–104.

"The Relation of Faith and Knowledge in the Lutheran Confessions." *CTM* 21 (1950): 321–31.

"Chalcedon after Fifteen Centuries." *CTM* 22 (1951): 926–36.

"Church and Church History in the Confessions." *CTM* 22 (1951): 305–20.

"The Temptation of the Church: A Study of Matthew 4:1–11." *CTM* 22 (1951): 251–59.

"Amerikanisches Luthertum in dogmengeschichtlicher Sicht." *Evangelisch-Lutherische Kirchenzeitung* 14 (1952): 250–53.

"The Eschatology of Tertullian." *Church History* 21 (1952): 108–22.

"In Memoriam: Johann Albrecht Bengel, June 24, 1687, to November 2, 1752." *CTM* 23 (1952): 785–96.

"Some Anti-Pelagian Echoes in Augustine's *City of God.*" *CTM* 23 (1952): 448–52.

"Some Word Studies in the *Apology.*" *CTM* 24 (1953): 580–96.

"The Doctrine of Creation in Lutheran Confessional Theology." *CTM* 26 (1955): 569–79.

"Tradition in Confessional Lutheranism." *Lutheran World* 3 (1956): 214–22. [Based on a paper presented to the Theological Commission on Tradition and Traditions—American Section—of the Commission on Faith and Order of the World Council of Churches.] German translation: "Die Tradition im konfessionellen Luthertum." *Lutherische Rundschau* 6 (1956–57): 228–37.

"Montanism and Its Trinitarian Significance." *Church History* 25 (1956): 99–109.

"The Tyranny of Epistemology: Revelation in the History of Protestant Thought." *Encounter* [Butler University, School of Religion] 18 (1957): 53–56.

"Kerygma and Culture: An Inquiry into Schleiermacher's *Reden.*" *Discourse: A Review of the Liberal Arts* 2 (1959): 131–44.

"Cosmos and Creation: Science and Theology in Reformation Thought." *Proceedings of the American Philosophical Society* 105 (1961): 464–69. [Paper presented at "The Influence of Science upon Modern Culture," Conference Commemorating the 400th Anniversary of the Birth of Francis Bacon.]

"Fathers, Brethren, and Distant Relatives: The Family of Theological Discourse." *CTM* 33 (1962): 710–18.

"The New English Bible—The New Testament." *Criterion* 1 (1962): 25–29.

"The Christian as an Intellectual." *The Christian Scholar* 45 (1962): 6–11.

"The Theological Library and the Tradition of Christian Humanism." *CTM* 33 (1962): 719–23.

"An Essay on the Development of Christian Doctrine." *Church History* 35 (1966): 3–12. [Presidential Address, American Society of Church History.]

"Beyond Bellarmine and Harnack: The Present Task of the History of Dogma." *Theology Digest* 16 (1968): 299–309.

"Upon the Tercentenary of the Death of John Amos Comenius." *Yale University Library Gazette* 45 (1970): 66–68.

"Historical Theology: A Presentation." *Criterion* 10 (1971): 26–27.

"Dukedom Large Enough: Reflections on Academic Administration." *CTM* 43 (1972): 297–302.

"The Liberation Arts." *Liberal Education* 59 (1973): 292–97.

"Continuity and Creativity." *Saint Vladimir's Theological Quarterly* 19, no. 3 (1975): 1–7.

"A Decent Respect to the Opinions of Mankind." *Scholarly Publishing* 8 (1976): 11–16.

"The Research University and the Healing Professions." *Criterion*, Autumn 1976.

"The Jewish-Christian Dialogue in Historical Perspective." *Bulletin of the American Academy of Arts and Sciences* 32, no. 7 (1979): 18–30.

"Negative Theology and Positive Religion: A Study of Nicholas Cusanus *De pace fidei*." *Prudentia* [University of Aukland], supplementary number (1981): 65–78.

"The Two Cities: The Decline and Fall of Rome as Historical Paradigm." *Daedalus* 111, no. 3 (1982): 85–92.

5

FOREWORDS TO WORKS
OF OTHERS

Introduction to *Protestant Thought from Rousseau to Ritschl.* Eleven chapters of *Die protestantische Theologie im 19. Jahrhundert*, by Karl Barth. Translated by Brian Cozens. New York: Harper & Brothers, 1959. Pp. 7–10.

Introduction to *The Mission and Expansion of Christianity in the Three First Centuries*, by Adolf von Harnack. Translated and edited by James Moffatt. New York: Harper & Brothers, Torchbook Edition, 1961. Pp. v–vii.

Foreword to *The Impact of American Religious Liberalism*, by Kenneth Cauthen. New York: Harper & Row, 1962. Pp. vii–x.

Preface and additional bibliography to *Protestant Thought before Kant*, by A. C. McGiffert. New York: Harper & Brothers, 1962. Pp. vii–xi.

Foreword to *The Structure of Lutheranism: The Theology and Philosophy of Life of Lutheranism Especially in the Sixteenth and Seventeenth Centuries*, by Werner Elert. Translated by Walter A. Hansen. Saint Louis: Concordia Publishing House, 1962. Pp. vii–xi.

"The Basic Marian Idea." Introduction to *Mary, Archetype of the Church*, by Otto Semmelroth. New York: Sheed & Ward, 1963. Pp. vii–xiv.

Introduction to *Luther and Aquinas on Salvation*, by Stephen Pfürtner. New York: Sheed & Ward, 1964. Pp. 5–11.

Introduction to *History of the Reformation: A Conciliatory Assessment of Opposite Views*, by John P. Dolan. New York: Desclee, 1965. Pp. ix–xvii.

Foreword to *The Promise and the Presence*, by Harry N. Huxhold. Saint Louis: Concordia Publishing House, 1965.

Introduction to *The Reformation: Causes and Consequences*, by John A. O'Brien. Rev. ed. Glen Rock, N.J.: Paulist Press, 1966. P. 4.

Foreword to *The Church in the Churches*, by James O. McGovern. Washington, D.C.: Corpus Books, 1968. Pp. 7–10.

Introduction to *The Church in the Modern World in the Words of Albert Cardinal Meyer*, edited by Michael P. Dineen. Waukesha, Wis.: Country Beautiful, 1968. Pp. 10–13.

Foreword to *The Anabaptists and the Czech Brethren in Moravia 1526–1628,* by Jarold Knox Zeman. Paris: Mouton, 1969. Pp. 5–7.

Foreword to *Christus Victor: An Historical Study of the Three Main Types of the Idea of the Atonement,* by Gustaf Aulén. New York: Macmillan Company, 1969. Pp. xi–xix.

Foreword to *Portrait of the Elder Brother: Jews and Judaism in Protestant Teaching Materials,* by Gerald S. Strober. New York: American Jewish Committee and National Conference of Christians and Jews, 1972. Pp. 5–7.

Foreword to *The Christian Trinity in History,* by Bertrand de Margerie. Translated by Edmund J. Fortman. Studies in Historical Theology, vol. 1. Still River, Mass.: Saint Bede's Publications, 1981. Pp. xi–xiii.

Introduction to *Martin Luther: An Illustrated Biography,* by Peter Manns. Translated by Michael Shaw. New York: Crossroad, 1982. Pp. 6–9.

Foreword to *The Secular Mind: Transformations of Faith in Modern Europe: Essays Presented to Franklin L. Baumer.* Edited by W. Warren Wagar. New York: Holmes & Meier, 1982. Pp. xi–xiii.

Preface to *The Triads,* by Gregory Palamas. Edited by John Meyendorff. Translated by Nicholas Gendle. Classics of Western Spirituality. New York: Paulist Press, 1983. Pp. xi–xiii.

6
ARTICLES AND ADDRESSES OF
GENERAL INTEREST

"Luther after Four Centuries." *The Cresset* [Valparaiso University] 4, no. 4 (1946): 14–18.

"The Spell of Saint Thomas." *The Cresset* 10, no. 6 (1947): 13ff.

"History as Law and Gospel." Parts I and II. *The Cresset* 12 (1949) 4:12–17; 5:19–23.

"The Marxist Heresy—A Theological Evaluation." *Religion in Life* 19 (1950): 356–66.

"Four Questions at Evanston." *The American Lutheran* 37, no. 7 (1954): 6–9.

"Flying Is for the Birds." *The Cresset* 21, no. 10 (1958): 6–9.

"Luther on the Word of God." *The Minnesota Lutheran* 34, no. 10 (1965): 16–25. [Essay delivered to convention of the Minnesota District of the Lutheran Church—Missouri Synod, 1958.]

"Catholics in America." *The New Republic* 142, no. 12 (1960). [Symposium with John C. Bennett and Arthur Schlesinger, Jr.]

"The American Church in the Church Universal." *The Atlantic* 210, no. 2 (1962): 90–94. [Part of special supplement, "The Roman Catholic Church in America."]

"Karl Barth in America." *The Christian Century* 79 (1962): 451–52.

"That the Church May Be More Fully Catholic." *The Catholic World* 198, no. 1185 (1963): 151–56.

"A Scholar Strikes Back." *The Catholic World* 200, no. 1197 (1964): 149–54.

[Adapted from an address delivered to the American Book Publishers Council.]

"Thine Alabaster Cities Gleam—The Secularization of a Vision." *A.I.A. Journal* 42, no. 2 (1964): 37–43. [Address delivered to the American Institute of Architects 1964 Convention.]

"In Memoriam: Paul Tillich." *The Cresset* 28 (1965): 24–25.

"Theologian and Thinker [Albert Schweitzer]." *Saturday Review* 48, no. 39 (1965): 21–22.

From "After the Campus Turmoil: A Plea for Reform." *Panorama—Chicago Daily News*, 15 June 1968.

"Faculties Must Reassert Powers They Defaulted." *Los Angeles Times*, 16 June 1968.

"The Pope and the Jews." *New York Times*, 28 October 1970. [Fifth anniversary of the Vatican II Declaration.]

"Paul M. Bretscher, Christian Humanist." *The Cresset* 37, no. 9 (1974): 4.

"What Gibbon Knew: Lessons in Imperialism." *Harper's* 253, no. 1514 (1976): 13–18.

"The Circle of Knowledge in Historical Perspective." [Address delivered on behalf of the Library of Congress Council of Scholars during a celebration of the Library, 6 December 1979.]

"A Gentleman and a Scholar." *The Key Reporter* [Phi Beta Kappa] 45, no. 2 (1979–80): 2–4.

"The Research Library, an Outpost of Cultural Continuity." *Imprint of the Stanford Library Associates* 6, no. 2 (1980): 5–10. [Address delivered at the dedication of the Green Library, Stanford University.]

"From Reformation Theology to Christian Humanism." *Lutheran Forum* 16, no. 4 (1982): 11–15.

"Special Collections: A Key into the Language of America." *Books at Brown* [Friends of the Library of Brown University] 29–30 (1982–83): 1–10.

"The Enduring Relevance of Martin Luther 500 Years after His Birth." *New York Times Magazine*, 18 September 1983, pp. 43ff.

7
ENCYCLOPEDIA ARTICLES

"Paths to Dialogue." In *1966 World Book Year Book*. Chicago: Field Enterprises Educational Corporation, 1966.

"Theology without God." In *Encyclopedia Britannica Year Book—1966*. Chicago: Encyclopedia Britannica, 1966.

"Confessions of Faith, Protestant." In *New Catholic Encyclopedia*, 1967 edition.

"Absolution"; "Agnosticism"; "Agnus Dei"; "Anointing"; "Atheism"; "Atonement"; "Baader, Franz Xavier von"; "Bampton, John"; "Baptism, Christian"; "Barclay, Robert"; "Baur, Ferdinand Christian"; "Bible"; "Bidding Prayer"; "Biddle, John"; "Burnet, Thomas"; "Butler, Joseph"; "Case,

Shirley Jackson"; "Catechism"; "Chalice"; "Chapel"; "Charity"; "Christianity"; "Communion, Holy"; "Confirmation"; "Congregation"; "Creationism and Traducianism"; "Dogma"; "Ernesti, Johann August"; "Eucharist"; "Excommunication"; "Exegesis and Hermeneutics, Biblical"; "Faith"; "Frommel, Gaston"; "Gichtel, Johann Georg"; "Grace"; "Hengstenberg, Ernst Wilhelm"; "Hope"; "Idolatry"; "Inspiration"; "Jesus Christ"; "Mary"; "Monophysites"; "Mysticism"; "Predestination"; "Religion"; "Sacrament"; "Sins, Seven Deadly"; "Theology"; "Trinity." In *Encyclopedia Britannica*, 1967 edition.

"Luther, Martin"; "Lutherans." In *World Book Encyclopedia*, 1970 edition.

Index of Names

Abelard, Peter, 107, 108, 109, 110, 111
Ailly, Pierre d', 120
Alcuin, 90–93, 94, 102
Alexander of Jerusalem, 52
Amalric of Bena, 113
Ambrose of Milan, 33, 92
Ambrosius Autpertus, 92
Ames, William, 125–26, 130, 137
"Anonymous of Melk," 97
Anselm of Canterbury, 108, 109, 118
Anselm of Laon, 95, 101
Anthony the Younger, 81
Apollonius of Tyana (pseudo), 23
Aristotle, 81, 83, 88 n. 14, 109, 113–14, 116, 117, 118
Arno (bishop of Salzburg), 92
Augustine of Hippo, 4, 31–32, 33–34, 35, 36, 38, 41–43, 44, 45–47, 68, 90, 92, 108, 117, 164
Aurelius of Carthage, 34
Averroes, 117, 118
Avicenna, 116–17

Backus, Charles, 127, 135, 145
Bacon, Francis, 141
Bacon, Leonard, 132
Bardy, Gustave, 17
Barlaam the Calabrian, 72
Baronius, Caesar, 8
Barré, Henri, 99

Barth, Karl, 5, 13, 153, 164, 168–69, 176 n. 114
Bauer, Bruno, 161
Baur, Ferdinand Christian, 10
Baxter, Richard, 133
Becket, Thomas, 113
Bede, 90, 91, 92, 94
Bellamy, Joseph, 126–27, 128, 131, 135, 136, 137, 139–40, 144
Bellarmine, Robert, 8
Berger, Peter, 168
Bernard of Clairvaux, 108, 109
Bismarck, 162
Boethius, 110, 111
Bonaventure, 116
Bonhoeffer, Dietrich, 169–70
Boniface VIII, 120
"Bordeaux Pilgrim," 60–61
Bossuet, J. B., 8, 9
Brown, Peter, 55
Bruno of Chartreux, 100
Buonaiuti, Ernesto, 11
Burton, Asa, 127, 129

Caecilian of Carthage, 40
Calvin, John, 5, 8, 9, 76
Candidus (pupil of Alcuin), 92
Cato, 24
Celsus, 52
Chadwick, Henry, 18
Chapin, Calvin, 147
Charlemagne, 91, 102
Charles the Bald, 95
Chemnitz, Martin, 9

189